RACE AND DRUG TRIALS

To the memory of my mother,
Grace Nwobiara Kalunta
and
the long and fruitful life of my father,
Chief Dr Ariwodo Kalunta

Race and Drug Trials

The Social Construction of Guilt and Innocence

ANITA KALUNTA-CRUMPTON
Institute of Criminal Justice Studies,
University of Portsmouth

Ashgate

Aldershot • Brookfield USA • Singapore • Sydney

Published by
Ashgate Publishing Ltd
Gower House
Croft Road
Aldershot
Hants GU11 3HR
England

Ashgate Publishing Company
Old Post Road
Brookfield
Vermont 05036
USA

British Library Cataloguing in Publication Data
Kalunta-Crumpton, Anita
    Race and drug trials : the social construction of guilt and
    innocence. - (Interdisciplinary research series in ethnic,
    gender and class relations)
    1. Trials (Narcotic laws) - Great Britain 2. Great Britain -
    Race relations
    I. Title
    345.4'1'0277'0269

Library of Congress Cataloging-in-Publication Data
Kalunta-Crumpton, Anita, 1962-
    Race and drug trials - the social construction of guilt and
    innocence / Anita Kalunta-Crumpton.
        p. cm
    Includes bibliographical references and index.
    ISBN 1-84014-396-7 (hc)
    1. Discrimination in criminal justice administration--Great
    Britain. 2. Trials (Narcotic laws)--Great Britain. 3. Sentences
    (Criminal procedure)--Great Britain--Social aspects. 4. Blacks-
    -Great Britain. I. Title.
    KD7876.K35 1998
    345.41'0772--dc21   98-31705
                                                                 CIP

ISBN 1 84014 396 7

Printed and bound by
Antony Rowe Ltd, Chippenham, Wiltshire

Contents

Foreword   *vii*
The Series Editor's Preface   *ix*
Acknowledgements   *xi*
Introduction   *xiii*

Part 1   The Background   1

1   The Problem of Disproportion: The Debate   3

2   Drugs, Response and Race   24

3   Social Construction and Claims-making:
    Theory and Methods   55

Part 2   The Substance   73

4   Establishing Guilt   74

5   Defending the Defendant   129

6   In Response: The Judge   156

7   The Verdict   196

Bibliography   *209*
Index   *225*

Foreword

This book illuminates one recurrent debate in criminology: the influence of race for defendants in the criminal justice system. It does so through a detailed analysis of the nuances of the process of 'doing justice' in court. A very public event, the trial serves as a display of its neutrality. After all, if evidence is aired in public, does this not reassure that the process is monitored and accountable to all? So why has there been so much attention paid to debates about the high proportion of black people in prison, for instance, without careful attention to the processing of such defendants during a trial? Can we be assured that legal procedures in any English criminal court have no trace of 'institutional racism'?

Anita Kalunta-Crumpton's book opens up a novel way of viewing the processing of defendants - both black and white - who are charged with possession and sale of drugs. What she shows is that prosecution, defence, the witnesses and the judges seem to agree on the use of language that crystallises popular beliefs about black and white people as racial groups. And these racial groupings absorb common sense discourses that confer the naturalness of such characteristics as 'deprived', 'unemployed', 'possibly violent', 'unclean', and 'sexually promiscuous'. This social context in effect embeds 'race' and possibly 'racism' within the contours of each aspect of the criminal justice process. Kalunta-Crumpton's analysis must prompt us to look at more creative ways of exploring and challenging racism in the criminal justice system.

This book will extend the debates about race in the criminal justice system. It is a readable, accessible, straightforward account of trial strategies in drug cases. Kalunta-Crumpton's analysis deserves to be read by criminal justice practitioners and theorists alike.

Professor Elizabeth A. Stanko
Director, ESRC Violence Research Programme
Brunel University
Uxbridge, Middlesex

The Series Editor's Preface

This book raises serious issues for modernist and neo-modernist accounts that privilege the role of facts and values in the explanation of the evolution and practice of penal juridification. The book does not argue that these accounts are wrong but suggests that procedural requirements are less important than the practice of 'claims-making' by social actors with power based hierarchical credibility who interact symbolically in the court process, from the beginning to the end and not just at the more researched point of sentencing, thereby sociallyconstructing the meaning of guilt and innocence in drugs trials involving an increasing proportion of black defendants.

The Author argues that attempts to explain the over-representation of black people in custody fail to focus on the symbolic interactionism of the court process itself which she studied with the appropriate methodology of direct observation. Anita also looked beyond the trial process and reviewed relevant literature on policing, sentencing and prisons against a historical background of government drugs policies from the distant past to the present. As successive governments relaunch the war that was presumably lost by their predecessors, the war against drugs, the theory of claims-making could serve as a warning to drugs Tsars and drugs courts that the social construction of guilt and innocence in court works against black people who possess relatively fewer power resources. Hence, a neglected reason why black people are being over-represented in prisons is being analysed here by the author as the power-loaded discourse of claims-making in drugs trials.

Biko Agozino, Liverpool

Acknowledgements

I thank all those whose contacts and involvement provided access to materials valuable to this book but for reasons of confidentiality, they cannot be named.

To my friends, I owe praise for their understanding and reassurance.

To my colleague, friend and 'brother', Dr Biko Agozino, I thank for being such a strong shoulder to lean on.

To Professor Elizabeth Stanko who supervised the Doctoral thesis on which this book is based, I thank for her understanding, commitment and professional help throughout the term of the thesis.

To my family, I owe gratitude for their encouragement and moral support.

To my best friend and confidant, David, I will forever remain grateful.

Most of all, I owe my sincere and humble thanks to God for giving me the strength and inspiration that guided me throughout the entire work.

Introduction

Over the years, there has been a growth in concern over the position of black[1] people as suspects, defendants and offenders in the criminal justice system in Britain. Questions have arisen about the overrepresentation of black people in the arrest, conviction and prison statistics and an extensive research literature has provided theoretical and empirical evidence as to the relationship between black communities and the police (Lambert, 1970; Humphrey, 1972; Stevens and Willis, 1979; Gordon, 1983; Smith and Gray, 1985; Pitts, 1986; Osborne and Bright, 1988; Day, 1989; Hall, 1989; Solomos, 1988a, 1989, 1993; Jefferson, 1988, 1991; Smellie and Crow, 1991; Cashmore and McLaughlin, 1991; Keith, 1991; Smith, 1994), the pre and post conviction processing of black people (Fludger, 1981; Kettle, 1982; Cain and Sadigh, 1982; McConville and Baldwin, 1982; Gordon, 1983; Crow and Cove, 1984; National Association for the Care and Resettlement of Offenders (NACRO), 1986; Hall, 1989; Walker, 1988; Day, 1989; Smellie and Crow, 1991; Hood, 1992; Home Office, 1992; Smith, 1994; Penal Affairs Consortium, 1996; Agozino, 1997; Mhlanga, 1997), and the possible link between black people and crime (Lea and Young, 1984, 1993).

McClintock (1963) conducted the first systematic study which sheds light on the high proportion of black people in the criminal statistics when compared to their number in the national population shown in the 1961 census. The study which focused on violent crime observed that in London, the proportion of persons (mostly West Indians) born in the Colonies and the Commonwealth who were convicted of violent crime increased from 6.2 per cent in 1950 to 13.0 per cent in 1960. Evidence of disproportionate arrest rates for black people is shown in various studies, for example, a Home Office study by Stevens and Willis (1979) on *Race, Crime and Arrests* in the Metropolitan Police District (MPD) indicates that for every category of offence, the arrest rate for black people was disproportionate in comparison to their number in the London population, and it was also higher than that for other racial groups. Further Home Office studies (1983, 1984, 1989a) in the MPD reveal that for all indictable offences, black people made up about 14-17 per cent of those arrested from 1977 to 1982, a proportion higher than their total London population of about 5 per cent. Arrest figures for 1981 to 1987 also showed that about 17 or 18 per cent of black people were arrested whereas their London population was still estimated to be 5 per cent. In contrast, the proportion of white people who were arrested was less than their London population of approximately 86 per cent according to MPD statistics. These variations are applicable to the ethnic distribution of those found guilty or cautioned for indictable offences in the period 1980 to 1983 which reveals that the proportion of black people in these categories compared unfavourably to their population figure (Home Office, 1984).

Particular attention has been drawn to the overrepresentation of black people in penal institutions including the remand prison population. On 30 June 1985 when the prison population of England and Wales stood at 47,503, about 8 per cent of male prisoners and 12 per cent of female prisoners were black which compared unfavourably to their general population of England and Wales of between 1 per cent and 2 per cent; for whites, the prison population was made up of 83.1 per cent males and 77.8 per cent females, and they accounted for about 93 - 94 per cent of the general population (Home Office, 1986a). Of the total male prison population of 46,776 in England and Wales on 30 June 1989, 10.7 per cent were black males and similarly black females constituted 20.1 per cent of the 1,756 female prison population (Home Office, 1993). By 1990, the figures had increased to 10.8 per cent for males and 22.9 per cent for females (ibid.); in 1992, the proportions for males and females were 10.2 per cent and 20.1 per cent respectively, and in 1993 when the resident population of black people in England and Wales was estimated to be 1.9 per cent, the prison figures were 10.8 per cent for males and 19.6 per cent for females (Home Office, 1994a).

Since the issue of race and drug offences is of particular relevance here, it is important to note that prison establishments are made up of a high proportion of black people, especially, females, and this is greatly influenced by the high numbers of foreign nationals sentenced for drug offences (Home Office, 1993, 1994a). In the period 1 July 1984 to 31 March 1985, the proportion of black males received under sentence was relatively high for drug offences - 19.1 per cent as against 67.7 per cent for white males; for females, the highest proportion of blacks received under sentence was for drug offences - 30.7 per cent whilst the proportion for whites was 58.8 per cent (Home Office, 1986a). In 1990, a higher proportion of blacks than whites were received under sentence for drug offences. For males aged 21 and over, 16.1 per cent blacks and 4.7 per cent whites were received under sentence for drug offences and for females in the same age range, the figures were 29.1 per cent for blacks and 10.8 per cent for whites (Home Office, 1994a). Evidently, a significant number of male and female prisoners in the United Kingdom are foreign nationals charged or convicted for importing illegal drugs (Green, 1991; Richards et al., 1995). Green's study on *Drug Couriers* (1991) show that two-thirds of the research sample are foreign nationals (72 per cent) with 30 per cent coming from Nigeria. Other foreign national prisoners commonly represented are Jamaicans/West Indians, Colombians and Pakistanis. Drug offences, particularly, drug trafficking form a category for which black people are more likely than other racial groups to be arrested, charged, convicted and sentenced to custody (Mair, 1986; Crow and Cove, 1984; Hudson, 1989; Home Office, 1989a).

The disproportionate representation of black people in the crime statistics has remained a subject of controversy as research studies have produced mixed explanations for this problem. In relation to the question of black disproportionate presence in the official criminal record for drug offences, nowhere has it received a specific or full and exhaustive notice as far as analysis is concerned, instead, it has been incorporated in the general explanations suggested for the problem of disproportion and racial variations as a whole which have, broadly speaking, been held in two fields of thought. One explanation suggested is that crime is disproportionately prevalent amongst black people given the high levels of socio-economic deprivation suffered by this group (Lea and Young, 1984; Pitts, 1986; Stevens and Willis, 1979; Box and Hale, 1986). There have been theoretical justifications for taking this line of argument which principally stem from criminological and sociological theories that associate criminality with societal members who are at the periphery of the stratification system (Cloward and Ohlin, 1961; Cohen, 1955; Merton, 1957; Downes and Rock, 1988). Lea and Young uphold this popular view in their argument that police crimin.' statistics are accurate indicators of real black crime rate which is explained in terms of black people being more likely to make the crime choice in response to their deplorable socio-economic conditions in society.

The claim that black overrepresentation in the crime statistics results from their disproportionate engagement in crime has been met with criticisms, for example, Gilroy (1987a, 1987b) strongly express doubts as to the accuracy of official statistics and argues that it is impossible to say what real black crime rates are with certainty (also see Blom-Cooper and Drabble, 1982). Other criticisms have highlighted limitations in research findings which show that it is problematic to empirically account for any possibility of a disproportionate involvement of any racial group in crime (Stevens and Willis, 1979). Arrest figures, according to the Home Office, do not fully reflect the extent to which crimes are committed by non-whites as opposed to white offenders, and available information on criminal statistics 'have limited value as measures of ethnic minority criminality' (Home Office, 1983). Even for conviction rates, limitations in findings clearly depict the difficulties embroiled in attempts to correlate criminal statistics with a possibility of disproportionate black involvement in crime (ibid., 1983, 1984). That black people are more prone to crime because of their deprived circumstances, however, remains a theoretical inference drawn from arrest, conviction and imprisonment statistics which imply that the black community - whose socio-economic position is on the whole that of the most deprived and marginalised group (Cross, 1982; Scarman, 1981, 1982; Solomos and Rackett, 1991) - have a higher crime rate. This line of thought, although widely acknowledged, has also been made questionable by studies of white-collar and business crimes (Sutherland, 1961; Levi, 1987; Clarke, 1990; Leigh, 1982) which have shown that economic and social necessities are not wholly useful in explaining criminality. Crime is not necessarily confined to those who are on the margins of society.

The 'black criminality-deprivation' theory is further undermined by the second field of thought which views criminal statistics as a reflection of selective criminal justice practices by the police and other criminal justice agencies. Several studies have drawn attention to the differential modes of criminal justice response received by individuals on the basis of their racial background with emphasis placed on the discriminatory and racist practices of criminal justice agencies as a fundamental explanation for the overrepresentation of black people in the crime statistics (Gilroy, 1982a, 1982b, 1987a, 1987b; Cain and Sadigh, 1982; Gutzmore, 1983; NACRO, 1986, 1989; Smellie and Crow, 1991; Mhlanga, 1997; Agozino, 1997). An additional argument that being black and over-represented in the lower socio-economic group make black people more vulnerable to arrest and more liable to criminalisation (Carlen, 1988; Box, 1971, 1981; Jefferson, 1988, 1991) is solidified by the preponderance of evidence which suggests that when people from various social classes commit crime, those that occupy the lower socio-economic position are more likely to be criminalised (Mays, 1970; Chambliss, 1969; Becker, 1963; Quinney, 1970; Manis, 1976), and are more likely to 'perceive criminal injustice' (Hagan, 1988). Individuals who are unemployed, socially and economically disadvantaged have more chances of being arrested, prosecuted and imprisoned since such socio-economic variables as unemployment and homelessness can critically influence arrest, prosecution, bail and sentencing decisions (Smith and Gray, 1985; Taylor, 1982; McBarnet, 1983; Box and Hale, 1986; Chigwada, 1989; Crow and Simon, 1987; Solomos, 1988a; NACRO, 1993a). Invariably, inner city areas characterised by deprivation and inhabited by most black people attract high-profile policing (Demuth, 1978; Blom-Cooper and Drabble, 1982; Benyon, 1984; Cain and Sadigh, 1982) resulting in a high arrest rate for those most vulnerable - the unemployed, the black population. And at other stages of the criminal justice process, the influence of race is also evident, for example, in decisions pertaining to prosecution (Landau and Nathan, 1983; Landau, 1981), bail (Gordon, 1983;

Home Office, 1992), committals (Smellie and Crow, 1991), the use of social inquiry reports (now pre-sentence reports) (Whitehouse, 1978; Voakes and Fowler, 1989), and sentencing (Tipler, 1985; Walker, 1988; Hudson, 1989; Runnymede Trust, 1990; Hood, 1992; Shalice and Gordon, 1990).

In the next chapter, these varied explanatory arguments relating to the disproportionate representation of black people in the criminal statistics are addressed in more detail with a view to posing questions vis-à-vis the racial discrepancies in the conviction rates and prison population for drug offences. In presenting these arguments, the intention is not to judge or critique the different studies from which the lines of reasoning are extracted as they have done well in their own right in explaining the problem of disproportion. However, as will be shown, these approaches are limited in the sense that they have failed to assimilate specific aspects of the criminal justice process in their analyses. There are arguments embedded in the general explanatory accounts for the overrepresentation of black people in the criminal statistics which have not been advanced, at least empirically, thereby rendering them less useful to a detailed examination of the problem of disproportion. For example, the overall court processing of offences and its influence on criminal statistics has been ignored and invariably, differentials in decisions relating to remand, prosecution, jury verdicts, convictions and so forth have not lent themselves to an exhaustive scrutiny in relation to how they affect criminal statistics. What this study examines is the influence of race in the trial process with focus on drug offence cases. Even though it provides a new approach that unveils how the trial process can affect the higher representation of black people in the criminal statistics, each of the existing explanatory accounts given is intelligible in its own right and lays a foundation for the approach adopted in this book.

Note

1   Refers to people of African and Afro-Caribbean origin.

PART 1

THE BACKGROUND

1 The Problem of Disproportion: The Debate

'Black Criminality'

As previously noted, black disproportionate presence in the criminal statistics has been examined within the context of 'black criminality' (Stevens and Willis, 1979; Lea and Young, 1984, 1993; Reiner, 1985). Of the many theoretical explanations for 'black criminality', the significant role of economic and social factors in determining the involvement of black people in criminal activities has dominated the debate. Studies and Official statistics have indicated that black people are more socially and economically marginalised than other racial groups and are over-represented in the lower socio-economic class (Brown, 1984; Solomos, 1988a, 1988b, 1989; Hiro, 1992; Pitts, 1986; Lawrence, 1982; Stevens et al., 1988, Brooks, 1987; Rankin, 1991; Box and Hale, 1986; Penal Affairs Consortium, 1996). On comparing such indicators as the employment, housing and educational conditions of black people with those of other racial groups, the conclusion has been that the circumstances of black people are worse than those of their counterparts in other racial groups (Runnymede Trust and Radical Statistics Race Group, 1980; Brown, 1984; Field and Haikin, 1971; Hepple, 1968; Day, 1989). For example, the rate of unemployment for black people is higher than that of their white counterparts and black people are mostly concentrated in unskilled and semi-skilled jobs. Black families often reside in inner cities or ghetto areas and this certainly introduces an element of educational disadvantage because these areas are worst served by the education system. And ultimately, as Donald (1956, p.42) points out, 'lack of education stands in the way of economic success and the achievement of social status...'. In relation to housing, the overall quality 'of the housing of black people is much worse than the quality of housing in general in this country' (Brown, 1984, p.305) since they are housed in the worst accommodation in deprived residential areas of the city.

One line of argument set out in the deprivation-criminality theory is that which emphasises the existence of fundamental defects in society and argues that society has failed to provide adequate societal institutions, and has through social injustice and unfair treatment been unable to equally distribute resources and satisfy the expectations and demands of certain groups of people (Benyon and

Solomos, 1987; Benyon, 1984; Cohen and Bains, 1988; Brown, 1984; Solomos, 1988a, 1988b). Consequently, the ethnic minority population 'occupy a marginal role in education, employment and other spheres of social and economic life' (Cross, 1982, p.35). Brown's view that the circumstances of black people in all spheres of life 'continue to be worse than that of white people' (1984, p.315) is explained in relation to the social injustice that exists within societal institutions:

> First, it is clear that racialism and direct racial discrimination continue to have a powerful impact on the lives of black people. Second, the position of the black citizens of Britain largely remains, geographical and economically, that allocated to them as immigrant workers in the 1950s and 1960s. Third, it is still the case that the organisations and institutions of British society have policies and practices that additionally disadvantage black people because they frequently take no account of the cultural differences between groups with different ethnic origins (ibid., p.318).

Scarman (1981, 1982) shares a similar view about racial discrimination when he described the Brixton riot of 1981 as a product of deprivation and acknowledged the negative impact of racial discrimination on the socio-economic life of black people. In providing the social background to the Brixton riot, he described the population of Brixton as being composed of a combination of a high proportion of deprived and vulnerable groups in the population as a whole, residing in an inner city area at its late stage of social and economic decay in the form of high unemployment levels, poor educational standard, appalling housing conditions, poor environment and lack of recreational facilities and so forth. This is a community mostly made up of unskilled and semi-skilled manual workers. This general deprivation is suffered most by ethnic minorities, especially, the black community of Brixton who experience higher rates of unemployment. Scarman (1981, para. 2.35) summarises the deprived circumstances of black people thus:

> ...overall they suffer from the same deprivation as the 'host community' (i.e the white population), but much more acutely. Their lives are led largely in the poorer and more deprived areas of our great cities. Unemployment and poor housing bear upon them very heavily; and the educational system has not adopted itself satisfactorily to their needs. Their difficulties have internalised by the sense they have of a concealed discrimination against them, particularly in relation to job opportunities and housing. Some young blacks are driven by their despair into feeling that they are rejected by the society of which they would wish to enjoy the same

opportunities and accept the same risks as everyone else. But their experience leads them to believe that their opportunities are less and their risks are greater. Young people feel neither socially nor economically secure.

The argument that racial discrimination in the education system affects black people's educational life has been used to dispute the assertion that black people are educationally under-achieving (Carby, 1982; Field and Haikin, 1971). To Carby (1982, p.205) the 'educational policy and practice actually constitutes black children as an alien group that present "problems" that are external to "normal schooling"'. Field and Haikin (1971, p.65) further add:

> The fault does not of course lie in any ineducability in the children themselves. The sad fact is that, if a child attending school in this country today is coloured, there is a high probability that the child will also fall into the category of educationally underprivileged or deprived children.

The scenario outlined by interpretations that focus on societal dysfunction is that of a likelihood of criminal behaviour stemming principally from deprivation (Scarman, 1981, 1987). This argument predicated upon Mertonian and Marxist frameworks, and echoing the views of the Chicago School depicts the deplorable socio-economic condition of certain individuals as produced by external forces beyond their control. According to this line of thought, individuals who find themselves pressurised by their position in the social structure inevitably stray from conventional lifestyles. Marxists, Mertonians and Chicagoans uphold that deprivation is synonymous with crime, and view the difference in socio-economic circumstances in the context of factors created by the malfunctioning of the social structure. From a Marxist perspective, society cannot attain a state of equilibrium if the social system fails to distribute resources equitably and accordingly, criminal behaviour is explained within the realm of the political and economic structure of society - in the form of capitalism - which creates deprivation and poverty and in turn lead to crime (Reid, 1979; Haralambos and Holborn, 1990). High levels of unemployment, for instance, emerge from a breakdown in the material structure of a capitalist society - resulting to crime. Merton (1957) also argues that crime emerges when the social order is incapable of providing opportunities for people to enhance their life chances or improve their status. Limited legitimate avenues of achieving conventional success, solidified by a class structure, explain the choice of illicit means to economic success among members of the lower socio-economic class:

Of those located in the lower reaches of the social structure, the culture makes incompatible demands. On the one hand, they are asked to orient their conduct toward the prospect of large wealth...and on the other, they are largely denied effective opportunities to do so institutionally. The consequence of this structural inconsistency is a high rate of deviant behaviour (ibid., p.146).

The Chicago School attributes criminal behaviour to the economically peripheral sections of society - the inhabitants of city areas referred to by the Chicagoans as the 'transitional zone'. This zone, mostly occupied by the immigrant population, is characterised by weak social organisation and harbours poverty, crime and delinquency (Carey, 1978; Downes and Rock, 1988; Haralambos and Holborn, 1990). Deficient social organisation originates principally from structural and cultural circumstances (such as high levels of population turnover, unstable standards of life, weak social control and diversity in values) which lead to high levels of unemployment, poverty and crime.

'Black criminality' theory favours the view that crime lend itself most commonly to poor life conditions and social problems in lower class areas (Cloward and Ohlin, 1961; Clinard, 1968; Miller, 1986). That the black community suffer an adverse and complex form of deprivation not experienced by other racial groups, and reside in inner cities characterised by economic, social and physical degeneration, is stressed as a fundamental cause of their criminality. Lea and Young have argued that 'black people have a higher crime rate than would be expected from their numbers as a proportion of the population' (1984, p.165), and add that the black community are more likely to commit crimes than other racial groups because they are economically disadvantaged and also experience racial discrimination. Pitts (1986, p.121) acknowledges the direct relationship between 'black criminality' and economic deprivation in his observation that crimes committed by blacks are opportunistic in nature, often 'concerned with procuring small amounts of money - what have been described as crimes of poverty'. According to Pitts (ibid., p.143), 'young black people who live in the most crowded homes, whose parents have the lowest income, who go to under-resourced schools and have the poorest educational and employment opportunities, are engaged in crimes of poverty'. Scarman (1981, para. 2.23) observes that it is the social and economic circumstances of young black people that force them out in the street and into the 'seedy commercially run clubs of Brixton'; it is there that they meet 'criminals, who appear to have no difficulty in obtaining the benefits of a materialist society'. Box and Hale (1986) also note that during periods of increasing unemployment, economic and social deprivation are more severely felt by the young and ethnic minority groups and many amongst these already reside in declining inner cities. Unemployment, they add, falls heaviest on the black population, especially, the black youth, and the likelihood is that those who suffer acute deprivation and economic deprivation in particular would find crime an alternative means of survival.

The supposed disproportionate black involvement in crime has also been highlighted by further attempts to analyse 'black criminality' in relation to certain forms of disadvantage believed to be relative to the black population (Gilroy, 1987a; Solomos, 1988a; Cohen and Bains, 1988). Instead of prioritising racial discrimination or failure of social policies to accommodate black people's needs, this line of argument pinpoints the impact of racial disadvantage on the lives of black people by focusing on, for instance, weak family structure, language difficulties and educational underachievement as fundamental preconditions of 'black deprivation' (Lea and Young, 1984; John, 1980, 1981; Cashmore and Troyna, 1982) and subsequent involvement in crime. This approach places the blame for deprivation on the deprived by portraying the various problems experienced by black people as originating from certain inadequacies and incapacities relative to the black community. It is argued that those who are deprived are unable or unwilling to provide adequately for their well-being and on this basis, neither political arrangements nor society in general are accountable for the deprivation suffered by such people. Black people are therefore blamed for causing their own handicaps and creating their own socio-economic conditions which in turn have reproduced poverty and deprivation, thereby making them victims of their own circumstances. This approach is referred to as 'blaming the victim' (Ryan, 1976) or 'social pathology'. Ryan has claimed that this individualistic approach is often used to hide the injustices suffered by the deprived in society.

Amidst the ascribed handicaps, the black family has received a very strong criticism for inadequate socialisation of black youth and subsequent black youth involvement in unlawful acts (Cross, 1982). 'Black criminality' is viewed as an expression of a family breakdown and pathological character of black families (Lea and Young, 1984; Humphrey and John, 1971; Pitts, 1993). The issue of a single parent, most times, the failure of the family to instil fatherly responsibility in the black males, has notably been thought to explain the likelihood of young black males engaging in all sorts of criminal activities, hence the increased vulnerability to arrest. Cashmore and Troyna (1982) reveal similar view in the account that a lack of social control exerted by the West Indian family, due historically to the fragmentation of the family structure in slavery, leads to a greater black youth involvement with the police. Black families make up the highest percentage of one-parent households (Hall, 1989) headed by black women (Chigwada, 1991) and the popular ideology is that as single parents, black women violate the traditional English family norms, thereby paving the leeway for their young ones to be crime prone (ibid.). The relationship between the assumed deficiencies in the social organisation of black people and the supposed black involvement in crime has a bearing on what Gilroy (1987a) referred to as the 'biological culturalism of conservative explanation'.

Looking at the 'deprivation-black criminality' link from a cultural perspective is the notion that black deprivation stems from black people's cultural beliefs which presumably do not emphasise upward mobility values (Sherman and Wood, 1979). Again, the black population are perceived as having linguistic problems and being educationally underachieving (Hiro, 1992; Hall, 1989; Solomos, 1988a, 1988b). Whilst Asians who, like black people, came to Britain with similar expectations made their way into the commercial sphere and advanced educationally, black people show apathy towards education and employment (Cashmore and Troyna, 1982). Failure at school and the lack of interest in education culminated in what Cashmore and Troyna (ibid., p.4) describe as:

> successive rounds of unqualified school-leavers recruited to the lower
> orders of the occupational world or registered with the Department
> of Employment. The 'twilight activities' of thieving and hustling are
> seen by some as 'strategies of survival', almost inevitable alternatives
> to mainstream existence.

Whether the marginalised position of black people is self-inflicted or originates in socio-economic forces beyond their control, the identification of black people with crime is perceived as a consequence of their membership of a disadvantaged group. Their peripheral position in society is popularly believed to make them more likely to resort to crime if they are unable to fulfil their aspirations through legitimate channels.

Policing and Arrest

> Being young, male, black, unemployed and economically
> disadvantaged are all associated with a higher probability of being
> stopped, searched, arrested, charged, making complaints against the
> police (especially of assault), and failing to have these complaints
> substantiated (Reiner, 1985, p.128).

That black people are over-represented more than other racial groups in the criminal statistics has been attributed to police use of discriminatory practices against them. This explanation is equally shared by studies which view the problem of disproportion within the realm of 'black criminality' and deprivation. According to Stevens and Willis (1979), the overrepresentation of black people in the arrest rate is partly due to differential rates of offending - attributed to the socio-economic deprivation faced by black people, the age-profile of the black population and police discrimination. Lea and Young's (1984, p.167) evidence also point in a similar direction - relating the disproportionate black arrest rate to two key factors: 'increased...black crime and police predisposition to associate blacks with crime'. In Reiner's (1985, p.132) observation, 'it seems clear that the disproportionate black arrest rate is the product of black deprivation, police stereotyping and the process by which each of these factors amplifies the other'.

Black people face a greater chance of being stopped, arrested and charged by the police than other racial groups (particularly whites) (Hiro, 1992; Smith and Gray, 1985; Willis, 1983; Benyon, 1986; Dholakia and Sumner, 1993; Smith, 1994; Norris et al., 1992; Walker et al., 1990) somewhat on the basis of police assumption rather than evidence (Smith and Gray, 1985). A police officer's decision to 'arrest, warn, caution, assist...a suspect' is not simply made 'by taking into account the legal facts of a case' (Box, 1981, p.171). Box adds:

> he has to introduce other criteria: these usually reflect his personal values, beliefs and prejudices, and those of the social group with whom he identifies. It is the covert and routine introduction of non-legalistic considerations that raises the issue of bias, for they normally influence the police-suspect encounter in such a way that lower strata suspects are frequently arrested (ibid.).

Smith and Gray (1985) draw attention to how the police associate black people with crime and, *inter alia*, view their deprived socio-economic condition as a symptom of their criminality. A popular police conception of black people is that of a poverty stricken, disorganised and alienated group, usually on the way to committing a crime (ibid.); their residential areas are perceived by the police as crime ridden (Institute of Race Relations, 1979; Blom-Cooper and Drabble, 1982). It becomes a self-fulfilling prophecy when people who fit the stereotype of likely offenders are indiscriminately harassed, arrested, prosecuted and so forth resulting in a vicious cycle of deviance amplification (Young, 1971). Those areas of deprivation attract saturation policing (Demuth, 1978), and as Cain and Sadigh (1982) state, offences that arise out of proactive policing bring many black people before the court. Therefore, the difference in offences for which blacks and whites are charged is possibly 'brought about by differential patrolling and charging practices on the part of the police' (Cain and Sadigh, 1982, p. 88). Police charging practices demonstrate less likelihood of blacks receiving a police caution than their white counterparts; instead, blacks are more likely to be charged even as first offenders and whites with more previous convictions than blacks are more likely to be cautioned by the police (Landau, 1981; Landau and Nathan, 1983). Steven's and Willis' study on *Race, Crime and Arrests* (1979) had earlier shown evidence of police bias in arrest. Although the researchers were careful coming to a definite conclusion, they highlighted that arrest rates for black people were so disproportionately high as to raise the question of whether black arrest rates actually reflected their involvement in crime. Whilst their findings suggest the role of police discriminatory practices, there are also suggestions that the demographic profile of the black population (black people have a young age profile) and their disproportionate representation among the lower socio-economic group equally account for their involvement in crime.

Complaints have been made by blacks (mostly young) about police antagonistic and discriminatory behaviour towards them (Smith and Gray, 1983; Solomos, 1988a; Jefferson, 1991). Solomos (1988a, p.95) pinpoints:

> First, complaints by young blacks that they were being categorised as a 'problem group' by the police, and that they were therefore more likely to be questioned or arrested. Second, allegations that the police used excessive physical violence in their dealings with black suspects. Third, it was argued that such attitudes and forms of behaviour by the police were helping to fuel popular rumours about the involvement of young blacks in crime, and to drive a wedge between the police and the black communities (also see Solomos, 1993).

Such police attitude towards the black community was expressed by the Institute of Race Relations (1979) when it called attention to the use of unnecessary violence by the police on black people, several cases of arbitrary arrests of black people made by the police and how certain arms of the police force sometimes overstep their boundaries, for example, the involvement of the Special Patrol Group (SPG) in indiscriminate stop-and-search activities in inner cities with the principal intention of arresting black people - leading to a high proportion of black arrests for obstructing and assaulting the police. In 1981, the final report of the Working Party on Community/Police Relations in Lambeth stated that the London Borough of Lambeth always remained the prime target for such SPG attacks carried out on the people of Lambeth between 1975 - 1979, and each time the SPG tactics followed a similar pattern - road blocks, early morning raids on black people's homes, random and aggressive street checks. Hunte's (1966) *Nigger Hunting in England* which concentrated specifically on the London Borough of Lambeth had earlier cited numerous cases of police discrimination against black people which included racist abuse of black people by the police, intentional harassment on black people's social life and overall police criminalisation of black people. Gus John's (1970) report on *Race and the Inner City* further described the relationship between the police and blacks in Handsworth (Birmingham) as suffering from a massive breakdown, and attributed the appalling relationship to the racist behaviour of the police - characterised by their constant suspicion of all black people, the over-policing of black areas and the use of the 'Sus' law to initiate arrests.

The use of the 'Sus' charge as 'an essential aid to deterrence and the prevention of more serious offences as part of the vital need to defend the streets from the rising amount of crime' (Roberts, 1982, p.108) was, some argue, an area of police discrimination against black people (Philips, 1976; Solomos, 1993). The 'Sus' law and its implementation was one instance in which any black youth was assumed to be criminally inclined (Gilroy, 1982a), and such suspicion warranted an 'unlawful and racially prejudiced conduct of police officers' (Gordon, 1983). Arrest figures for 'Sus' reveal that blacks, unlike whites, were more frequently arrested, for example, in 1975, the Metropolitan Police District arrest figures for 'Sus' according to ethnic group showed that blacks formed 40.4 per cent of all 'suspected person' arrests; of the total 2,112 persons arrested in 1976 for 'Sus' in the MPD, blacks made up 42 per cent of this figure; in 1977 and 1978, 44 per cent and 43 per cent of 'Sus' arrests respectively, were of black people (Roberts, 1982). Demuth (1978) in her survey based on information derived from 170 'Sus' cases involving 299 defendants noted that certain areas were prime targets for 'Sus' arrests. These areas referred to as high crime areas and mostly inhabited by black people are classed as decaying inner-city localities characterised by high levels of unemployment and poverty. Police assumption that 'black criminality' is synonymous with these images has warranted increased police power and activity which is more prominent with an increase in unemployment (Benyon, 1984). An increase in policing in turn leads to a high increase in reported and recorded crimes (ibid.).

Areal association between crime and black settlements has remained common: various crimes, especially, street crimes are attributed to inner city localities like Brixton (London) - an area particularly viewed by the police as 'unique' due to its alleged violent street crime (Blom-Cooper and Drabble, 1982). In 1980, for example, when the number of serious offences in the Lambeth district was 30,805, Brixton alone had 10,626 (ibid.) and the assumed high crime rate in this area was thought to justify saturation policing (ibid.). It has been argued that over-policing in itself generates crime in as much as certain crimes come into existence with the presence of the police, that is, crimes that never occurred and never would have occurred prior to police arrival (Cain and Sadigh, 1982; Pitts, 1986). In a sense, saturation policing does not necessarily have anything to do with the detection and prevention of crime in black areas rather it involves an ongoing process whereby the police escalate black arrest rates and make criminals of groups of black people (Humphrey, 1972).

High-profile policing was applicable to the period of violent street crimes when blacks were ambiguously defined as potential muggers, and black localities were classed as principal centres of violent street crime (Hall et al., 1978). Official statistics at the time revealed that blacks made up a high number of those convicted of mugging offences (ibid.). Subsequent crime statistics showed an overrepresentation of black people in violent crimes such as robbery and other violent theft (Home Office, 1983, 1984). Such official crime statistics have been criticised as a fabrication or construction of police prejudice which is seen as being consistent with the subjection of blacks to false attributions of criminality (Gilroy, 1987b). This is justified with claims that police discretionary practices in categorising and recording offences constitute an amplifying factor in crime statistics for blacks: minor charges brought against blacks are framed, exaggerated and treated more seriously (Humphrey and John, 1971); charges such as petty theft and handbag snatching are sometimes recorded as 'mugging' with the offenders viewed in the same light (Hall et al., 1978); and the police have been known to record as black in cases where the victim was unsure of the race of the attacker. Gordon (1983) cites a case of a victim of mugging who told a TV journalist that she had been attacked from the back and was too shocked to see her assailant but the police had recorded the assailant as black. Another justification is that white victims of such crimes are less likely to hesitate to report the crimes to the police when offenders are black (Bottoms, 1967; Bottomley and Pease, 1986), and where there is uncertainty about the racial identity of an offender, there is more likelihood of claiming that he is 'coloured' rather than white (Sparks et al.,1977). Although white youths were involved in mugging (Ramsay, 1982) and mugging escalated in areas with no recognisable number of black people, the impression that blacks and mugging are interlinked had been deeply rooted in both official and public consciousness (Hall et al., 1978). As Solomos (1988a, p.117) asserts:

the phenomenon of street crime particularly mugging was a symbol
of a broader process through which young blacks were constructed
both in policy and popular discourses as caught up in a vicious circle
of unemployment, poverty, homelessness, crime and conflict with
the police. This was encapsulated in Enoch Powell's statement in
1976 that mugging was a 'racial crime', with black youth as the
main actors.

Indeed the social construction of the issue of mugging, 'black crime' and black youth as being permanently linked was popularised by media coverage, public debates and official reports, and the image of criminal areas with all the characteristics of deprivation obtained an obvious racial dimension within the official arena (Solomos, 1988a). Two decades after the emergence of the mugging phenomenon in the 1970s, the terms - mugging and 'black crime' - remain synonymous as evident in the extensive media coverage, political and official debates on mugging that followed Sir Paul Condon's public statement in 1995 that a significant proportion of those arrested during Operation Eagle Eye (a drive against street crime) were young black males.

It was as a police response to street crime that Operation SWAMP 81 came about in Brixton (Cashmore and McLaughlin, 1991). The purpose of the operation was to detect and arrest violent criminals. Part of the instruction given to the large numbers of uniformed and plain clothes police officers dispatched to Brixton reads:

> The purpose of this operation is to flood identified areas on L district
> to detect and arrest burglars and robbers. The essence of the exercise
> is therefore to ensure that all officers remain on the streets and
> success will depend on a concentrated effort...based on power of
> surveillance and suspicion proceeded by persistent and astute
> questioning (Lea and Young, 1982, p.63).

The aftermath of SWAMP 81 was the 1981 Brixton riot (Cashmore and McLauglin, 1991) which to black people was precipitated by constant police harassment of the black community (Scarman, 1982). Whilst the underlying conditions were popularly related to political, social and economic deprivation experienced by the black community (Benyon and Solomos, 1987; Scarman, 1981; Roberts, 1984), others explained the riot in a biological context. Clare (1984, p.52) quoted Sir Kenneth Newman in the American *Police Magazine* as stating: 'In the Jamaicans, you have people who are constitutionally disorderly. It's simply in their make-up. They are constitutionally disposed to anti-authority'.

However, the purpose of the operation which was to arrest violent criminals was not achieved: most arrests (which were basically the outcome of stop-and-search activities) made by the police were for non-violent crimes such as possession of cannabis, obstructing police, insulting behaviour and carrying an offensive weapon (Pitts, 1986; Blom-Cooper and Drabble, 1982). Whilst few arrests were made for snatch thefts and so forth, virtually none was made for robbery or burglary (Blom-Cooper and Drabble, 1982).

Allegations of police bias against black people, including brutality and general ill-treatment, have been denied by the police who have defended their operational methods as being important and useful to combat crime and effect general crime prevention, especially, in areas with a 'high crime' rate (Humphrey, 1972; Gordon, 1983, Jefferson, 1988). A similar allegation brought against the police for indiscriminately using the 'Sus' law to arrest black people has also been denied (Gordon, 1983). Instead, the police have argued that the over-representation of black people in the 'Sus' figure was due to their greater involvement in crime and so disproportionately came to the attention of the police (Roberts, 1982). Claims have been made by the police that black people are frustrated and tend to vent their frustration, anger and hostile feelings, which originate from their deprived conditions, on the police (Simpson, 1969). Such claims have also referred to black people as hostile, aggressive, abusive and insolent towards the police. Humphrey (1972, p.221) states, 'it is now almost textbook knowledge in police circles that West Indians are argumentative, rowdy, excitable and arrogant' (also see Gordon, 1983; Jefferson, 1988; Pitts, 1986). Similarly, Keith (1991, p.193) cites Banton (1972) as noting:

> West Indians are sometimes regarded as more difficult to deal with, being disputatious and very ready to register complaints against the police. They are also regarded as more violent than English men.

According to Chigwada (1991, p.139), black women, unlike their white counterparts, are believed by the police to be disruptive, aggressive and hostile - these attributes, the police feel, are consistent with their 'innate racial characteristics'.

Such racist beliefs identified as prevalent in the police force (Young, 1991; Graef, 1990) are upheld and reinforced in other racial stereotypes such as those which portray black people as dirty and filthy (Hiro, 1992). According to Hiro (1992, p.83), a 1981 study by Andrew Colman, a Psychology lecturer at Leicester University, not only showed that 'police recruits and probationers were significantly more conservative and authoritarian than the public at large and that racial attitudes of experienced officers were markedly illiberal', he cites a probationer as saying to Andrew Colman: 'fifty per cent of the trouble caused today is either by niggers or because of them. Most of them are just dirty, smelly people who will never change in a month of Sundays...'. Police bias and prejudice against black people is seen to be widespread as Reiner (1985, p.101) observes in his exploration of racial prejudice within the police force. He quotes a uniformed police constable as saying: 'the police are trying to appear unbiased in regard to race relations. But if you asked them you'd find 90 per cent of the force are against coloured immigrants. They'd never want you to do that research and come up with that sort of finding'.

Much evidence point to police bias and discrimination as resulting to black people's subjection to police malpractice and brutality, the confinement of saturation stop-and-search practices to black communities and above all, the indiscriminate police arrest of blacks and the resultant disproportionate appearance of this racial group before the court as well as their overall high representation in the criminal statistics.

The Court and its Practices

Much of the in-depth research studies of the courts and the disproportionate number of black people in the criminal statistics have focused on the sentencing patterns of the courts. Except for the limited data which reveal the disproportionate presence of black people in the conviction rate, no detailed account appears to exist regarding the link between conviction or acquittal decisions made by the courts and the overrepresentation of black people in the criminal statistics. Findings have merely shown that black people are more likely than other racial groups to be convicted (Hood, 1992; Hudson, 1989; Dholakia and Sumner, 1993) or that their acquittal rate on the basis of insufficient evidence is more likely to be higher (Walker, 1987, 1988). In any case, a notable claim is that blacks receive little justice when their cases appear before the court (Cain and Sadigh, 1982; Smellie and Crow, 1991; Gordon, 1983; Smith, 1994; Agozino, 1997) which have also been substantiated with evidence of complaints made by black people about the disparate treatment embedded within the court system (King and May, 1985). In Smellie and Crow's (1991) account, blacks envisage the possibility of receiving a hostile court response at any time they appear in court, and as defendants, their confidence in the court system is lost. Blacks, suggest Smellie and Crow, are surrounded by nervousness, confusion while expecting the possibility of a severe sentence - on the basis of their race.

Research studies of court disposal of defendants according to race have, nevertheless, produced mixed findings. Whilst some studies have disclosed that differential treatment permeates the court system, others have given a different picture which has portrayed the court as adopting similar sentencing patterns for different racial groups (McConville and Baldwin, 1982; Crow and Cove, 1984; Moxon, 1988). Based on their survey on *The Influence of Race on Sentencing in England*, McConville and Baldwin (1982, p.658) hold that the judicial system does not permit such variables as race to influence sentencing decisions. In conclusion they note:

> What emerges from our analysis is a single, tentative but important finding: that there appears to be no evidence of direct, systematic bias on racial lines in sentencing in the crown court. The implication is that defendants are treated equally once they attain the status of convicted persons: not necessarily fairly or appropriately, but equally.

Like McConville and Baldwin, Crow and Cove (1984) observe that the racial background of defendants do not determine the courts' sentencing decisions. After conducting a research on *Ethnic Minorities and the Courts* in London, the Midlands and the North, they conclude:

> The present study is re-assuring as far as it goes, in suggesting that once they appear in court, whether juvenile, magistrates or crown court, offenders from different minority groups who are convicted are treated equally. This may serve to contribute to the development of confidence amongst ethnic minorities (p.417).

McConville and Baldwin have indicated that although injustice or bias in sentencing does not exist in the courts, racism could be practised at other stages of the criminal justice process for example, 'in connection with policing, arrest patterns, bail status or jury selection' (1982, p.658).

Other studies have produced indications of unequal treatment in the courts, which as already noted, is usually reflected in the trend of sentencing. The view is that when cases involving both black and white defendants are considered, the sentencing pattern is to the disadvantage of black defendants who are more likely to receive a custodial sentence than white counterparts (Dholakia and Sumner, 1993). This observation applies to juvenile courts (Tipler, 1985), magistrates' courts and Crown Courts (Hudson, 1989; Walker, 1987, 1988; Hood, 1992). When important sentencing criteria such as type and severity of offence, previous convictions and so forth are taken into account, black defendants, unlike their white counterparts, have less chances of receiving other sentencing options such as a conditional discharge and a probation order, but more frequently receive a custodial sentence (Voakes and Fowler, 1989; Hudson, 1989; Runnymede Trust, 1990). Whilst white defendants receive probation or fines for offences similar to those committed by black defendants, the latter receive community service or a custodial sentence instead (Hudson, 1989). Hudson (1993, p.10) adds: 'one of the undisputed facts about race and criminal justice is that black offenders are less likely than their white counterparts to be made the subject of probation orders'. This claim had earlier been made by probation officers (Whitehouse, 1978). Hood's (1992) findings that black offenders are less likely to have social inquiry reports prepared on them and less likely to be recommended for probation than whites contradicts earlier observations made by probation officers that the non-placement of black defendants on supervision, as an alternative to incarceration, does not emerge from social inquiry reports and recommendations made on them (Inner London Probation Service, 1982). West Indians in particular, the Inner London Probation Service claims, are more likely to receive recommendations for supervision but in spite of that, they are still more likely than whites to receive a custodial sentence. A survey conducted by the West Midlands Probation Service in 1986 argues that although white defendants had a higher proportion of the serious offences (for example, murder, robbery, sexual offences, assault/wounding) than black defendants, the latter were less likely than the former to be placed under supervision or fined. Non-custodial recommendations were made in 90 per cent and 86 per cent of the reports written on black and white defendants respectively, however, more than half of the recommendations on blacks were not followed; for whites, less than half of the recommendations were not adhered to, resulting in blacks receiving more custodial sentences. In all cases where there were no recommendations on black defendants, a custodial sentence was given, but not all white defendants that had no recommendations made on them received a custodial sentence. The survey further reveal that black defendants were more likely to get a custodial sentence at once and also more likely to get a suspended sentence (West Midlands Probation Service, 1987).

When past criminal record is taken into consideration, white defendants on average have more previous convictions than black defendants (Hudson, 1989), however, black defendants with fewer previous convictions are more likely to be imprisoned than white defendants with strings of worse criminal offences (Voakes and Fowler, 1989; Day, 1989). In relation to offence seriousness, Hudson (1989) notes how black defendants receive more custodial sentences than whites for offences which can be considered as minor. Although Hudson observes that factors such as age and other social circumstances could determine the difference in custody rates, she suggests that injustice still surfaces, especially, with the ordinary offences against the person and minor robbery offences. Hood's study on *Race and Sentencing* (1992), which observes that 56.6 per cent of black offenders sentenced by the courts were given a custodial sentence compared with 39.6 per cent of Asians and 48.4 per cent of whites, further shows that there is a race effect in sentencing in some circumstances independent of other factors such as black defendants being more likely to enter a not guilty plea and opt for trial at the Crown Court where there is a high possibility of a custodial sentence. This observation had earlier been made by Walker (1988) although subsequent studies have also related the high imprisonment rate for black people to a likelihood of being tried and sentenced at the Crown Court for offences triable on indictment (Jefferson and Walker, 1990; Brown and Hullin, 1992; Hood, 1992; Smith, 1994) which places black defendants in a more likely position of being convicted of offences which more easily attract a custodial sentence (Hudson, 1989; Hood, 1992). Nevertheless, it has been claimed that black defendants are more likely to be committed to stand trial at the Crown Court (Dholakia and Sumner, 1993; Smellie and Crow, 1991) - even when cases are triable either way (Home Office, 1992).

This discrepancy has been known to occur at the point of remand decisions which work to the disadvantage of black defendants who are more likely to be refused bail and remanded in custody pending trial (Home Office, 1989a, 1992; Shalice and Gordon, 1990). The proportion of black defendants remanded in custody by the magistrates to stand trial at the Crown Court (Walker, 1988; Home Office, 1989a; Day, 1989; Hood, 1992) and those on police remands (Walker, 1988) are higher than of white defendants. This racial disparity occurs in the magistrates' courts 'even when seriousness of offence and other relevant factors are taken into account' (Home Office, 1992, p.15). Even when fewer black defendants are granted bail by magistrates, they are more frequently placed on conditional bail (Gordon, 1983; Runnymede Trust, 1990).

The courts' sentencing practices are further characterised by a response to economic crisis which means that during periods of economic recession, the unemployed or those in the lower stratum tend to be perceived by those in positions of power as potentially or actually disruptive and as having the capabilities of destabilising the social system by committing a crime (Box and Hale, 1986). Accordingly, the courts are empowered to use coercive means (that is, imprisonment) when necessary to restrain and control those who disrupt society through criminal behaviour. More often than not, the unemployed and socio-economically deprived face liability of punishment and penal severity (Hudson, 1996). In studies of black people and criminal justice, the socio-economic factor has formed a notable subject. Variables such as unemployment and homelessness have been known to have a direct bearing on sentencing, bail and prosecutorial decisions (Box and Hale, 1986; McBarnet, 1983; Carlen, 1988; Crow and Simon, 1987; NACRO, 1993a). Once an offender is unemployed, the court visualises the possibility of such an offender committing further crimes and will pass a custodial sentence as punishment. Chigwada (1989, p.104) states:

> Sentencers often take into account employment status when determining which sentence to impose. Employment increases the chances of avoiding custody, as the courts do not wish to jeopardise income. Similarly housing situations are also considered. However, bad housing has been found to cause depression which can result in sentencing to psychiatric hospitals.

In like manner, defendants with no employment are more likely to be subjected to custody on remand (Crow and Simon, 1987; McBarnet, 1983; Matthews and Young, 1986). This sentencing practice mostly affect black people who form a large section of the unemployed. As Taylor (1982) states, black defendants in the Crown Court are three times more likely than whites to receive a custodial sentence principally because they experience high levels of unemployment and usually have no fixed home address.

Evidence of discriminatory practices of the court is not only reflected in sentencing practices and remand decisions. In a study by Cain and Sadigh (1982, p.93), they point out 'the possibility of institutionalised and hidden racism among court officials, and the reasonableness of black defendants who claim that the courts are prejudiced against them'. Their findings show that court cases involving black defendants were intentionally allocated by the list office to the magistrates reported as being 'tough' and noted for using abusive language and for not granting bail. They added that the various attitudes of the magistrates included in their research were universal and applicable to all defendants irrespective of race but the situation could have been interpreted by blacks as racist.

Explaining the Discrepancies: An Alternative Approach

The approach adopted in my analysis of the specific problem of the disproportion- ate presence of black people in the criminal statistics for drug offences is a departure from those so far employed in the explanatory accounts of the problem of disproportion in general. Rather than uncritically accept the existing explanations, this approach which focuses on the court,[1] has concerned itself with specific social processes which although have not received in-depth research, nonetheless, play a vital role in determining the production of criminal statistics.

In examining the role of the court on the overrepresentation of black people in the criminal figures, research studies have neglected a significant area of the criminal justice process - the trial process. Little or no light has been cast on the whole processing of cases in court from the point that a defendant appears for trial or hearing to the stage of conviction or acquittal. Instead of exclusively concerning ourselves with sentencing which represents the greatest part of research in this area, this approach explores how collective forms of human actions characterise the conviction or acquittal forming process. The problem of disproportion of black people in prison may become intelligible at the point of conviction. The approach adopted here locates the study within a theoretical perspective which analyses rather than obscures the court process: it gives prominence to the beginning and end of a case prior to sentencing and examines how legal members participate in the production of a 'case' outcome through the process of *claims-making*.

The conviction or acquittal forming process takes place within the court - an arena where 'the conflicting claims of diverse groups are presented and resolved' (Quinney, 1970, p.139). For the explicit purpose that the court serves, it requires a host of occupational roles for its existence and functioning. The court is bureaucratically organised and each role, though specific and distinct, operates in relation to others. Only authorised members occupy role positions and specific structured positions from which they can speak or remain mute, question or be questioned, authorise or be authorised. It is through the diverse but collective work of authorised members that drug trials are heard. We are concerned with the legal work roles and claims-making activities of legal members in the court process. We have the prosecution who demands that a defendant be adjudged responsible for an alleged drug offence; the defence, on the other hand, claims that the defendant is innocent. Such claims-making process is supervised and guided by the judge (and the magistrate in the lower court) who, for instance, undertakes the sentencing decision once a guilty verdict is defined in the court. In the Crown Court, the jury, individuals drawn from different ranks of society, play a fundamental role in the process for its decision determines the outcome of a case. Cases are presented by lawyers, 'stories' are told about the arrest of defendants, varied decisions are made by the judge (the magistrate in the lower court) and jury based on the information produced in court; legal actors respond to each other's statements and actions, and they employ their theories in the construction of 'criminal reality'. This process reveals what Best (1987) describes as the dynamics of claims-making.

In the process of claims-making, race remains a vital element. This study represents an inquiry towards an understanding of the role of race during events that take place in the court process, and how race affects the production of events which subsequently create the problem of disproportion. In describing how race is reconstructed in court and how the problem of disproportion may arise, a comparative analysis of how the court process operates vis-à-vis defendants of two racial backgrounds - black and white - is considered vital. From my observations of drug offence trials, these two racial groups of defendants do not have their cases perceived and dealt with in a similar manner in the sense that legal members concerned with the processing of drug offence cases act in ways that are detrimental to black defendants. This disparity does not necessarily lie in the offence type or offence seriousness, neither does it bear any relevance to the socio-economic and criminal characteristics of the defendants and so forth. These factors, even when similar in black and white defendants' cases, are not accorded a similar degree of significance in the assessment of a case. This is not to say that legal actors are not guided by the formal rules of the criminal procedure which outline what lawyers and judges (and magistrates) are legally allowed to do. This fact is not to be ignored because the legal rules and procedures are there and it is upon them that they act (McConville et al., 1991), however, as McConville et al. (ibid.) point out, criminal cases are constructed in the utilisation, manipulation and interpretation of legal rules. Cooney (1994, p.838) quotes Lafree (1989) as stating:

> In actual practice, evidence is not a fixed commodity but a purposefully constructed set of documents, testimony, and material objects.

This indicates that legal evidence is not devoid of social effects and so is able to have a discriminatory influence in court cases. It is the lack of uniformity in the way in which cases concerning black and white defendants are defined (legally) that is the burning issue.

Discrepancy on the basis of race surfaces in the social construction of drug cases in the courtroom - whereby racially imbued knowledge, stereotypes and ideologies permeate the discourses of drug trials and inform the presentation of the defendants' cases. The language in use in court subtly represent racial elements implicit in the wider society - pertaining to black and white racial groups. Although the existing literature on the problem of disproportion does not altogether answer my question as to the reason behind the overrepresentation of blacks, and not whites, in the criminal statistics, much of it is relevant to my analysis of how the court process reproduces race as a category of criminality and consequently creates disproportion. On looking at strategies by which information about a drug offence case is constructed and communicated within the courtroom, and how such information is manipulated through language, we see how the various arguments raised in relation to the issue of disproportion are proliferated in the courtroom to fathom claims and counter claims regarding the probable guilt or innocence of a defendant. An instance is the popular argument which views illegal drug use and drug dealing (like crime in general) as outstandingly the preserve of the lower class and linked to deprivation (Parker et al., 1986; Haw, 1985; Hartnoll, 1989; Burr, 1987; Peck and Plant, 1986; Pearson et al., 1987; Dorn et al., 1992). In the courtroom, this dominant ideology is further propagated. We shall also see how studies of deprivation and 'black criminality' and other literature on the issue of overrepresentation bear resemblance to the language used by all participants - legal members and witnesses - during drug trials. These participants demonstrate an awareness of the existence and relevance of popular images of race, crime, drugs and criminal justice practices, and as it appears, such information implicitly gives justification and solidity to the assertions that they uphold in drug cases.

The analysis reveals that the guilt or innocence of a defendant is an outcome of social construction and in the first section of Chapter three, it sets out the theoretical framework which locates the social construction of an alleged drug offence within the process of claims-making whereby legal actors, in the process of interacting with each other and with victims of social control, inject their legally provided discretion and extra-legal aspects into the interpretation of black and white defendants' cases. The second section of Chapter three addresses the research methodology adopted. Chapter four introduces the prosecution and demonstrates with case studies the significance of race in the prosecution's grounds and justifications for a drug offence allegation. In Chapter five, the defence provides justifications for refuting a drug offence allegation and in the process, drug cases are differentially described and presented with race as an underlying element. Race also remains a vital factor in judges' (and magistrates') response to claims made by the prosecution and the defence in drug cases. Chapter six specifically illustrates how judicial response relegate black and white defendants to separate positions. Chapter seven concludes by summarising the social construction and claims-making activities of legal members; it then places the jury within the social construction process and examines what conditions the juries' decisions based on the varied pieces of evidence provided in court. In doing so, the overrepresentation of black people in the criminal statistics is put into perspective by highlighting the fundamental influence of indirect discrimination as an issue that needs to be addressed in criminal justice practices.

The following chapter will assist us in our understanding of the problem of disproportion in relation to drug offences. It discusses how the issue of drugs has been viewed for decades - and how legal restrictions on drugs slowly emerged. A description is given of how images of race became gradually absorbed into the discourses of drugs.

Note

1   Drug cases were observed at one Crown Court and one magistrates' court in London but the analysis derives its principal substance from information gathered at the Crown Court.

2 Drugs, Response and Race

The Development of Present Drug Controls

An examination of the history of drugs in the 18th and 19th centuries is a first step towards putting into perspective the contemporary drug problem, its control and the conceptions of drugs within the context of race. Usually, the debate on the present drug problem projects a distorted picture of its development and gives a limited insight into the conditions of its emergence. Whitaker (1969, p.10) was probably right when he noted that:

> In fact if pressed, most people without doubt would note that narcotic addiction is some contemporary perversion, an unfortunate by-product of 20th century progress, like air pollution or juvenile delinquency....Both the psychedelic cultists and the crusaders against the dope menace seem to be united on the assumption that the whole drug affair is something radically new and hitherto unheard of.

Pearson (1995, p.279) further observes

> Nineteenth-century Britain was therefore certainly not in a state of innocence about drug issues. Its notorious role in the Opium Wars and the promotion of opium markets in Southeast Asia is, in any case, legend.

Before restrictions and controls were attempted on opium use for instance, the opium poppy as indicated by Whitaker (1969) had been known to mankind for thousands of years (also see Stewart, 1987), although where its use first became known can no longer be exactly determined (Whitaker, 1969). Opium was widely used as a medical and recreational drug for centuries (Berridge and Edwards, 1981; Willis, 1973), and so were Indian hemp and leaf from coca bush (Deedes, 1970; Berridge and Edwards, 1981). The drug phenomenon eventually developed into a world-wide problem as reflected in the Indo-Chinese opium trade and the widespread consumption of opiate-type drugs in some western countries in the later half of the 19th century (Musto, 1973). What followed in subsequent years were international and national efforts to control the opium trade and drug use.

Contemporary legislation and policies relevant to drug control in Britain grew out of previous world-wide economic interest in the opium trade and later attempts in the 19th century to control drugs. By 1715 when Britain had taken over the opium trade from the Dutch, the British East India Company organised poppy cultivation in India for the Chinese market (Lindesmith, 1965). Criticisms were received by Britain for exporting opium to China but that made no change due to the high demand for opium and the deep involvement of Chinese officials in the profit making illicit traffic (ibid.). Prior to this period, China who has often been associated with opium smoking, only grew the poppy principally as an ornamental plant (Stimson and Oppenheimer, 1982; Inciardi and Chambers, 1974). Although all European powers with interest in the Far East were blamed for Chinese misery from opium addiction, the main responsibility for deliberately introducing opium to the Chinese fell more on Britain (Lindesmith, 1965; King, 1974; Stimson and Oppenheimer, 1982).

The market in opium was heightened in South Asia in the 19th century 'with the emergence of modern capitalism and its attendant need for labour, profits and international markets' (Lewis, 1985, p.17). As there grew an international demand for Chinese items such as silk, tea and spices, Britain was anxious to find a product that would trade for these items, and so offered opium, alongside gold and silver. Continuous efforts made by the Chinese authorities to suppress the trade pursued by Britain, led to the two opium wars (Willis, 1969) between 1839 and 1858 (Berridge and Edwards, 1981). Prior to this time, China had promulgated her first prohibitionary laws in 1729 against the sale and smoking of opium but 'despite efforts to control its usage, opium was extensively smuggled into China with the help of the British East India Company' (Stimson and Oppenheimer, 1982, p.14). The opium trade carried on throughout the 19th century due to Britain's insistence on continuing the trade in order to maintain her business interests.

Moving into the 20th century, the drug phenomenon witnessed a serious international involvement in the discussion on drug prohibition (Lindesmith, 1965). In 1909 an international opium conference, which was attended by the major European colonial powers, China, Japan and the United States of America (Britain only attended after pressure from America), was held in Shanghai to discuss anti-opium measures in the Far East (Hartnoll, 1989). The conference was largely initiated by the United States who had no economic interest in the opium trade unlike the major European colonial powers, and subsequently led to three conferences in Hague in 1911-12, 1913 and 1914 (Berridge, 1984). It was at the Hague Convention of 1912 (the most notable being the first International Opium Convention), to which Britain was one of the signatories, that the

European policy of gradual suppression of drug abuse (agreed at the 1909 Shanghai Conference) was implemented (Bean, 1974; Lindesmith, 1965) thus placing international drug trafficking under regulation. It was decided at the Hague Convention that the use of opium, morphine and cocaine be confined to legitimate medical purposes. China who advocated immediate and complete prohibition found this concession unfavourable as it was believed to result in a total government monopolisation of the legal production and distribution of opium by the European countries who were only concerned in raising revenue rather than solving the problem. The struggle still continued. But in the second world war period, government monopolies were eliminated and prohibition of opium smoking enforced in the Far East following, amidst other influences, pressure on colonial powers (with interest in the Far East) by the United States, the United Nations and the League of Nations (Lindesmith, 1965).

Although opiate use had infiltrated Britain by the 19th century, it principally served medical purposes. Cannabis, just like opium and morphine, was mainly adopted for medical practice (Deedes, 1970). These drugs, however, were also used recreationally by some sections in society, for example, western intellectuals. Berridge (1989, p.23) cites cases of the existence of opium use as far back as the 19th century. An instance was the use of 'opiates - chiefly laundanum, the camphorated tincture known as panegoric elixir, and raw opium, sold in pills and penny sticks' which were 'widely used both on medical prescription and, more usually, as self medication by those who had no access to medical treatment'. However, the use of opiates for whatever reason was normal and acceptable for much of the 19th century to those involved in the use and sale of the drug, and was viewed neither as a medical nor social problem but just a 'bad habit' primarily practised by respectable middle-class citizens.

Towards the later part of the 19th century, the spread in the use of opium amongst the working class in many cities in Britain became a matter for growing concern (Berridge and Edwards, 1981). It was then that the issue of drug controls began stressing the link between the drug and the drug taker. A different interpretation emerged which no longer viewed addiction as a habit but a problem due to the working class involvement in the consumption of opium, which was attributed to the ease at which such a drug could be procured even after the 1868 Pharmacy Act. The Pharmacy Act did put opium, cannabis and morphine under strict restrictions and legal controls thereby preventing their easy procurement over the counter but these drugs were still available since they could be bought from pharmacists without a prescription, and grocers still sold opium based patent medicines without restrictions (Berridge, 1989). The recreational use of opium by the working-class assisted in justifying the Act's first restriction on the drug (Berridge and Edwards, 1981). However, the 'disease' theory developed in the late nineteenth century by the medical profession to explain alcoholism was later applied principally to explain the middle-class addiction to opium - a view which called for treatment and cure involving gradual withdrawal and maintenance prescribing on low dosages of opiates. The drug habit amongst the middle class was more tolerable than it was within the working class whose addiction was blamed on the availability of drugs, and the cure focused on the need to curtail supplies.

This explains the class basis to the call for greater control over opiates by the medical profession who did not see the working class involvement in opiate use as a problem of habituation but a problem of drug use for recreational reasons. As Berridge and Edwards (1981, p.xxviii) note, 'the problem of opium use was in this sense the outcome of the class bias of Victorian society. It was in part a question of social control'. Similarly, Conrad and Schneider (1980, p.275) observe:

> As a particular kind of deviance becomes a middle-class rather than solely a lower-class "problem", the probability of medicalization increases. There seems to be a historical proclivity to define deviance that is thought endemic to lower-class life as badness, but when it becomes evident that it is also a middle class phenomenon, it is likely to be defined as sickness.... Similarly, when opiate addiction left the ghetto and became a middle-class problem in the late 1960s, there was a rapid increase in medicalization....In short, as public perceptions move from a lower-class problem to a middle- class problem, deviance designations tend to change from badness to sickness.

Other views were that the self-indulgence and recreational use of opiate was a vice, a deviance and a social problem meant to be eradicated through methods of penal control. The medical perception of drug use as a disease started losing its popularity in the early part of the 20th century and that was because the use of the law emerged as a remedy for the drug problem. The first step taken by the Home Office was to introduce Regulation 40B under the Defence of the Realm Act (DORA) 1916, which was geared towards controlling the trafficking and misuse of cocaine (Plant, 1987; Tyler, 1986). By the early part of the 20th century, Britain had started going through 'a cocaine tremor' (Tyler, 1986). Cocaine was quite common amongst prostitutes and service personnel during the first world war (Plant, 1987; Willis, 1973), however, recreational cocaine use in the British scene did not really develop fully until around 1916 and even then, its use was not widespread but limited to few areas of London. A good deal of cocaine use took place in aristocratic circles but the young working class, prostitutes and male criminals made up the street users (Tyler, 1986). But under the Defence of the Realm Regulation 40B (DORA 40B), the possession of cocaine was made illegal (with the exception of members of the medical, veterinary and pharmaceutical professions) unless prescribed by a doctor (Dorn et al., 1992). Yet, it was almost impossible to purchase cocaine other than through illegal means because unlike some other drugs like morphine, it was rarely prescribed by medical practitioners. Resorting to illicit cocaine use, in effect, made the lower-status section of the society more vulnerable to arrest and prosecution unlike the aristocrats or the middle class who had the connections to avoid law enforcement agencies. By the 1930s, the illicit drug scene in cocaine seemed to disappear, probably, due to the emergence of new types of drugs - such as barbiturates and amphetamines - in the drug market (Tyler, 1986). Amphetamines, a legal drug at the time, acted as a substitute for cocaine but by the 1950s, cocaine re-emerged into the drug scene and was made available through illegal trade, prescription by doctors, theft from hospital pharmacy and so forth.

The early 20th century was a remarkable period in the drug scene. Unlike previous times when laws were not made against drug use (Morris, 1989), it was the first time that the Home Office stepped into a territory that had previously seemed to be falling into the hands of the medical profession. The drug use issue was no longer viewed solely as a medical problem but a vice, a criminal problem that needed state and penal intervention. Britain's 1920 Dangerous Drugs Act (which was an extension of DORA) promulgated the criminalisation of drug use because of the move towards penal reaction, and laid the foundation for subsequent legislation. This Act which was primarily motivated by international commitment following the Hague Convention of 1912 conformed to the guidelines outlined by the Hague Convention and extended controls to cover drugs addressed at the convention. To possess (without a doctor's prescription), distribute or import cocaine, heroin and morphine became an offence (Dorn et al., 1992). America had already adopted the prohibitive system reflected in the Harrison Narcotics Act 1914 that only allowed medical prescribing of opiates by physicians (Stewart, 1987). These two Acts are similar as both were based on the Hague Convention and its decision to regulate opiate use (Glaser, 1974).

The British 1923 Dangerous Drugs and Poisons (Amendment) Act increased the penalties imposed by the courts for illegal possession and supply of drugs. In addition, police powers of search were increased. Meanwhile, members of the medical profession maintained that drug addiction was a disease as against the vice and social problem model of addiction pursued by the Home Office. In 1926, the Rolleston Committee (composed of members of the medical profession) Report, through its recommendations, finally established what became known as the 'British system' of maintenance prescribing for dealing with drug addiction. Doctors were allowed to prescribe maintenance doses of heroin, morphine and other dangerous drugs to addicted patients. At the same time, illegal possession of drugs was within the realm of the criminal law.

Race and Drugs : The Emergence of a New Drug Perspective

Drug use developed another meaning in Britain in the late 1940s and in the 1950s with the arrival of West Indian (and Asian) immigrants into Britain, and Britain, it was alleged, had her first experience of reasonably large numbers of people smoking a 'new' type of drug - cannabis (Plant, 1987). Cannabis came under international control under the Dangerous Drugs Act of 1925 (Dorn et al., 1992), and in 1929 Britain effected her legislation on cannabis (Stimson and Oppenheimer, 1982). Because the major dangerous drugs policies passed in Britain between 1920 and 1964 were meant to meet international demands, cannabis, like other dangerous drugs, had already been prohibited even before its use came into full force during the 1960s (Bean, 1974). This dangerous drugs legislation on cannabis was enacted not principally because cannabis posed any domestic problem, but rather, world-wide perception of drug use, such as opium, as an international menace that was growing out of hand demanded criminalisation as a rightful response to cannabis use (Willis, 1973).

Although cannabis use had been criminalised, prosecutions for drug offences between 1929 and 1948 concentrated mainly on opium and cocaine, and this could be attributed to the little attention that cannabis drew during those periods (Stimson and Oppenheimer, 1982). The government, satisfied that cannabis was neither extensively used nor causing any grievous harm, was able to claim in its report to the League of Nations in 1932 that 'the illicit use of and traffic in the drug appears to be confined to Arab and Indian seamen'; and in 1935 stated that 'such cases of illicit import of drugs as were discovered were individual attempts on the part of seamen, mainly orientals, to bring in small quantities for the use of compatriots in the United Kingdom' (Spear, 1969, p.249). A year after the second world war, the government's annual report on drugs observed that 'it is known that the traffic in Indian Hemp is practically confined to two negro groups in London and those attempting to import the drugs have generally been coloured seamen' (ibid.). Towards the later part of the 1940s and in the 1950s, cannabis use was on the increase (Willis, 1973). This was reflected in the rapid rise in the prosecutions and convictions for cannabis offences, for instance, there were 1,269 prosecutions from 1946 to 1959 as against 93 from 1929 to 1945 (Stimson and Oppenheimer, 1982). The situation was reported by The Times (2 July 1955) which stated that with the exception of cannabis which was 'largely confined to Africans, Asiatics and West Indians...', heroin and cocaine addiction was not common in the 1950s - and so were drug offences relating to heroin and cocaine.

Alongside drugs were issues of sexual immorality. Not only were blacks associated with cannabis use and dealing, they were also believed to be living off the immoral earnings of white prostitutes (Hiro, 1992; Solomos, 1989). The issue of sexuality was centralised as the police identified black people with immoral activities (Cashmore and MacLaughlin, 1991; Hall et al., 1978). According to Hiro (1992, p.36), many Britons

> considered West Indians as indolent blacks, draining the National Assistance Funds while simultaneously living off the immoral earnings of white women. By 1958 this image of West Indians was past the stage of grapevine, pub talk, occasional newspaper headline or readers' letters. It was echoed at the highest level of government.

The supposed involvement of black men in prostitution and drugs had made up some of the main areas of concern in the 1950s and the black community came to be identified with a particular range of petty crimes of which the most common were brothel-keeping, living off immoral earnings and drug pushing. In 1957 a newspaper headline announced: 'Black men, Brothel-Keeping and Dope' calling for a tighter control on the frequent number of clubs growing up in the West Indian localities (Howe, 1973). By the 1960s, 'the stereotype of the black pimp, ostentatiously dressed and driving a flash car, was becoming a fixture of popular mythology' (Hiro, 1992, p.36).

However, the use of cannabis in the 1950s was not limited to the ethnic minority population alone; jazz musicians and delinquent youngsters of different races were all involved in this drug (Glatt, 1974). The early 1950s was when the Home Office Drugs Branch officials appeared to realise that 'cannabis was a drug with a certain amount of appeal' to the 'indigenous population' (Spear, 1969, p.249). This statement apparently suggests that prior to the early 1950s, whites were not exposed to the use of cannabis, and that all those prosecuted and convicted for cannabis offences were purely minority ethnic groups. It is surprising that cannabis was believed to be alien to the indigenes before the 1950s considering that cannabis served recreational purposes in the 19th century (Berridge, 1988) - although its existence in Europe can be traced back to the 5th century (Whitaker, 1969). With a black presence, cannabis became associated with the practices of black people and whilst law enforcement agencies probably never looked to white communities for cannabis offences, it was common for the police, particularly in the 1960s, to conduct drug raids in black areas (Roach Family Support Committee, 1989).

The Chinese population had a similar experience in Britain when they were criticised for engaging in opium use. In the 1920s, opium use with the exception of a few artists was said to be almost exclusively confined to Chinese communities and invariably, the majority of drug offences occurred in towns where the Chinese mostly resided. Likewise, 'opium traffic' was reported by The Times (2 July 1955) to be 'largely confined to Chinese'. With the arrival of significant numbers of black immigrants into Britain in the late 1940s and in the 1950s, the attention which was previously focused on the Chinese communities became redirected to cannabis use and to blacks and parts of the country with large black populations. Mr Anslinger (of the U.S Federal Bureau of Narcotics) remarked that the British government confined the traffic in opium and cannabis to the Chinese, blacks and Indians (Lindesmith, 1965). The more black immigrants moved into Britain, the more conscious and alert the police became, and the more arrests were concentrated within the black community. This vigilance on the side of the police may have accounted to a large extent for the sudden rise in prosecutions and convictions for cannabis offences after the second world war.

The law against cannabis use has been justified by claims that cannabis and crime are causally related and that its use could progressively lead to heroin addiction - but these justifications are not backed up with sufficient evidence (Norman, 1971; Stewart, 1987; Deedes, 1970; Willis, 1973; Willis, 1969). It was not a drug covered by the 'British system' of treating drug addiction which is consistent with the fact that it does not produce physical dependence (Willis, 1969; Willis, 1973) and so its use does not require treatment programmes. Yet, it is classified as illegal, equating its harm with that of heroin and cocaine. The 'British system' covered 'hard' addictive drugs, especially, heroin which was known within the white community. The heroin addict population was made up of therapeutic (mostly middle-aged people) and non-therapeutic addicts (mostly middle-class citizens) including those in the medical profession who became dependant due to the availability of these drugs (Plant, 1987; Hobson, 1975). It has been argued that the 'British system' was enforced to the advantage of the middle class (Berridge, 1984; Stein, 1985). This is not surprising as prohibition laws are to a high degree determined by influential groups in the society, especially, when that which is being prohibited is common among low-status segments of the population (Glaser, 1974). But when a particular drug is used by the influential groups, such as alcohol, prohibition of such a drug is almost ignored. Such drugs are subject to very minimal control and these groups of people are favoured (ibid.). The United States Marijuana Tax Act of 1937 was precipitated by prohibitionists who emphasised that the drug was a menace deeply connected with crimes such as rape, murder and other crimes of violence - committed by those who come from the lower class back-ground (Whitaker, 1969) - and who are usually black. Britain took a similar step of imposing penalties for the use of cannabis, a drug far less harmful than heroin and cocaine.

How do we explain the fact that drinking alcohol - common amongst the white indigenous group, particularly, the working class - is quite acceptable in our society while cannabis use is illegal? Lindesmith (1965, p.226) has argued:

> Denunciations of the weed come characteristically from persons of those classes which prefer whisky, rum, gin and other alcoholic beverages and who do not themselves use marihuana. Such persons, overlooking the well-known effects of alcohol, commonly deplore the effects of hemp upon the lower classes and often believe that it produces rape, murder, violence and insanity. Despite the prevalence of these beliefs among the drinkers of rum and whisky and the upper classes generally, impartial investigations invariably have shown no such results.

Alcohol can equally 'produce rape, murder, violence and insanity'. The negative effects of alcohol are so numerous (MacGregor, 1989a; Stewart, 1987; Willis, 1973). Whilst cannabis has not been proved to be physically addictive, alcohol produces physical dependence and can be addictive. Alcohol just like cannabis can cause psychological harm. All accusations levelled against cannabis are applicable to alcohol (Lindesmith, 1965; Willis, 1973) but meanwhile these two drugs are poles apart under the law.

Drugs: The 1960s and 1970s

The 'British system' of treating drug addiction came to a halt in the late 1960s when the authority to prescribe addictive drugs for maintenance of physical and psychological dependence was restricted to a limited number of medical facilities, and more emphasis was placed on persuading addicts to either use less addictive drugs or abstain completely (Glaser, 1974). What emerged in 1968 was the setting up of 'clinics' which were special hospital-based drug dependency treatment centres (DDUs) (Jamieson et al., 1984; MacGregor, 1989b). More than 500 hospital-based doctors were granted a special licence by the Home Office to prescribe heroin and cocaine, and most of these doctors were within the field of psychiatry (ibid.). The decision to end the 'British system' was reached after the drug situation had been reviewed by the Brain Committee. The committee set up in 1960 published its first report in 1961 and in 1965 published a second report, *Drug Addiction*, which pointed out the sharp increase in drug misuse and suggested the need for tighter controls on prescribing by the medical profession. The restriction was implemented by the 1967 Dangerous Drugs Act (Plant, 1987) and the prescribing of cocaine and heroin was therefore limited to a few specially licensed doctors at certain clinics.

The striking change that took place in the nature of the drug scene in Britain from the 1960s and into the 1970s prompted 'calls for a new response from the government' (Jamieson et al., 1984). Drug use aroused great anxiety and received considerable attention, especially, from the media which publicised the widespread and adverse effects of drug misuse. What probably instigated strict measures to be taken was the rapid involvement of young people in drug use and the rapid emergence of youthful drug cultures that revolved around drugs. In reference to the late 1960s, MacGregor (1989b, p.170) notes:

> a new form of drug-taking appeared, involving increasing numbers
> of young people 'espousing an alternative way of life', dropping out,
> seeking pleasure, gravitating to London and its West End.

The early 20th century impression of drug use as an exclusive privilege exercised by middle-aged and middle-class therapeutic addicts and in the 1950s by professionals and other middle-class non-therapeutic addicts (Willis, 1969) changed once the problem was perceived as affecting other classes and groups of people. Jamieson, Glanz and MacGregor (1984, p.6) referred to these groups of people as:

> less respectable characters, more often members of the underclass
> and petty criminal underworld, obtaining their drugs from other
> addicts, the grip of the medical profession over their care began to
> loosen.

The rapid rise in the incidence of drug misuse among youths was parented by a host of factors: peer pressure, hedonism, political radicalism and social pressures, and according to Deedes (1970, p.12) 'curiosity, devilment, self-indulgence or group loyalty...'. Availability, Plant (1987) adds, contributed greatly to the increase in illicit drug use among youngsters. Newly invented drugs and drugs from abroad which flooded the country attracted more recreational drug users. Amphetamines, for example, were recreationally used due to large amounts of the drug being procured either through prescription or theft. As of 1966, 160,000 people were estimated to be abusing amphetamines and the habit was said to be widespread amongst adolescent delinquents (Bewley, 1966). This was also the case with heroin. Of the 2,240 registered heroin addicts in Britain in 1968 (King, 1969; Norman, 1971; Stimson and Oppenheimer, 1982) about one-third were in their teens and a reasonable number of them were of a lower status (King, 1969). Like other drugs, the use of cocaine came on the increase during the second half of the 1960s, which was attributed to the arrival in Britain of many Canadian cocaine addicts with the hope of getting legal cocaine from medical practitioners (Tyler, 1986).

The 1970s also witnessed a rapid rise in heroin use and heroin dependence (Dorn et al., 1987). Plant (1987, p.41) notes that 'this upsurge in youthful heroin use in the 1960s' and later in the 1970s was aggravated by 'over-casual prescribing so that "spare" supplies could be passed on to others eager to experiment'. An illicit heroin market - sustained by the sale of legitimately prescribed heroin - was in existence in Britain since the mid-1960s. After 1968, there gradually grew a black market in illegally imported heroin and as Lewis (1985, p.42) states, 'by the end of the 1970s, there was an established and growing black market in imported heroin in the United Kingdom'. However, the rise in illegal heroin use and the massive growth in the illicit heroin traffic and market did not witness as many prosecutions and convictions as would have been expected. In 1968 for instance, only 73 people were prosecuted and convicted for heroin offences but there were 2,240 registered addicts and 2,232 non-therapeutic heroin addicts known to the Home Office (Stimson and Oppenheimer, 1982). Prosecutions and convictions for cannabis offences numbered 3,071 in 1968 (ibid.) - a far cry from the recorded heroin offences in the same year. The widespread use of cannabis in Britain has been attributed to post-war West Indian and Asian immigration (Plant, 1987). Cannabis use among blacks and Asians was extended to the 'host' community and rapidly increased so that the offence superseded other drug offences (Stimson and Oppenheimer, 1982)).

More stringent restrictions were placed on controlled drugs under the 1960s and 1971 drugs legislation. Under the Dangerous Drugs (Prevention of Misuse) Act 1964, unauthorised possession of LSD, amphetamine drugs and similar substances was an offence punishable by imprisonment of up to six

months on summary conviction and two years on indictment (King, 1969). It was in 1966 that the Act was extended to include LSD, DMT and mescaline (Plant, 1987; Dorn et al., 1992). The Act proscribed the permitting of premises to be used for smoking and dealing in cannabis. To import any illegal drugs without a licence became an offence so that manufacturers and wholesalers were required to be registered. Greater powers were given to the police to control drugs and such powers authorised them to arrest without a warrant a person who is committing, or 'reasonably suspected' of having committed, a drug offence (Deedes, 1970), and to search premises if there was evidence that a drug offence was being committed (Plant, 1987). The 1965 Dangerous Drugs Act made illegal possession of cocaine, heroin and cannabis punishable by up to twelve months imprisonment on summary conviction and ten years on indictment (King, 1969). The 1967 Dangerous Drugs (Prevention of Misuse) Act extended police powers. The police, under this Act, were authorised to stop and search without a warrant, persons, vehicles and vessels 'reasonably suspected' of unlawfully possessing or carrying illegal drugs (Plant, 1987; Deedes, 1970). The police were also empowered to search any premises for drugs with or without a warrant (a search warrant is required when entry is refused by the occupant). With a search warrant the police are legally authorised to enter any premises by the use of force if necessary.

To consolidate previous legislation and bring Britain in line with post-war international conventions, the 1971 Misuse of Drugs Act (Home Office, 1989b) was passed and has since formed the basis of present drug control in Britain. The Act further increased police powers. And under this Act, prohibited drugs were categorised into three sections in relation to their harmfulness and in each of these categories, different maximum penalties were specified for illegal possession, production, importation, exportation, supply and sale of the drugs. At present, the Medicines Act of 1968 and the Misuse of Drugs Act of 1971 remain the two main statutes regulating the availability and misuse of controlled drugs.

The circumstances surrounding drug misuse in the 1960s and 1970s attracted both statutory and non-statutory intervention. Whilst legal restrictions were placed on controlled drugs, statutory services controlled by the medical profession provided treatment and rehabilitative services to drug dependants. Within the voluntary sector, social work and related practices developed in various community projects and rehabilitation agencies that sprang up at the period - offering rehabilitation, counselling and advisory services to both drug users and addicts (Dorn and South, 1985).

Race and Drug Offence Laws

Pryce (1979) has observed that some black youths in the 1970s were involved in drugs but those blacks used such drugs as marihuana (which was usually peddled), pep-pills and other amphetamine tablets rather than heroin which was almost unknown to them. In 1972, the Select Committee on Race Relations and Immigration further pointed out that only a limited number of blacks featured in the drug circle (Gilroy, 1987b). Nevertheless, there was already in existence a notable association of black people with drugs. Writing about Rastafarianism and criminality in English cities, Dodd (1978, p.600) referred to 'the emergence of a black street sub-culture in the working class slums' in which 'there is meaning in music, there is meaning in ganja and there is meaning in crime'; and Brown (1977, p.8) had provided a description of Rastafarians thus:

> Deprived and disadvantaged, they see themselves as victims of white racist society and attracted by values and lifestyle of alienated dreadlock groups, drift into lives of idleness and crime, justifying themselves with half-digested gobbets of Rastafarian philosophy.

But Miles (1978, p.7) sees the conception of a 'Rastafarian as a man with long flowing dreadlocks, unkempt beard, high on ganja, unemployed and unemployable' as a stereotype. There are Rastafarians who do not fit this description whilst others do, and there are many black youths who exhibit the symbols and practices of Rastafarianism but are not genuine Rastafarians (ibid.).

By the late 1970s, black residential areas were noted for drug dealing and prostitution (Hiro, 1992), and had become prime targets for police drug raids. The relationship between the police and black people was strained with the implementation of drug offences legislation in the 1960s and 1971. Humphrey and John (1971, p. 36) observe how the police allegedly used the drug laws to discriminate against black people:

> In Moss Side the police had upset the blacks by making a drive on illicit drugs and using their powers under the Dangerous Drugs Act 1965 to stop and search people in the street or at house parties. Black people felt that they were being singled out for these searches and some retaliated leading to charges of assault on the police.

The police took advantage of the Act and intentionally went out of their way to single out blacks who were frequently stopped, searched, framed and arrested. Black people were already popularly identified by the police with drugs -

justifying such police activity - which in turn amplified the link between race and drugs. This process demonstrates a 'self-fulfilling prophecy' or what Jock Young (1971, p.171) describes as 'the translation of fantasy into reality'. Young (1977, pp 121-122) argues:

> the negotiation of reality by the policeman is exhibited in the widespread practice of perjury. This is not a function of the Machiavellianism of the police, but rather a product of their desire in the name of administrative efficiency to jump the gap between what I shall term theoretical and empirical guilt. For example, a West Indian who wears dark glasses, who has no regular employment, and who mixes with beatniks, would quite evidently satisfy their notion of a drug pusher. If he is arrested, then it is of no consequence that no marihuana is found in his flat, nor is it morally reprehensible to plant marihuana on his person. For all that is being done is aiding the cause of justice by providing the empirical evidence to substantiate the obvious theoretical guilt. That he might actually have only sold marihuana a few times in the past, that he mixes with hippies because he likes their company, and that he lives in fact from his National Assistance payments is ignored; the stereotype of the pusher is in evidence, and the reality is unconsciously negotiated to fit its requirements.

Many black youths interviewed by Humphrey and John (1971) in Handsworth held that black people in some cases were planted with drugs and dangerous weapons. In his book *Police Power and Black People* published in 1972, Humphrey cited cases of alleged drug planting by the police on black people. Referring to the involvement of the police in drug planting and brutality, a woman police officer in Liverpool commented:

> In certain police stations, particularly in the city centre, brutality and drug planting and the harassing of minority groups take place regularly. On one occasion, I witnessed a police sergeant attack a teenage youth who had reported to the station while on parole. The sergeant poured insults on the youth, picked him up by the coat lapels and banged his head against the wall several times, before throwing him into a chair. The youth was then dragged out to the police jeep and driven away. After hearing the word 'agriculture' used on a number of occasions I asked what it meant. The reply was 'planting', but you can leave that to us (Humphrey, 1972, p.18).

Humphrey and John (1971, p.7) further drew attention to blacks' experience of police powers when they stated:

> Not a week went by during my nine months in Handsworth without my hearing of at least one instance of someone being taken, or having to go to hospital for treatment as a result of injury sustained at the hands of the police. Youths and their parents complain about the police's indiscriminate use of handcuffs, of police insults to black women who they regard as 'only black and therefore not to be respected as women', of men being put against the walls of the police station and searched, at the same time being asked 'where are the drugs, you dirty black bastard?', 'you don't work, you scum', 'you live off our women', 'I am going to make damn sure you will get put inside for good'.

The relationship between black people and the police degenerated at any stage more powers to control drugs were given to the police under a Drugs Act. With the implementation of the 1967 Dangerous Drugs Act, black people were subjected to systematic harassment by the police (Humphrey, 1972). Under such powers, the police were enabled 'to use their specialised force for vice and drug detection, and for the surveillance of suspects' which invariably enabled 'the police to abuse discretion and infringe the law as a means to that greater end' (ibid., p.116). The relationship between black people and the police probably worsened even further as soon as additional powers of arrest were given to the police under the 1971 Misuse of Drugs Act. Criticisms were made against the police for indiscriminately picking out blacks for drug offences. Clifford Lynch who spoke on behalf of the West Indian Standing Conference criticised the police for their engagement in 'blackmail, drug planting, trumped-up charges and physical assaults' and their 'systematic brutalization of black people' (Guardian, 28 January 1972).

Drugs: From the 1980s Onwards

> Illegal drug menace is like a medieval plague (The Times, 19 May 1989).

> Drug abuse is making victims of all of us (News of the World, June 22 1997).

Similar views were constantly expressed in the mass media in 1980s. With evidence of a high increase in drug use (particularly heroin) and its spread in parts of the country in the 1980s (Haw, 1985; Parker et al., 1986, 1988)), the drug problem once again became top of Britain's social concern agenda. As Gay (1989, p.8) observed, the 1980s drug problem became an epidemic that 'was no longer confined to certain localities or defined groups' because 'the problem could clearly affect any family anywhere'. It was feared that the situation posed a threat to the social order and that the society was undergoing a process of disintegration. Several questions were raised as to the cause of the problem, the nature of the drug problem in the past, the policy changes that have taken place in the past, and the next possible step to take in order to control the drug problem.

Of the drugs abused in the 1980s, the misuse of heroin, cannabis and cocaine caused the greatest concern. In relation to cocaine, the previous popular impression of the drug as being too expensive for the 'ordinary' individual, and being virtually limited to the higher echelons changed in the 1980s as soon as its abuse penetrated different parts of the country and social classes. Hansen (1989, p.8) notes:

> In well-to-do and professional circles, cocaine is an increasingly popular 'additive' at parties, both for the 'high' that the drug itself produces, and for the added excitement of doing something 'different' and 'dangerous'.

She adds that the use of cocaine has become more widespread and no longer limited to the wealthy sections of the society, one reason being that the drug is not as exorbitant as it used to be since the price has started to drop.

The accompanying health related problems, negative effects on families and the wider community highlighted the intensity of the drug problem. A notable cause for concern was the causal relationship between drug use and other forms of criminality. Drug users are known to engage in various types of criminal activities geared towards procuring supplies of drugs. The general stereotype of a drug user or addict is one who is forced into a life of crime to meet his psychological and physical craving for the drug (Burr, 1987). Those addicts who are medically protected may lead a stable and law-abiding lifestyle whereas, illegal drug addicts (unless they are well-off) who are into 'expensive' addictive drugs usually turn to crime to finance their drug habit - an option which seems to be the only way out for the low income-group or unemployed. Burr (1987) in her study on *Chasing the Dragon*, highlighted the relationship between drug use among the socio-economically deprived and criminality. She argues that the majority of heroin users, irrespective of their sex, commit burglaries in the suburbs and even on their own estates; stealing from cars or offices and shoplifting were common amongst some, and a few indulge in cheque and credit card fraud. In spite of the risks involved in drug use and criminality, this group of people feet secure in the world of crime and more alienated from a law-abiding lifestyle. According to Burr (ibid., p.352):

> the demands of supporting a long term heroin habit have turned a hard-core of delinquents into sophisticated adult thieves at a remarkable early age, often by the age of 19. Regular thieving to support their habit has taught both those who did not work and those who held regular jobs prior to taking heroin, that they can earn a great deal of money from thieving. Not many are willing to return to conventional, poorly paid jobs, even if they could find them, and with their delinquent past and lack of local employment opportunities, few are able to do so.

The rapid involvement of young people in illicit 'hard' drug use was another issue that drew public and official attention to the 1980s drug problem - similar to the drug situation which aroused great anxiety in the 1960s and 1970s. Pearson (1987a, p.4) has stated that '...the new heroin users are more likely to be young men and women in their late teens and early twenties'. As soon as the drug problem began to raise public interest in the 1980s, concern was particularly shown about young people described by MacGregor (1989a, p.11) as 'that new generation whose integration into the social order would, as ever, be necessary if society was to continue much as it had done in the past'. Several studies conducted in parts of Britain such as London, Edinburgh, the Wirral and Glasgow, produced evidence of a widespread use of heroin among young people (Newcombe, 1987; Parker et al., 1988). Parker and his colleagues (ibid., p.7), on the basis of their research in the Wirral, commented that the

> Local Radio claimed that 50% of young people between 14 and 25 were using heroin regularly.

They add:

> Wirral was singled out with headlines about many babies being born addicted to heroin in Wirral's maternity units and moving stories about local families wrecked by heroin addiction (ibid.).

The Home Office (1985) had previously observed that the majority of reported drug addicts were between 15 and 35 years, whilst an increasing number were getting younger and younger. Overall, official evidence highlighted a drastic increase in the number of drug users. The number of drug addicts known to the Home Office rose over the years, for example in 1980, 2,846 drug addicts were known to the Home Office and this number increased to 5,079 and 7,052 in 1983 and 1985 respectively (Plant, 1989). Such figures are far from typical of drug users in general as the majority are probably not notified to the Home Office so that the Home Office record represents a small proportion of the number of drug users and addicts. In most cases, drug addicts do not bother to seek medical treatment but prefer to procure drugs through illicit means. With the growing number of drug users and illegal drug users in particular, a sample survey of general practitioners in England and Wales suggested a possibility of between 30,000 and 40,000 'new addicts' every year (Glanz and Taylor, 1986), with a greater percentage of these new addicts being more likely to be unknown to official agencies.

Whilst it was feared that the problem was becoming uncontrollable in the 1980s, the 1990s seem to be witnessing even more complex drug problems. There has been a rise in the growth rate of drug use and all the drug associated problems of the 1980s have continued into the 1990s. According to NACRO (1993b, p.17), '24,700 drug addicts were notified to the Home Office in 1992 (19% more than in 1991), including 9,663 new addicts'. Notified heroin addicts increased from 14,500 in 1990 to 18,920 in 1993 and in the same periods, there was an increase of notified cocaine addicts from 1,090 to 2,460 (Home Office, 1994b). Cannabis remains the most widely used drug in the United Kingdom (ibid.). The increase in youth involvement in drug continue to arouse fear. A police officer was reported in the Guardian (21 March 1991) as stating:

> The most worrying part of our operation as far as I am concerned is
> that there were increasing numbers of 14 and 15 year olds charged
> with possession and intention to supply.

Such fear has also been expressed by drugs squad officers regarding the spread of different types of drugs - such as ecstasy and crack - among young people (Guardian, 10 Sept.1992). By 1997, the concerns of politicians and government officials about the threat posed by drugs on the lives of youths had deepened, initiating support for a campaign conducted by the News of the World (July 6 1997) to 'halt the drugs explosion'.

What seems to become obvious in the 1990s is the rise of poly-drug misuse whereby a variety of illegal and legal drugs are used by drug users alongside their favourite drug. The poly-drug culture followed the emergence of the 'rave' scene among youths in the late 1980s. 'New' drugs such as Ecstasy have become fashionable with previously scarce drugs such as cocaine and crack becoming increasingly available (Mirza et al., 1991a); meanwhile, LSD and Amphetamine remain popular. This widespread availability of various types of drugs is featured in the poly-drug scene.

The significance of the drug problem is not only reflected in the general trends in drug misuse but in the number of seizures made by Customs and the police, and the number of persons dealt with for drug offences. In 1983, 26,200 seizures of controlled drugs were made (Home Office, 1985) unlike 17,617 in 1980 and 19,428 in 1981 (Plant, 1987). These figures increased to 28,560 in 1984 (ibid.) and in 1992, a total of 76,341 seizures of classes A, B and C drugs were made. Recorded drug offences by the Home Office has been on the increase. In 1983, approximately 23,300 persons were found guilty of, or cautioned for, drug related offences; this figure is roughly 3,000 more than in 1982, and 11,500 more than in 1975 (Home Office, 1985). In 1985, there were 26,596 cautions or convictions for drug offences (Plant, 1989). Most of these drug offences were related to cannabis (Home Office, 1985; Plant, 1987, 1989). The number of persons found guilty, cautioned or dealt with by compounding rose to 47,616 in 1991 (NACRO, 1993c) and in 1992, increased to 48,924 (Home Office, 1994b). This increase is also applicable to drug trafficking. Metropolitan Police (1990) figures showed that in 1986, 1,969 drug trafficking offences were recorded; the number increased to 2,415 in 1988 and 2,643 in 1989, and in 1991 and 1992, rose to 11,379 and 13,809 respectively (Home Office, 1993).

Various explanations for the cause of the drug problem have arisen but are, broadly speaking, categorised into two lines of thought. One relates the problem to the demand for drugs (with deprivation popularly viewed as the major reason behind the demand for drugs) and the other focuses on the supply of drugs. Each is discussed below but none can be specifically identified to account for the problem.

Demand

A popular contention exists which links drug use to socio-economic deprivation. Several studies that analysed the 1980s drug problem associated a high concentration of drug use with deprived localities and people who experience high rates of socio-economic deprivation in the form of unemployment, substandard housing, poor residential environment, homelessness, poverty and so forth (Pearson, 1987b, 1989; Pearson et al., 1987; Peck and Plant, 1986). Parker et al. (1986, p.143), based on their research in the Wirral, described a 'typical heroin user' as 'a young unemployed man or woman, aged between 16 and 24, living in a relatively densely populated town with higher than average levels of socio-economic deprivation'. Burr's (1987, p.338) research in South London also linked drug use and criminality to economic deprivation. She states:

> Job loss generally resulted in an increase in criminal activity and size of habit. It gave youngsters an incentive to steal. Also, they now had time on their hands, and the companionship of other like-minded delinquents in a similar position. They encouraged each other's criminality.

These analyses associating drug use, particularly, amongst youths to deprivation were welcomed by state officials and politicians. Allan Roberts, Labour MP for Bootle, held the view that 'the Thatcher years' are 'the hard-drug years' whereby a 'whole generation is being sacrificed'. Holding the government directly responsible, he added that 'unemployed youngsters and teenagers with no hope or stake in their future are easy prey to the evil drug pusher'(Yorkshire Post, 29 June 1984). Contrary to the deprivation and drug use conception, there is a correlation between middle-class areas and drug use, and low rates of drug use and areas of high levels of deprivation (Pearson et al., 1987). Other studies have argued that the use of drugs is not confined to any particular group or class of people; drug use has no boundary but cuts across different classes and groups in society (Hansen, 1989; Gay, 1989). Keith Hellawell, Chief Constable of West Yorkshire was reported in the News of the World (July 6 1997) as stating that the drug 'curse is in the leafy suburbs and our schools', contrary to the popular perception of drugs being confined to the inner cities. He adds, 'No parents can think they are immune'. Despite the obvious indications that drug use does not necessarily reflect socio-economic circumstances, theoretical explanations linking drug use to deprivation have received more popularity in academic, official and public discourse. It is generally believed that drug spread is common amongst the lower class, who form the symbol of economic marginalisation and are therefore classed as a delinquent population. The 'logic' is that the poor socio-economic circumstances of this section of the society make them more likely to follow the path of long-term drug use. This popular image is similar to Finigarette and Hasse's (1978, p.168) description of a drug addict. Having noted that 'a person who has developed roots in conventional society and skills for leading a productive life is substantially less likely to find a meaningful social identity in the drug culture and such a person can more readily abandon addiction as it develops', Finigarette and Hasse portrayed a picture of drug addicts as:

> young, psychologically immature, occupationally un-skilled, socially uprooted, poor and disadvantaged....Young people who are disadvantaged and alienated may find the foundation of a socially authenticated identity in addiction. For such persons, drug use provides at last a "constructive" focal activity in life, generating its own occupational responsibilities, opportunities for success and achievement, social status and ideological, philosophical or religious meaning.

The consequence, therefore, is that the internal official response to the drug problem in this country has stressed the link between the drug and the drug taker, so that some drug policies and laws are enforced with the 'deprived' as the prime target.

Supply

In 1994, the former Prime Minister, John Major was cited by the Home Office (1994b) as stating:

> Drugs are a menace to our society. They can wreck the lives of individuals and their families. They are a frequent cause of crime. That is why we have toughened laws against drugs and why we have given the police and Customs the powers and the resources to enforce those laws effectively. Those efforts are delivering results....Strong enforcement action has gone hand in hand with measures to reduce demand....In spite of these efforts, the drugs menace remains and the trends are worrying....Everyone's aim must be to put the drug barons out of business and protect our people from the misery and waste that drugs produce.

In 1997, the Prime Minister, Tony Blair commended The Sun newspaper's campaign against the drug problem. He was reported by The Sun (14 June 1997) as stating:

> We must all work together to make sure there is no hiding place for the pushers at the school gate who peddle filth or the "Mr Bigs" who grow rich on the back of their vile trade.

Much of the blame for the drug problem has been placed on the drug trafficker. The drug trafficker bears the brunt of society's contempt; s/he is a menace who sells drugs to drug users purely for profit. Drug traffickers are viewed in the same light as terrorists - as social outcasts - by the government and the courts (Green, 1991). In the 1980s, drug traffickers were described by Baroness Cox as 'merchants of death' and as '...despicable people who exploit and who profit handsomely from the misery of drug addiction' (cited in Green, 1991, p.18). Dorn and South (1987, p.122) described the 1980s Conservative government's portrayal of drug traffickers as 'serious criminals akin to terrorists, and drug users...as helpless victims, reduced to moronic social garbage'. Drug trafficking, its pattern, and nuisance nature has been a popular subject in official debates. The press has given it prime exposure, proclaiming to the public its dangerous existence, a criminal and deadly image of the drug trafficker and above all, the ongoing war against drug trafficking. These impressions are exemplified in the following newspaper headlines:

> Crack Wars: Drug Dealers Are Fighting For The Right To Sell This To YOUR Children (South London Press, 19 July 1991).

> Evil Drugs Godfather Gets 20 Years (The Sun, 18 December 1991).

> New Team For War On Drugs (Streatham and Clapham Guardian, 10 September 1992).

> Cops Swoop On £70m Drugs Factory (News Of The World, 25 July 1993).

> Bid To Crack Down On Drugs (Lewisham and Catford News Shopper, 21 June 1989).

> Drug Mob Youths Get 80 years (The Sun, 26 March 1992).

Several views have perpetuated the myth that the domestic drug problems are largely caused by foreigners. As Dorn et al. (1992, p.153) have observed, the 'combination of drugs intelligence and immigration intelligence reflected a perception (which recurred in the 1980s) that it was immigrants, legal and/or illegal, who were responsible for much of the importation of illegal drugs into Britain'. Green (1991, p.21) also noted that the 'constructed drugs "crisis" is seen as a principally imported crisis - imported by West Africans, Asians or

South Americans, fuelled by Third World supplies rather than domestic demand'. Accusations are levelled against foreign countries for intentionally causing harm to vulnerable young British people who fall prey to drugs that are imported from such countries. Highlighted here is race as a visible feature of the popular perception of drug trafficking at the international level which probably accounts for the longer prison sentence that drug couriers from countries such as Pakistan, Nigeria, Jamaica and Colombia receive in British courts (Green, 1991, 1996; Heaven, 1997).

Since the late 1970s, the increase in heroin use was associated with the increase in the supply of the drug from South West Asia. Pakistan, according to MacGregor (1989a, p.7) had for some time 'borne the brunt of criticism because of its "lawless frontiers" which were thought to have contributed to the supply of heroin to the west'. In relation to cocaine, Mirza et al. (1991b, p.117) provide a similar view:

> Where cocaine was concerned, however, Britain had neither a history of colonial involvement in Latin America nor a tradition of trade and other forms of social intercourse. But here the question of the Caribbean reared its head - both in fact and public fantasy - as a region with which Britain had considerable links of history and peoples, and as a possible entrepot for cocaine trafficking between Latin America and Britain.

It has been argued that cocaine traffickers have decided to divert their supplies to the Western European market as soon as there was an excess supply of cocaine in the North American market by South America. Douglas Hurd described this point thus:

> The evidence is plain: the North American market having been saturated, the cocaine barons of Latin America are now driving their product into Europe (The Times, 19 May 1989).

Like heroin and cocaine, most of the cannabis that is abused in Britain is illegally imported into the country. Cannabis, according to the Home Office (1985, p.4), 'is grown in many areas including the "Golden Crescent" (Pakistan, Afghanistan and Iran), the Middle East and North Africa'. Such drugs as LSD and amphetamines whilst illegally produced in this country and abroad are, like other drugs such as barbiturates, 'mainly obtained by diversion from the licit market in this country' (ibid.).

Before drawing conclusions on the role of foreign countries in perpetuating Britain's drug problem, we need to place the issue of drugs in varied contexts. Drug misuse is not a problem that is limited to the British society alone; the abuse of drugs is an international problem. Likewise, drug trafficking involves a world-wide network of drug distribution; it is a lucrative illicit business that attracts people from various groups and classes. Basically, the drug phenomenon links various countries into a network of production, supply and consumption of illicit drugs. But, as Lewis (1985, p.42) rightly noted, the press portrayal of drug trafficking fails to see the illicit drug trade in terms of 'an articulated world economy' that also incorporates a whole network of an organised Western-based drug traffickers. Instead it is seen in the context of 'unscrupulous foreigners dumping "white death" on innocent British kids'. Henman et al. (1985, p.2) argue that the popular portrayal of the production of heroin, cocaine and cannabis as being 'sufficiently distant to promote the idea that the threat is alien and external' is questioned by contrasting views held by producing countries, which see 'the drug business as something inspired by the insatiable markets of the industrialised, metropolitan world'. For example, in a response to criticisms from the West, a letter to the Guardian (7 January 1984) by the Pakistan Embassy in London related to 'the follies of the rich, heroin consuming West'. The Pakistan Embassy noted that 'if the demand for heroin and cocaine in Britain and the other countries of the West can be stamped out, there will be no supply'.

Obviously, economic factors underlie and sustain the global drugs trade. Aside the lucrative nature of drugs which apparently favours the trafficker, drug production for producer countries provides a profitable means of subsistence and is an attractive option for peasant farmers who lack access to more adequate sources of income, so that in spite of a series of international meetings and treaties geared towards international enforcement of controls, policies are still patterned by definite internal domestic circumstances. Opium, for instance, is a traditional cash crop in opium producing countries and constitutes a major source of income for farmers and tribal groups. Any attempt to control cultivation would more likely elicit a negative response - a condition which has a lot to do with economic contingencies rather than the 'reality' of danger embedded in the use of the drugs. To a large extent, this situation has contributed to the lack of uniformity in policies which in turn fosters the weakness and ineffectiveness of international controls. Opportunity enhanced by contradictory policies is exploited by the international drug trafficker.

Government intervention: law enforcement

Government response to the domestic drug problem has gone through a number of phases and has taken various forms of external and internal controls of both demand for, and the supply of, drugs. The drug policies which have been adopted since the mid 1980s are clearly outlined in *Tackling Drug Misuse* (Home Office, 1985) which gives a summary of the government's strategy for dealing with the drug problem. The strategy addresses five main areas (Home Office, 1994b, p.21) which are:

> improving international cooperation to reduce supplies from abroad;
> increasing the effectiveness of police and Customs enforcement;
> maintaining effective deterrents and tight domestic controls;
> developing prevention publicity, education and community action;
> and improving treatment and rehabilitation.

Amidst the drugs policies from the 1980s, of particular relevance is the policy on law enforcement through the police and the courts which involves the use of the law as a remedy for the drug problem, particularly, in relation to drug trafficking.

In the 1980s, the emphatic reference to drugs supply as a major cause of the drug problem was supported by publicised calls from politicians and government officials for the implementation of stringent punitive measures (including the death penalty) for drug trafficking. Leon Brittan, then Home Secretary, thought it was necessary to 'deter and punish very severely those whose trade is in other people's misery' (News of the World, 15 January 1984). It could, however, be argued that harsh penalty on its own cannot deter any distribution because such penalties only succeed in eradicating relative amateurs and at the same time harden the drug trade. But, the response from the government called for more severe punishment, and law enforcement has so far been strengthened more towards surveillance and pro-active policing, and increased penalties, in order to fight the battle against drugs. The recent appointment in 1997 of a 'Drugs Czar', Keith Hellawell (a top police officer) by Tony Blair to target drug pushers and suppliers highlights the main focus of law enforcement on drug trafficking.

Police   It is the main responsibility of the police to detect and investigate drug offences, as well as to arrest and charge those involved in such offences. The 1971 Misuse of Drugs Act, as already noted, has given the police wider powers of stop-and-search and arrests in cases relating to drugs. By the mid-1980s, the issue of curbing drug offences has taken a high priority within the police force as stated by the Police Commissioner for the Metropolis in his strategy for 1985.

Drugs law enforcement by way of policing witnessed a new organisational structure based largely on the recommendations of the 1985 Broome Report which mapped out three broad levels of drugs policing consisting of (a) regional crime squads to focus on major drug trafficking business involving a network of importers and distributors on both national and international levels; (b) force drugs squads to address mid-level traffickers in the drug distribution system; and (c) divisional level enforcement which involves the policing of localities by police officers in the normal course of their duties (Home Office, 1994c; Dorn et al., 1992; Foy, 1996). As at 1994, the drugs wings of the regional crime squads in England and Wales employed about 345 police officers and about 60 per cent of the work of the 85 police officers attached to the Scottish crime squads was related to drugs (Home Office, 1994b).

Policing drugs at divisional level is considered a vital pattern of drugs enforcement due to its demand and harm reduction approach to drug misuse. It involves street level surveillance and stop-and-search practices which concentrate on specific areas such as council estates, streets, public houses and private flats, and geared towards detecting retail drug markets. High-level drugs enforcement has been known to be problematic amidst complexities involved in intercepting drug traffickers at the upper reaches of the drugs economy, which makes it limited in its cost effectiveness. Although this does not imply ineffectiveness at the higher levels of police operational response to drugs, it does highlight why divisional-level policing has remained prominent in its focus on drug traffickers, buyers and users in select areas, usually in inner cities, with the aim of disrupting low-level drug transactions and in turn reduce the availability of, and demand for, drugs. A disturbing consequence of its significant use in inner city areas is the likelihood of a high proportion of inner city residents, mostly the lower class and black people, being apprehended and prosecuted for a low-level drug trafficking offence, more so with its escalating utilisation given the relatively unsuccessful top-level drugs enforcement.

Courts The 1980s brought new changes in the sentencing policies on drug offences. It was claimed by the government that the existing penalties for drug offences at the time did not have an adequate deterrent effect on drug offenders, especially, drug traffickers who became the prime-target of the 1980s drug control laws. The lucrative nature of the drug business was seen as the main motivating factor behind the trade and invariably, sentencing policies devised by the state concentrated principally on drug trafficking rather than illegal possession of a controlled drug.

Under the 1985 Controlled Drugs (Penalties) Act, a maximum penalty of life imprisonment for trafficking in class A drugs was imposed (Green, 1991; Black, 1991). Previously, the maximum penalty for trafficking in such drugs was 14 years imprisonment and an unlimited fine. But, as the Home Office (1985, p.15) argues:

> The introduction of life imprisonment will enable the courts to impose even longer sentences in cases where, for example, the offender has been responsible for trafficking drugs worth several million pounds.

To deprive convicted drug traffickers of the profits made from their illegal dealings, a new legislation was enacted under the 1986 Drug Trafficking Offences Act giving courts powers to confiscate assets belonging to convicted drug traffickers, which are believed by the courts to be the proceeds of drug trafficking unless proven otherwise (Sallon and Bedingfield, 1993). Any default of payment or refusal to comply with confiscation orders would mean an added prison sentence commensurate with the assessed value of the proceeds from drug trafficking.(Plant, 1987; Dorn et al., 1992). The justification for this additional penalty is put by the Home Office (1985, p.15) thus:

> Lengthy sentences of imprisonment may not in themselves be an adequate deterrent. Many drug traffickers make vast profits from their illicit activities. Because of shortcomings in the existing law, they are often able to enjoy these illegal profits on their release from prison. The Home Secretary has decided to introduce legislation in this parliament to make it easier to trace, seize and confiscate the profits of drug trafficking (and other crimes).

The provisions of the 1986 Drug Trafficking Offences Act have been strengthened by other measures aimed at deterring drug traffickers, for example, the International Mutual Legal Assistance Treaties binding several countries authorise law enforcement agencies to provide each other with mutual assistance and permit mutual search and seizure powers (Murji, 1996); and under the 1990 Criminal Justice (International Cooperation) Act, drug trafficking money which is being exported from, or imported into, the United Kingdom is authorised to be forfeited (Home Office, 1994b).

Race, Drugs and Law Enforcement

One would have thought that the analyses linking illicit drug use to deprivation was a move towards focusing attention on the problem of deprivation, however, the various drug control strategies devised to fight the drug problem within the United Kingdom seem not to view the issue of deprivation as the prime target. Instead, ideologies and theoretical explanations which place illicit drug use within the context of deprivation have indirectly criminalised those who fall within the lower socio-economic stratum - composed of the majority of black people.

The issue of drugs has been incorporated into the analyses of black people and crime. For a long time as Gilroy (1987b, p.100) points out, 'drug use has been a background theme in the representation of blacks as a criminal group'. Similarly, Cashmore and Troyna (1982, p.12) had drawn attention to the characterisation of Rastafarianism as a 'mafia-style organisation dealing in prostitution and dope...'. This popular association of blacks with drugs is solidified by interpretations that relate their involvement in drugs to socio-economic deprivation. As Rex (1982, p.65) states, unemployed West Indians are believed to 'live by pimping, by cheating and thieving, and by peddling "ganja"...'. Subsequently, the economic and social circumstances of black people and the ideological association of these conditions to drugs have become rooted in policies and official justification for discriminatory law enforcement (Kalunta-Crumpton, 1996, 1998).

Drug use is not confined to any particular group or class of people as studies have shown. Hansen (1989, p.8) notes that 'almost anyone of any age or background may become a drug user' and she adds:

> The popular image of the young drug abuser as a child of a broken
> home, living in an underprivileged environment, is just not borne
> out by the evidence.

But whilst the working class involvement in illicit drugs receives negative official response, their middle-class counterparts who are considered as productive members of the society are carefully exempted from the bitter side of the law. The middle-class drug users, as Parker et al. (1986, p.143) state, 'can often pay, or manoeuvre, their way out of contact with NHS clinics, court appearances and the like...'.

When racial background is put into consideration, black people have been known to make up a small proportion of drug users when compared to both working class and middle-class whites (Pearson, 1995), even in areas with a flourishing irregular economy (Auld et al., 1986). In their observation, Awiah, Butt and Dorn (1990, p.14) indicate:

> Assumptions about black people and drugs in Britain are generally underpinned by stereotypes, over-generalisations and racist posturing, rather than by evidence.

Likewise, Mirza et al. (1991b, pp 120-121) note that 'although police arrests might suggest that cocaine and crack use was a black problem, the vast majority of these cocaine and crack users were white...'. They add that the evidence from their survey failed to verify the myth that lots of black people misuse drugs. A sample survey conducted by the Inner London Probation Service (1991) to compare the relationship between race and drug misuse within the Inner London area, revealed a higher drug abuse among whites than blacks. The findings showed a strong association between: (a) black drug misuse and cocaine and cannabis; and (b) white drug misuse and alcohol. Although heroin is less racially determined than cannabis, cocaine and alcohol, it was more likely to be used by whites than blacks. It was also shown that for the other drugs included in the study (for example, amphetamine, LSD, barbiturates, solvents and prescribed drugs), white misuse was more than black misuse.

The same can be said for drug trafficking. Unlike the prevailing popular perception of black people as 'drug barons', they occupy the lower levels of the drugs distribution chain in the drugs economy, whereas, white people are located at the top end of the drug trade as suppliers and distributors with access to the lucrative parts of the drugs market (Ruggiero and South, 1995; Bean and Pearson, 1992). In reality, domestic drug trafficking receive sensational media coverage, political reaction and high priority drug trafficking controls, in the form of law enforcement, which place blame on black involvement in drug trafficking as significantly responsible for Britain's drug problem. Drug trafficking became racialised in the 1980s (Dorn et al., 1992) and has since been particularly perceived within the context of black people and deprived inner city areas. Those deprived areas and communities are identified with drug trafficking noted to be at its lowest level involving a network of drug distribution to the lower levels of the market (Pearson, 1987b; Dorn et al., 1992). This grade of drug trafficking which attracts retailers including drug users who deal in drugs in order to support their own habit, has received widespread publicity, not only through the significant low-level law enforcement strategies which are directed at it but also through the media which in their prime and sensational exposure of drug trafficking activities in inner cities, accompanied with the image of the deadly drug trafficker, have maintained and perpetuated a connection between drug trafficking, race and inner cities. Black men are defined as the drug traffickers and represented in the image of professionals in drug trafficking activities; they have, in effect, remained key targets in the drugs law enforcement practices. Indeed, as Cashmore and McLaughlin (1991, p.11) describe:

> Throughout the 1970s and 1980s the concern about black youth and their supposed 'heritage of violence' as 'muggers', 'drug barons', 'steamers', 'Yardies' and 'posses' has been handled in such a way as to engender public support for police strategies, especially as most of the stereotypes have been uncritically accepted and, at times, supported by politicians and the mass media.

The above description is still demonstrated in the 1990s perception of drug trafficking. A description of a mafia-style drug market saturated by 'Big-Time' black professional drug traffickers is attached to black communities by the media; and over-policing operations in black areas has long been justified sometimes leading to police harassment of black people, allegations of drug planting (Chigwada, 1991) and similar unpleasant encounters between the two groups - exemplified in the 1981 Brixton disorder and the 1985 riots in Handsworth (Birmingham) and Broadwater Farm Estate (London). Drug raids and selective drug laws enforcement form part of the policing tactics employed to control blacks, particularly, in the 1980s when drug operations by the police involved military-style tactics in raids and surveillance in black settlements. The prevalent street level drugs policing is considered necessary to tackle inner city drug trafficking. In a report by the Advisory Council on the Misuse of Drugs (Home Office, 1994c, pp 3-4) this policing strategy is justified thus:

> An important element of street level policing is the tactic of stop and search of individuals suspected of involvement in drug offences. A significant amount of activity involving drugs is concentrated in our inner cities, where ethnic minorities are also heavily represented. In turn, this can result in apparently disproportionate numbers of ethnic minorities being stopped and searched compared with the general population.

It could be legitimately argued that the image of black people as drug traffickers and black localities as drug areas is deeply embedded in official mythology. Even though such conception is based on illogical assumptions, it attracts the subjection of black people to frequent and indiscriminate drugs law enforcement strategies, and meanwhile, the spotlight is taken off the influential social categories that dominate the drug trafficking business. During a public seminar held on 18 September 1991 at the London Borough of Lambeth Town Hall, the police identified Lambeth, where a high proportion of black people reside, as a drug (especially Crack) trafficking area. Thus, in an Annual Report of the Brixton Division of the London Metropolitan Police (Metropolitan Police, 1991, p.1), the high level of importance given to drugs policing in such inner city area was addressed:

> The sale and distribution of illegally obtained drugs continues to be
> one of the principal priorities for police activity.

Complaints made by black people reflect the extensive use of low-level policing in drugs associated areas. Day (1989, p.11) comments on the feelings of blacks 'that the police are quick to label them as criminals, concentrating on areas of so called "black crime" such as mugging and drugs'.

What seems clear is that blacks form a group and class of people who remain vulnerable targets, easy prey and ideal scapegoats for stringent law enforcement, given the failure of law enforcement agencies to control the powerful forces in the drug market. The disproportionate representation of black people in the criminal statistics for drug offences is therefore not surprising.

3 Social Construction and Claims-making: Theory and Methods

Theoretical Perspective

Here, how an alleged drug offence is socially constructed in the courtroom by legal actors through the process of *claims-making* is placed in a theoretical context. According to Spector and Kitsuse (1977, p.78), claims-making 'is always a form of interaction: a demand made by one party to another that something be done about some putative condition'. In applying this conception to the court process, claims-making takes the form of demands and assertions made in an interaction setting whereby what is or is not a drug offence is described and defined - a defendant is perceived as either guilty or innocent. The social problem of drug offence is therefore a human construction; it does not come into existence until it is perceived, described, constructed and defined as such (Spector and Kitsuse, 1977; Kitsuse and Spector, 1975). Its 'reality' emerges from the diverse social constructions placed upon it in an ongoing interaction situation between legal actors who engage in the categorisation of presumed attributes as indications of a drug offence - a social problem (Best, 1989; Pfohl, 1977; Conrad and Schneider, 1980).

Court proceedings are dramatic events staged with actors assuming their varied roles and positions in the interaction process. Goffman's dramaturgical model (Gouldner, 1970) is apparent here in the sense that a courtroom arena is like a stage, a theatre and the interaction process depicts a drama. Participants in the claims-making activities are actors engaged in an ongoing drama. And the outcome of a drug trial depends on the collective work of these actors. As Blumer (1971, p.301) observes, the formation of social problems 'from the initial point of their appearance to whatever may be the terminal point in their course' is located in the process of collective definition. In examining how legal actors and other participants in drug trials collectively define their situation and attach meanings to events that take place in the courtroom, we can explore the meaning of 'a crime' as it is constructed within the 'fact finding' process of court inquiry.

Legal actors' aim in drug offence trials is to establish the guilt or innocence of black and white defendants, and in doing so, subjectiveness surround the collective constructions placed upon the objective facts of a drug case. This means that the end product of drug offence cases involving black and white defendants emerges principally from the subjective definitions given to factual or assumed characteristics of defendants' cases by legal actors in a claims-making activity. Evidently, the objective facts of a drug offence case form the bases of the claims-making activity; they underlie the lawyers' claims and the judicial response to the claims. However, the existence of the facts does not in itself constitute the guilt or innocence of a defendant; instead, the facts form part of the rhetorical activity of legal actors in the claims-making process; they form part of the process through which drug offence cases involving black and white defendants are subjectively described (kalunta-Crumpton, 1998). In the process of claims-making, the absoluteness of drug cases becomes diluted; the objective facts get distorted in the rigmarole, legal niceties and bartering between members. Drug trials reveal that phenomena often appear inconsistent, confusing and uncertain, yet a 'real' picture is afterwards constructed and formed. And although a plurality of interpretations is given to the *same* supposed condition, its definition is however created; that which lacks clarity is eventually 'made sense of' through the process of negotiation; ambiguities are filtered out in the processing of a case and what initially appeared amorphous is shaped into a definite construct. Thus, the transformation of an inconsistent phenomenon into a 'fact' in the social process is, therefore, a social construction, a negotiated 'reality', and not something that develops in a vacuum - as Conrad and Schneider (1980, p.21) note:

> "Reality" is defined not as something that exists "out there" for the
> scientist or anyone else to discover but as a social construction that
> emerges from and sustained by social interaction.

Likewise the 'reality' of a drug offence is not a glaring and fixed phenomenon 'out there' awaiting discovery, rather it results from the debate, lobbying and negotiation between actors making claims; it emerges from the varied human elements that penetrate the legal procedure; its formation is influenced by discretionary practices and power positions of actors (Becker, 1963; Davis, 1971; Carlen, 1976; Eaton, 1986).

Justice is negotiated (Cicourel, 1976). The negotiating nature of justice in drug cases reflects, for example, the discretion, personal values, moral standards, knowledge, taken-for-granted assumptions and conceptions of competing legal actors and other members involved in the problem. The situation in the courtroom is pluralistic and characterised by an organisation of differences. All parties involved in the trial process act, as Quinney (1970, p.158) states, 'according to their own pasts, their present perspectives, and their future expectancies; and their actions are oriented to the behaviour of others'. We witness a scene composed of lawyers, judges, (and magistrates), juries and witnesses with diverse values, beliefs and so forth competing and negotiating to create or prevent the creation of a drug offence. The process involves a struggle and bargaining between these actors; it is also shaped by conflict - conflict between the prosecution and the defence to prove guilt or innocence; between lawyers and the judiciary over their interpretation of the law; and among the jury to ascertain what they consider the 'actual facts' of the alleged drug offence. This opposition which goes on at various points in the process is not based solely on values, nor is it based upon ideologies and similar human criteria alone. It is also concerned with the exercise of authority. Conflict is almost inevitable where there is a differential distribution of authority or where power positions indicate superordination and subordination (Dahrendorf, 1959).

In essence, a defendant's guilt or innocence emerges from ambiguous social interaction, particularly, involving legal actors or 'protagonists' (Giddens, 1991) or 'imputational specialists' as Pfohl (1978) would describe them. Legal actors' interpretation of what is wrong or right is relative and lacks universality. In any case, the validity or falsity of legal actors' perspectives and definitions regarding an alleged drug offence is irrelevant (Spector and Kitsuse, 1977), as what matters in the social construction process is how members in the legal setting negotiate shared knowledge, beliefs and so forth, and how they logically engage in an interpretative process in their encounter with each other. What this means is that participants' representations of social problems are similar to those popularly shared in the society and correspondingly, drug cases are placed within the realm of the wider society, revealing that the court is part of the society and as such it is an institution that operates with reference to the social structure (Eaton, 1986; Quinney, 1970). Stereotypes, myths and beliefs which are inherent in the wider society form part of the process through which claims are made about black and white defendants' cases. Cashmore and McLaughlin (1991, p.40) have similarly observed that 'stereotype images' and 'convenient myths' rather than 'empirical facts or scientific observations' often determine the construction of realities. Invariably, the objective facts about a presumed drug offence are most times not presented and described by legal actors as the *governing* issue, instead, details that are not directly related to the alleged drug offence in question become the central focus of the debate, and the facticity of 'the case', although important, receives minimal attention. In the process, what is demonstrated is how the awareness of legacies is embedded in the 'fact establishing' process, resulting in differential descriptions of black and white defendants' cases - in a form tantamount, for instance, to stereotypical images of race, drugs and crime, and beliefs about race and policing.

The pattern that claims-making activities takes does not necessarily reflect the idealised form of the written law but is constructed within a situational context, and this is because legal actors (and other participants involved in the court process) as members of society are not dominated by learned rules (Worsley, 1970). Even though rules are made to be followed by members, patterns of interaction are not fixed but are unstable; they develop and change depending on various factors including the context within which the interaction process occurs. The law, like other normative rules, in itself is partial. From the standpoint of ethnomethodology normative rules witness 'essential incompleteness' (Mehan and Wood, 1975) no matter how well codified they are. In the perspective of symbolic interaction, those 'rules which are learned do not completely and precisely specify the details of individual conduct. The rules of society are often vague, ambiguous and quite unclear in their implication' (Worsley, 1970, p.545). To this extent, the law as a system of rules, well laid out and codified does not cover the personal facts of participants in the legal setting; it does not incorporate situational factors, or new informal rules that emerge as new situations arise in the day-to-day activities of members. Consequently, the 'essential incompleteness' of the rules of law is 'filled in' by informal rules which Garfinkel (1967) refers to as the 'et cetera clause'.

In such instances, negotiation and particularism manifest in the activities of legal members, contrary to the definiteness and universality that the rules of law illustrate. For in spite of the presence of 'legislative or judicial norms', Gusfield (1981, p.133) argues:

> common behaviour may adhere to other standards, other values. All of these facts and values seem to be at work in the ways in which practical contingencies, accepted social norms, interests, and powers operate in daily life.

What we are presented with during court proceedings is a legal process that contradicts the principles of justice, and in any case, such deviation from the due process principles is institutionalised in the law itself (McBarnet, 1983). Yet, we are not to assume that legal actors do not act with reference to the normative order - the rules of law. The argument, instead, is that underneath such adherence to the law is a gradual process of negotiation whereby the law is open to varied considerations; whereby a new less formal set of rules, a different realm of law is created but not included in the general written rules of law governing the administration of justice; whereby the objective nature of drug offence cases is coloured by the subjective influences of legal actors.

Both formal and informal ('hidden') determining factors are unveiled in the course of justice For example, legally provided discretion is brought into existence in the routine day-to-day legal practices of legal actors; also, legal members employ their own 'et cetera clause' in the negotiation and construction of 'reality'. These factors as Gusfield (1981) would say, form 'part of the way in which a rough justice is meted out and a sense of fairness maintained'; they form part of the way in which race is represented in the claims-making activities of legal actors.

Claims-making and Discretionary Justice

> ...those who have comparatively more power in a society are typically more able to create and impose their rules and sanctions on the less powerful (Conrad and Schneider, 1980, p.2).

> ...in the process of registering criminals, or transforming normals into (official) deviants, state agents have considerable discretion (Box, 1971, p.169).

> Discretion is at the root of criminal justice practice (Sanders, 1994, p.776).

Claims-making activity, as already stated, has no fixed or definite pattern but occur within a situational context. The 'reality' of a social problem is influenced by the discretionary power of the definers or those whom Becker (1963) would refer to as 'moral entrepreneurs' to impose their definitions on others. Thus, the pattern of claims-making in drug trials reveals that power positions and discretion in their inter-related form are fundamental in the imposition or non-imposition of criminal definitions on assumed characteristics, or in the guilt or innocence producing process. The use of discretion by legal actors enables the conversion of fiction into 'fact'; it determines what qualities constitute a drug offence and how cases are interpreted by legal actors in drug trials of black and white defendants. At various stages in the court process, discretion is applied and utilised by legal actors within a complex of individual conceptions and social interactions. And throughout the transitional process, from the point a behaviour is observed and given a name to the point where it is either established as 'real' or 'unreal', discretionary power is exercised with the influential members structuring their actions in terms of meanings they give to situations. Their interpretations of events represent their reality. In any case, as Hawkins (1992, p.11) rightly points out:

> Discretion is a central and inevitable part of the legal order....Discretion is the means by which law - the most consequential normative system in a society - is translated into action....Discretion - which might be regarded as the space, as it were, between legal rules in which legal actors may exercise choice - may be formally granted, or it may be assumed.

It is the complex, ambiguous, inflexible and incomplete nature of legal rules that calls for the granting of discretionary authority to those who apply them (Schneider, 1992).

Not all presumed drug offences become defined and constructed as a social problem. In other words, the obvious existence of a drug offence is dependent on the reaction of others. As Becker (1963, p.14) observes:

> Deviance is not a simple quality, present in some kinds of behaviour and absent in others. It is a product of a process which involves responses of other people to the behaviour.

Quinney (1970, p.207) similarly states:

> No behaviour is criminal until it has been so defined through recognized procedures of the state. In this sense, "criminal behaviour" differs from "noncriminal behaviour" only according to the definition that has been created by others. It is not the quality of the behaviour, but the nature of the action taken against the behaviour that gives it the character of criminality.

The criminal label, in effect, is a product of 'collective action' (Becker, 1963). Conditions which become officially classified as a social problem are socially constructed phenomena that stem from the patterns of social interaction of which discretion is a major determining factor. In the presence of discretion, similar events can be viewed and interpreted differently and overall, constructed differently. Likewise, 'the same behaviour may be an infraction of the rules at one time and not at another; may be an infraction when committed by one person but not when committed by another' (Becker, 1963, p.14).

This image suggests that flexibility, relativity and inconsistency are embedded in the guilt and innocence forming process; that in the routine process of drug offence trials, justice is not uniformly administered. With no defined instructions as to the implementation of the law, discretion remains a crucial characteristic in the administration of justice. In black and white defendants' cases, the racial element reveals itself in the discretionary practices of legal members as they attribute meanings and definitions to the behaviour of the defendants.

Lawyers and Claims-making

The prosecution and the defence are the most active participants in the claims-making process. Claims-making is utilised as a tool by these legal actors in the court process and it is in their interest, in a confrontation between them, to make their respective assertions acceptable to the judge and jury (or the magistrate). Claims-making activities in the court process is a fight (see Frank, 1949) where the primary weapon used by lawyers is verbal. Claims are argued and debated, and what the supposed drug offence (which constitutes the claims) 'really is' is defined through a struggle to present claims effectively in order to persuade the judge and jury[1] to which they are addressed. Best (1987, p.102) describes claims-making as 'a rhetorical activity'. He adds, 'Claims-making is an act of communication....Claims-making attempts to persuade' (1989, p.1). Spector and Kitsuse (1977) have used the term 'values' in their analysis of social problem construction and as they have argued, the concept - 'values' 'are an important element' in the social problem producing process. 'Values' 'are the explanations people give in support of their claims, complaints or demands...'.; they are 'those statements that express the grounds or the basis of the complaints' (pp 92 & 93). 'Values' may be imputed by members to explain the actions and claims of other participants in the social problem producing activities. Best (1987) has also employed the terms 'Grounds' and 'Warrants' as vital rhetorical devices utilised in the persuasion process. 'Grounds' constitute the key facts of a condition which form the basis of an assertion and 'Warrants' are 'statements which justify drawing conclusions from the grounds' (p.108) - and are used to emphasise and solidify a line of argument. Whilst claims have grounds, the nature of the claims are justified by way of representation and accordingly, Best (1989) further identifies 'typification' as an essential component of claims-making in any social condition.

In the trial process, we see lawyers adopting any promotional strategy to realise their goal; they try to articulate their claims and 'make sense' of the cases by utilising various 'warrants' and 'typifications' that they *believe* would sound meaningful and convincing to the judge and jury (or the magistrate). In the process, lawyers' own sets of meanings, common-sense reasoning, stocks of knowledge and similar elements, embedded in the 'warrants' and 'typifications', are brought into the interpretation and assessment of circumstances surrounding the alleged drug offence. As the meanings they give to events are influenced by the realities in which they individually operate, the process of establishing a defendant's guilt or innocence will therefore reflect their bodies of knowledge and conceptions of phenomena in the interaction situation.. It is in this context that familiar imageries, stereotypes and so forth infiltrate lawyers' discourse in the representation of black and white defendants' cases. What *really* matters in the claims-making process is the ability to logically or reasonably describe, justify and portray events, and persuade through language - a primary symbolic medium through which members convey meanings to each other in social interaction; an important rhetorical device that competing members utilise to attract a required response. Such human interaction according to Herbert Mead also takes the form of non-verbal gestural practices (Adler and Adler, 1980) - another vehicle through which meanings are exchanged by members, and which sometimes remain as powerful as words (Giddens, 1991). It is the way in which language is used in presenting and describing a case rather than the facticity of the case that often justifies a claim. Mehan and Wood (1975, p. 18) rightly argue that 'the factual matters of a case comprise only a part of the apparatus which the courtroom participants employ to decide a case'. Put differently, the outcome of a case is not often determined by the factual evidence presented about the case. The significance of a claim lies in its justification which derives much of its intelligibility from the 'rationality' of the debate regarding the event. As McBarnet (1983, p.12) points out, 'justification lies not in any idealism that "the truth the whole truth and nothing but the truth" results, but in pragmatics'. In essence, what matters in the legal system is winning or losing and not truth or falsity (Matoesian, 1993).

The issues that prosecuting and defence lawyers raise to justify their assertions often reflect the positivist model. Positivism assumes a value consensus in society, discarding behaviours which violate this consensus as meaningless and unhealthy for the society. Criminality is one of such deviant behaviours that threatens 'the agreed upon' consensus. Since positivist explanations are facilitated by the existence of cause-and-effect statements, criminal behaviours are believed to be determined. Consequently, criminality has been given biogenic explanations as manifested in Lombroso's 'criminal type' (Taylor et al., 1973; Roshier, 1989); psychoanalytic explanations have ascribed criminal behaviour to psychological characteristics (Clinard, 1968); sociogenic theories explain criminality within the context of, for example, social structural factors such as socio-economic deprivation (Downes and Rock, 1988). Defendants are usually portrayed in such positivist fashion, for instance, in a language which relate their association or supposed association with drug offence to socio-economic factors. In like manner, the drug offence (or assumed) itself is analysed within a positivist framework in the sense that it is cognitively and morally assessed (Gusfield, 1981). In passing a cognitive judgement, theories and beliefs about the phenomenon are posited such as the 'fact' that deprivation leads to crime. The moral aspect, Gusfield (ibid., p.9) notes:

> is that which enables the situation to be viewed as painful, ignoble, immoral. It is what makes alteration or eradication desirable or continuation valuable.

It is common for claims to be 'buttressed by espousals of moral positions and assertions of value judgements' (Spector and Kitsuse, 1977, p.92). The language that these members popularly use in the court process is neither unique nor unfamiliar for it is analogous to that used in political and official discussions, throughout the mass media and in the works of academics. Statements and utterances revealed in lawyers' interrogations (and witnesses evidence), pleas of mitigation and bail applications - which demonstrate for instance, images of race, crime and drugs - derive their intelligibility from information provided and upheld by institutions that constitute a major source of knowledge and beliefs for members in society.

Lawyers' claims made against, or on behalf of, defendants are justified differently according to race: black and white defendants' cases are constructed in terms that are unsimilar in similar cases; explanations evoked to ground and justify assertions regarding the defendants differ regardless of similarities in circumstances surrounding the cases. Their arguments are dominated by racial stereotypes and beliefs, exhibiting the negotiation and construction of 'reality' to fit their theoretical pre-conceptions and perpetuate their ideologies. Ultimately, there appears to be a pattern of prosecution and defence which serves to keep the black defendants at a disadvantaged position before the judge and jury[2].

Response and Claims-making

Three groups of participants - the judge and the jury in the Crown Court and the magistrate in the lower court - engage in the responding activities. In a social problem producing process, all parties to the problem do not have the same ability to influence the formation or non-formation of a social problem; they as Gusfield (1981, p.8) argues 'do not possess the same degree or kind of authority to be legitimate sources of definition of the reality of the problem, or to assume legitimate power to regulate, control and innovate solutions'. Of particular relevance is the Crown Court setting where the judge and the jury are the most powerful in the social construction process; they impose their terms of reference and ultimately could determine or determine the finished product of a drug offence trial; they are invested with the authority to either define or not define an alleged drug offence as a social problem. It has been argued above that the ultimate goal of the contending participants - the lawyers - is to shape the opinion of the judge and jury to their (that is, the lawyers') advantage. I have also mentioned that in the bid to invite a favourable response, contending lawyers utilise all sorts of stratagems, and in their concerted effort to influence the responders, they invariably express their beliefs and so forth. In addressing the responding activities of the judiciary, we will see how some claims receive greater support than the others and how judges identify with either claimants or counter-claimants in the claims-making process. We shall be addressing what *conditions* judicial acceptance or negation of claims made by lawyers, and show how differential treatment by race arise from the responding activities of judges[3]. In the concluding part of this book, we shall ask what *governs* decisions made by the jury.

The success or failure of assertions depend upon the meaning and interpretations given to the differing claims by those whose right it is to assess them. As human beings, judges (and jurors) are not mere machines; they are not dispassionate, unemotional fixed objects. As members of society, they too have varied values, moral standards, cultural norms, stocks of knowledge, theories and typifications. Therefore, whether or not they treasure specific assertions will, to a reasonable extent, be determined by the world of discourse in which they belong (Griffith, 1985). Whilst judges in their routine practices may adhere to both the procedural and legal rules provided by the law, their decisions may also be based on their subjective reactions to the conflicting members' diverse information and actions. After all, the judge and the jury only know about the phenomenon through the oral testimony (which is open to fallibility) of opposing claimants and accordingly rely on the evidence presented before them. Similar to this viewpoint,

Frank (1949, p.37) states that the 'actual facts of a case do not walk into court, but happened outside the court-room, and always in the past'. What the court does, Frank adds 'is to reconstruct the past from what are at best second-hand reports of the facts'.

In drug trials, disagreement exists in the way judges understand and view drug offence cases and this inconsistency is reflected in the variations that underlie judicial interpretations of similar cases. What seems to significantly guide this group of responding members in the process is their subjective feelings, that is, what they individually believe to be the truth about a case. In the main, it is not the facticity of the phenomenon that solely matters but its subjective believability. As will be revealed, what judges believe to be real stems from their common understanding of some 'facts of life' and it takes the similarities in meanings given to events, the shared conceptions of persuaders and those being persuaded for a world of 'fact' to be created. For example, contending members' arguments capture a positive attention of a judge when racial stereotypes 'make sense' in a way to explicate a connection between an alleged drug offence and drug offender. This is because judges like opposing claimants, introduce what Box (1981) calls 'non-legalistic considerations' or 'irrelevant criteria'; or 'extralegal factors' in the words of Quinney (1970); and according to Bottomley (1973), 'extra judicial factors'; or still, 'extra-legal resources' according to Platt (1969)[4]. These factors reflect these members own moral standards, ideological orientations, their conception of the aetiology of criminality and their stereotypical image of criminals which are among a multitude of stimuli that provide the basis for their actions and decisions. By way of the rhetorical device - claims-making, an art of persuasion used to induce belief, judges' responding activities are carried out in reference to the meanings they attach to events; they interpret situations according to the ideas that they are exposed to and the type of knowledge they accumulate; and they bring their morals and values into play in their characterisation of guilt or innocence. In the definitional process, judges responding activities are not only effected verbally but are also carried out through their unspoken gestures. Non-verbal communications such as cynical smiles are used to interpret events and to 'make sense' of the situation to other members. Through these means, judges show their agreement with, or negation of, claims and justifications, and it is also in this pattern of response that their conceptions of issues regarding a drug case become patent.

The rhetorical strategy is subtly employed by judges in their commentaries and above all, in their instructions to their responding partners - the jury. Later in this book, we will take a more detailed look at the popular lines of argument that judges uphold in order to understand how the reaction of a jury may be shaped by how rhetorically persuasive a judge is. The views of judges often move along this line: members in society have a common-sense knowledge of the 'natural facts of life' (Garfinkel, 1967) that depict the real society which they are part of. They are expected to comply with their common-sense understanding of these 'facts of life' or 'expectancies' in order to uphold an interaction process between them. It becomes a breach of contract and a threat to the legitimate order when a member of society does not adhere to these 'known facts' which include 'known moral standards' or 'known values' legitimised and sustained by the dominant class to stabilise the social order. However, the understanding or knowledge of the 'facts of life' is not universal and varies in a pluralistic society. Some members of society may be unaware of the supposed known facts of life and others may not agree with them.

Nevertheless, in the course of claims-making, judges draw the attention of other participants to the 'agreed upon' behavioural patterns. They emphasise their perspectives on issues and invariably convey to other members, their beliefs in relation to what they consider the 'actual facts' of a condition. Fellow members are reminded of what they are expected to view as acceptable or unacceptable actions, and to perceive the alleged problem at hand within the realm of the pre-existing consensus. Judges express a dislike towards behaviours that prove a threat to the existing social order and to law and order which they aim to maintain (Griffith, 1985). They preach the need to preserve specific social and moral standards, and to maintain a stable society in the interest of the 'generalised other', an interest which reflects their own class interest, and which also coincides with the   interest of those in other positions of authority (ibid.). In their commentaries, the assumed social problem is imbued with an aura of consensus, thus exemplifying a conservative view and fostering the acceptance of their own ideologies. Through their statements, as shall be demonstrated, judges attempt to galvanise the jury into holding certain lines of reasoning and if what the jury decides about a case is coloured by a judge's beliefs, the latter's apprehension of the 'actual facts' of the case will prevail.

Within this context of the responding process, race emerges as a vital element in the accumulation of variations in the way in which similar drug cases are perceived - indicated in the language with which events are portrayed. Judges' use of terminology differ in the manner they understand, interpret and describe similar black and white defendants' cases; black and white defendants in similar circumstances are questioned differently. Seemingly, this disparity derives its strength from judges' subjective considerations, such as, what appears to be an adherence to the belief that crime is more prevalent amongst blacks[5]. Ultimately, it may be that the juries' decisions on the drug cases demonstrate different criteria in similar situations.

Methodological Approach

In 1991, I conducted a seven month field study of court proceedings involving black and white defendants charged with a drug offence. Data were derived from my observations of 104 drug offence cases at one Crown Court and one magistrates' court in London. The drug cases observed were not randomly selected were studied purely on their availability. This was because the practicalities of the research process precluded control over the selective process of cases. That notwithstanding, observations were carried out in different courtrooms thus providing me with a broad view of the social construction process as it occurred in the different cases involving different judges (and magistrates), lawyers and witnesses. This is a case study and it is not my intention to exhibit the cases described here as a basis for substantial generalisation vis-à-vis other courts and times. In like manner, I do not suppose that the recorded courtroom discourse represent the generality of the courtroom dialogue in the courts researched into during the period of observation. Oral statements were recorded in shorthand and notes were made of non-verbal behaviours, forming a wealth of qualitative material which will be used in this book to shed light on the role of claims-making in the court processing of drug offence cases.

By pre-arrangement between me and my contact at the Crown Court, days and times of observations were unspecified and unlimited but at the magistrates' court, I was allowed to attend on two specified mornings although on occasions I observed afternoon court proceedings when drug cases which could not possibly be heard in the morning were adjourned till noon. In relation to the specified days of observation, one difficulty that arose was that cases that were to be observed at the magistrates' court sometimes clashed with trials that were to start or had already started at the Crown Court. On such occasions, I observed proceedings at the Crown Court for the principal reason that Crown Court trials provided more detailed and descriptive information useful to the analysis of social construction and claims-making.

At no stage prior to a trial or appearance of a case in court was a defendant's racial background known to me, therefore, it was by visual categorisation that information on the defendants' race was obtained. The courts, I was told, did not keep records of defendants' ethnic or racial origin. Information that I received from the Crown Court about a trial due to take place was limited to the name/s of the defendant/s, the charge/s on the indictment, the time of the trial and the courtroom in which the trial was to take place. On many occasions, the cases were floaters meaning that those cases were not assigned to any particular courtroom, neither was a specified time mapped out for them to be heard. On some of those occasions, I had to constantly listen to the announcements made over the tannoy system for information leading to the whereabouts of floaters. At the magistrates' court, I had access to court lists which indicated such information as the name and age of a defendant, and the charge/s. My decision as to which courtroom to sit in was based on the number of drug cases on the court lists for the courtrooms, so that a courtroom with a greater number of drug cases on the court list appeared more promising to me. A notable difficulty encountered during the observations at the two courts was that many of the cases were not completely dealt with on the same day resulting in adjournments for days or weeks. In effect, the choice of court, courtroom and cases to observe was also influenced by the need to follow up cases to the end.

In addition to the observational methods, informal interviews and discussions were held with a sample of defendants and their relatives and friends, police officers, probation officers and court staff members, during recess (sometimes over a cup of tea) or after a trial.

Data Collected

The data collected comprise:

1. 40 drug cases that appeared at the Crown Court; 23 of the cases concerned 24 black defendants and 17 of them involved 20 white defendants. Some of the defendants appeared as co-defendants.

2. 7 of the 40 Crown Court cases involving 5 black and 2 white defendants respectively were adjourned during trial, leaving 33 complete cases of which the defendants comprised 19 blacks and 18 whites.

3. 71 cases involving 42 blacks and 30 whites were heard at the magistrates' court. One black and one white appeared as co-defendants.

A total of 31 informal interviews and discussions were held with 6 defendants, 12 defendants' relatives and friends, 5 police officers, 2 court staff members and 6 probation officers.

Data Analysis: Methods

The significance of the analysis lies in a detailed examination of information drawn from observations of particular court proceedings involving black and white defendants charged with a drug offence. The purpose is to address the issue of the social construction of an alleged drug offence in the public forum of a courtroom and in doing so, this book provides a comparative analysis of the quality of treatment that defendants from two racial backgrounds receive whilst going through the court system. As the primary focus is on the claims-making activities of legal actors including what conditions and sustains them - leading to the creation of guilt or innocence - the observed proceedings which form the main material of analysis will provide a descriptive account of an interactive process between concerned participants as it occurred in the natural setting of a courtroom.

Not all the drug cases that appeared in court during the period of observation resulted in a contested trial or a completed case. This was particularly the case at the magistrates' court where no contested trial was witnessed. Apart from cases where the defendants pleaded guilty and were dealt with there and then by the magistrate, the court was concerned with preparatory procedures to commit cases to the Crown Court. However, the interaction that took place between legal actors was revealing of the stages of social construction and the processes involved. For the sake of clarity, the focus of the observation at both the Crown Court and magistrates' court is categorised into three:

1. At the Crown Court, the primary focus was on events that occurred leading to a complete case whether or not there was a contested trial.

2. In cases where defendants pleaded guilty to a drug offence charge at the magistrates' court, the debate and negotiation surrounding plea of mitigation and sentencing formed the main issue.

3. In relation to drug cases that appeared before the magistrates' court for preliminary investigation or for committal for trial in the Crown Court, attention was principally focused on the debate and negotiation over bail.

The bulk of the claims-making activities relevant to the analysis in this book took place at the Crown Court so that throughout the book, events that occurred at the Crown Court remain the primary focus of attention for our comprehension of social construction vis-à-vis the problem of black disproportionate presence in the criminal statistics. Reference made to data from the magistrates' court aims to support and solidify specific arguments on the role of race in the processing of drug cases by legal actors' at the Crown Court. In analysing the Crown Court data, a sample part of the collective role of groups of members in the social construction process is unveiled. First, the prosecution counsel (and the prosecution witnesses) in relation to how they ground and substantiate their allegations against a defendant; second, the defence counsel (and the defence witnesses) regarding how they refute allegations brought against a defendant by the prosecution; third, the judge (and the jury) and how they respond or may respond to, and determine the outcome of, the claims-making activity of the prosecution and the defence. In the course of the analysis, how differential treatment according to race emerge in the process is revealed and so is the overall impact that the disparity may have on the outcome of a drug case. Whilst analysing legal members' varied contributions to the creation or non-creation of a drug offence, attention is placed on the comparable characteristics of the process as reflected in issues and arguments raised and how they were defined and responded to in relation to black and white defendants. These comparable characteristics are indicators that identify the existence of differential treatment - in legal members' mode of interrogation, comments, non-verbal actions and so forth.

My record of informal interviews and discussions, which revolved around issues on drugs, crime, criminal justice and individual cases that appeared in court, provides background information that identified or confirmed members' personal conceptions that underlie their role in the social construction process. Although the findings do not form part of the data used for detailed analysis, some illustrations add to the wealth of qualitative material described in the book.

Notes

1   At the magistrates' court, claims-making is used by lawyers at the sentencing stage and during bail applications.
2   Lawyers at the magistrates' court describe similar black and white defendants' cases differently with race as a significant factor.
3   Magistrates' response to claims regarding bail reveal differential treatment on the basis of race which could account for the overrepresentation of black people in the remand prison population.
4   Also applicable to magistrates.

5   Seemingly, magistrates' bail decisions reflect their belief in the link between race and crime.

PART 2

THE SUBSTANCE

4 Establishing Guilt

The first step in the social construction process in the courtroom is one taken by the complainants - the prosecution (and the police). This means that the court does not go through the complex process of a trial unless the prosecution along with the police declare the existence of an 'offensive' behaviour and define it as criminal requiring the court's attention (Gandy, 1988; Ashworth, 1994; Sanders, 1994). Both the police (Box, 1981; McBarnet, 1983; Smith and Gray, 1985; Sanders, 1994) and the prosecution (Stanko, 1977; Banks, 1977; McConville and Baldwin, 1981; Kalunta-Crumpton, 1996; Mackay and Moody, 1996) have ample discretion in making prosecutorial decisions, and their joint practices and decisions play a crucial role in the way the social construction process takes place. A defendant is brought before the court with the prosecution seeking the court's validation of the arguments in favour of finding the defendant guilty. However, once a case has appeared in court, the prosecution has the power to withdraw that case, drop a charge, modify or amend a charge (Wood, 1988).

In this chapter, we shall be looking at the manner in which the prosecution present their case: a drug offence allegedly committed by a defendant. Here, the concern is to examine firstly, the significant difference in drug offence charges - with similar backgrounds - brought against the defendants and secondly, the fashion in which the allegations are interpreted and presented by the prosecution. Primarily, this chapter demonstrates that in cases where there are similarities in circumstances, the prosecution's pattern of proving guilt is often inconsistent and racially differentiated. Alongside legal rules, a combination of knowledge and common-sense understanding (Frohmann, 1991) of issues surrounding drug offences or potential drug offenders seem to shape the way that the complainants' assertions are presented and supported. Illicit drug use is commonly associated with deprivation (Burr, 1987; Haw, 1985; Pearson et al., 1987) and in like manner, drug trafficking is linked to race (Dorn et al., 1992). Manifested during the prosecution's examination, cross-examination and re-examination procedures (and in the evidence given by the police), we encounter a subtle display of personal beliefs and typifications of drug offenders, for although blacks and whites are prosecuted, the former are more likely to be cast as the 'real' offenders.

The prosecutors are the 'providers of key information about the details and circumstances of the offence...'. (Parker et al., 1989, p.98). They have a personal choice of making an offence 'sound much worse...' or making it 'sound much less serious than it first appeared' (ibid.). During claims-making, questions raised and statements made by the prosecution differ in content and emphasis according to defendants' race, irrespective of similarities in cases. The pattern of proving guilt means tapping into knowledge which has as its ingredients elements of racial awareness, stereotypes and theoretical preconceptions (Kalunta-Crumpton, 1996, 1998). It is this knowledge that they communicate to other members in the courtroom which ultimately may work against the interests of black defendants. This chapter shows the extent that the prosecution go in pressing their search for incriminating information about black defendants, and how they use whatever means available and draw upon whatever information to justify allegations against black defendants. The discussions and interviews with the police, and record of interrogations by prosecutors in drug trials will provide illustrative materials on their conceptions of the phenomenon in question and elucidate their role in the social construction of guilt.

Grounds for Complaints

Drug offence charges brought against the defendants include (1) unlawful possession of a controlled drug; (2) unlawful possession of a controlled drug with intent to supply to another; (3) offering to supply a controlled drug to another; (4) supplying a controlled drug to another; (5) conspiracy to deal in a controlled drug; (6) concerned in supplying a controlled drug to another; and (7) importation of a controlled drug. Furthermore, the number of drug offence charges instituted against the defendants ranged from one to seven. In reality, the more the number of charges, the more likely it is to establish guilt, at least so the complainants believe. Thus, the following comment by a police officer, "I tell you, he's not gonna get away with it not with all those charges (four charges). He is better off pleading guilty", epitomises this point. In addition to the drug offence charges, a significant number of the defendants were charged with other offences that were drug-related or not drug-related at all. This was particularly the case with the defendants that appeared at the magistrates' court.

The most common drug offence charge brought against the defendants was unlawful possession of a controlled drug with intent to supply to another. Most committals to the Crown Court made at the magistrates' court involved this charge and most of the contested trials that took place at the Crown Court were in relation to this charge. The 'intent to supply' charge and other 'supply' charges fall within the realm of a drug trafficking offence (Home Office, 1986b, 1989b) which is considered 'extremely' serious and worthy of a 'severe' punishment. Such drug offence charges are subject to the provisions of the law meant for the control of drug trafficking and suspects charged with any of these offences face a greater likelihood of receiving a harsh penalty in the form of a custodial sentence, once convicted. For example, the defendants who were found guilty of 'intent to supply' at the Crown Court received a custodial sentence. In both courts, particularly the magistrates' court, white defendants were mostly charged with possession of a controlled drug and supplying a controlled drug to another; unlawful possession of a controlled drug with intent to supply was a charge mostly brought against black defendants. These charges were the most significant in number. In any case, the majority of the defendants who appeared in these courts during the period of observation were black. And unlike their white counterparts, the majority of the black defendants charged with 'intent to supply' in both courts were remanded in custody and at the magistrates' court were mostly committed to stand trial at the Crown Court, often, on the principal recommendation of the prosecution. Magistrates related their decision to remand defendants (who were mostly black) in custody or commit cases to the Crown Court to the seriousness of this particular drug trafficking offence charge.

Pre-trial custody is not a condition conducive to the projection of a favourable image of a defendant in the sense that it symbolises a presumption of guilt and could create in the minds of magistrates, judges and jury, a feeling associating a defendant with the offence even before the trial commences. Studies have shown, according to McBarnet (1983, p.13), 'that defendants who have been on bail stand a better chance of acquittal than those who have not perhaps because they have less opportunity to come smartly turned out for the occasion, perhaps because of the cues suggested by just being in custody'. Barnett (1977) has also noted that an accused on bail has a chance of preparing his case. The relatively few black defendants who were granted bail at the magistrates' court were placed on strict bail conditions such as surety of large amounts of money, imposition of curfew, conditions of residence, reporting daily at a police station at specified times, restrictions on movement and so forth.

During drug trials, the level of seriousness ascribed by the prosecution to such drug offences as 'intent to supply' and 'supplying drugs to another' seemingly varies according to the race of the defendants. There was no clear consensus that I could find as an observer between the prosecutors as to the charges instituted against defendants who supposedly committed similar offences. What had been anticipated was that a greater part of any discrepancy according to race would stem from differences in the gravity of the offence which is a legally-provided criterion for variations in charges. In drug cases with similarities in the bases for the charges, a disparity exists in the charges pressed against black and white defendants with the former charged with a more serious drug offence. In my interviews and discussions with police officers, they were asked what the bases are for charging a suspect with unlawful possession of a controlled drug with intent to supply. The explanations below, as given by two police officers from the drugs squad, are the sine qua non for instituting the charge against a suspect. One of the police officer claims:

> The quantity of drug in the person's possession is a strong incriminating evidence. Another thing is how the drug was broken up. For instance, if a person is in possession of several separate amounts of drugs separately wrapped, it will be fair to assume that that person is a pusher, especially, if he or she has a pocket full of money as well.

My question (to the police officer) as to what quantity of drug would constitute evidence of 'intent to supply' received the answer "a saleable quantity". On the basis of this answer, a saleable quantity could be any quantity. The second officer's version reads thus:

> It depends on a lot of things. If someone is caught on the street with a pocket full of dope, it's obvious that he is a trafficker, after all junkies, don't often walk about the streets carrying large quantities of the stuff on them, only the pushers. On the other hand, if you raid a suspect's flat, certain items in that flat can give you a good idea of whether you have got a pusher or not. These dealers have usually got plenty of you know little plastic bags, cling film and sometimes you may be lucky and find a set of scales.

These two quotations indicate the existence of objective or factual evidence reasonably believed by the police to be relevant to the institution of the aforementioned drug offence charge; they also show the existence of conjectural and discretional influences in police decisions to press a prosecution for a particular drug offence.

The reasons given by the prosecution in their submission for bringing the 'intent to supply' charge against a defendant also show that the bases for this charge include (1) the amount of drug found in the person's possession or control which in the terms of the complainants must be "a saleable quantity" or "a large quantity" or "a substantial quantity" (2) if the drug found in the person's possession or control was separated into two or more portions in which case it would be believed to be for sale (3) if the suspect had sums of money (especially if considered 'large' or 'substantial') or assets (if particularly considered 'huge') identified to be the proceeds of drug trafficking (4) if drug-related paraphernalia identified to be for the production and distribution of drugs were found in the suspect's possession or control. Such items as tin foil, baking powder, cling film, a set of weighing-scales and baking powder were classified as being related to drug trafficking.

Any of the above criteria in the eyes of the prosecution makes a suspect eligible for incurring this charge. These criteria are also relevant to other drug trafficking offence charges and they apply irrespective of the class of drug. At the Crown Court where the grounds for complaints are comprehensively stated, there is evidence that charges do not correspond to the grounds, in terms of their being racially universal, in spite of the resemblance in the overt reasons given for bringing the cases to court. Every complaint made against a defendant is grounded by the prosecution in his/her submission which takes the form of narrating a brief story as to why the alleged behaviour by a defendant is considered improper and criminal and why the case is brought before the court. The submission constitutes the substance of the case - the grounds for complaints. It is those grounds presented by the prosecution whilst making the initial complaint that will first be discussed, for it is during the submissions that a racially-underlined discrepancy in charges surfaces when the bases for the allegations are similar. Those grounds form the beginning and the bedrock of the social construction of guilt and innocence in drug trials. The following two examples are illustrations of differences in charges where grounds for complaints made by the prosecution are similar. Two defendants, one black and the other white, appeared in court on different occasions for committing a drug offence. The former was charged for being in unlawful possession of a class A drug with intent to supply, and the latter was charged for being in unlawful possession of a class A drug. In a description of why the black defendant was brought before the court, the prosecution states:

> ...the defendant was stopped by the police for committing a driving offence....His behaviour according to the arresting officers was suspicious when he was being questioned about the driving offence....Knowing that he had drugs on him, the defendant acted like he was in a hurry, claiming that he was going to pick up his son from school. He left his car and walked

off in a rush and on the way dropped something on the ground, an act that was noticed by the officers. He was again stopped...and one of the officers picked up what he dropped and it turned out to be a silver wrap containing 321 milligrams of cocaine, a class A drug. He was arrested and taken to the police station. He agreed that the drug was his and that it was meant for his own personal use. On being searched at the station, one hundred pounds was found on him which the defendant said was payment for a building job he did, but the police claim that the money was made from illicit drug dealing.

The prosecution in the white defendant's case states:

At about (time) on (date and year), the defendant, Mr A was arrested on X road for being in unlawful possession of a controlled drug, namely 418 milligrams of diamorphine - heroin. On the day of the arrest, there was a heavy traffic hold-up on X road and there happened to be several police officers on that road at the time trying to control the traffic. The defendant in an attempt to get away from the traffic jam, committed a traffic offence. He was approached by two officers who demanded that he got out of his car. His car was searched by these officers and inside the dashboard was eighty five pounds and a silver foil which was not concealed. The silver foil contained a rizzla paper which was used in wrapping the powdery substance, that is, the heroin. The defendant was arrested. In his interview with the police at the station, he told them that the drug belonged to him and that he was a heroin user. He also told the police that the eighty five pounds was part of his social security allowance. The defendant today is claiming that the drug which he without inhibitions told the police belonged to him was not really his.

In these two cases, similar grounds gave rise to the respective charges: both defendants were in possession of what criminal justice agents often describe as "a small amount" or "an extremely small amount" of drug; the drugs found on both of them were singly wrapped; in addition to the similar sums of money found in their possession which they both accounted for, none of them was associated with any item related to drug use or drug trafficking. The charges however differed.

What also came to notice in drug trials was the influence of plea status in the choice of charges pressed against defendants regardless of the resemblance in the circumstances surrounding the charges. Prior to my observations of court proceedings, I was made to understand by criminal justice agents, particularly probation officers, that black offenders, unlike their white counterparts, do not usually plead guilty to their offence which accounts for their accumulation of charges. Black defendants, they claim, contest their cases and in effect go through the adversarial trial in court, and expectedly, they face the hostility of the court and a greater possibility of incurring a severe sentence if found guilty. The following statement by a probation officer illustrates this point:

> Black defendants rarely plead guilty to the charges against them....They end up with several charges and that partly explains why they often receive a custodial sentence. Many of them that appear in court have quite a lot of charges facing them and it is so surprising that they don't plead guilty to any of the charges, at least to make it easier on themselves. I feel that their reluctance to plead guilty to an offence has a lot to do with lack of legal advice which itself has a lot of pitfalls....Drug offence cases appear in the magistrates' court where they are dealt with once and for all by the court so long as the cases are within the magistrates' jurisdiction and if the defendants involved agree to stand trial at the magistrates' court...and again if the defendants involved don't dispute the charges against them like most black defendants do. Otherwise, the cases are committed to a higher court where there is a greater likelihood of incarceration once a guilty verdict is reached.

The court observations reveal that guilty pleas are not uncommon amongst black defendants, neither are not guilty pleas rare in cases involving white defendants. But whatever the plea status, prosecutorial processing of cases are subjected to discretionary practices which subsequently create disparity in the charges. Again, guilty pleas do not necessarily attract a less serious charge, likewise, not guilty pleas do not entirely entail a more serious charge and the resultant contested trial. Apparently, the differential prosecution processing of cases irrespective of pleas reflect an outcome of prosecutorial discretion and negotiation that take place between interested participants in a case - as demonstrated in the following case studies.

Case 1: A Black Defendant

T was self-employed as a second-hand car dealer. He lived with his girlfriend and three children in a council flat. He had four previous convictions, none of which involved drugs. Acting on information, the police had called at the home of T where it was alleged that they discovered 84.14 grams of herbal cannabis, some cannabis seeds, a quantity of green herbal tea, three hundred and sixty pounds in cash and a set of weighing-scales. On the basis of these findings, T was charged with (1) unlawful possession of a class B drug, and (2) unlawful possession of a class B drug with intent to supply.

On the first day of the trial, T pleaded guilty to being in unlawful possession of a class B drug, that is, 84.14 grams of herbal cannabis and some cannabis seeds, and to the charge of being in possession with intent to supply, T pleaded not guilty. The prosecution's submission suggested that the large quantity of drug was meant for sale. The three hundred and sixty pounds was deemed by the prosecution to be his proceeds from drug trafficking. The quantity of green herbal tea, as was alleged, was used to mix with the cannabis in order to produce a larger saleable quantity. The set of weighing-scales was described as the method for weighing out the saleable drug quantities.

After a four day trial, T was found guilty of being in possession of a class B drug with intent to supply, and received a one year custodial sentence. On the charge of possession of a class B drug to which he pleaded guilty, he received a one day custodial sentence. The sentences were to run concurrently.

Case 2: A White Defendant

M had been unemployed since leaving school. He lived with his pregnant girlfriend in a council accommodation. He was in receipt of unemployment benefit. M had eight previous convictions, none of which concerned drugs. Acting on information, the police raided a public house in South London. All the patrons of the public house were searched. M was one of the patrons. The prosecution alleged that during the search, M had in his possession 73.15 grams of cannabis resin in 21 separate wraps and two hundred and twenty pounds in cash alleged to be his proceeds from drug trafficking. M was arrested and along with several other people escorted to the local police station. At the police station, a further 2.42 grams of cocaine in 5 separate wraps were found in his possession. The police made a search of M's home during which the police found what they termed to be drug-related items, that is, tin foil and cling film. M was charged with being in (1) unlawful possession of a class B drug, (2) unlawful possession of a class B drug with intent to supply, and (3) unlawful possession of a class A drug.

In addition, M along with his girlfriend, was charged with seven other offences, not drug-related. The offences were: affray, assault, assault occasioning ABH on victim, assault, criminal damage, assault on a police officer occasioning injury on nose, and threatening words. On the first day of the trial, M pleaded not guilty to the three drug offence charges. On the second day of the trial, complaint alterations were made by the prosecution regarding the case. The defendant had changed his plea from not guilty to guilty on the two charges of unlawful possession of a controlled drug. The prosecution dropped the charge of unlawful possession of a class B drug with intent to supply. Out of the other seven charges, M pleaded guilty to affray and assault on a police officer occasioning injury on nose, and not guilty to the remaining. After consultation with the Judge, it was agreed that all the not guilty pleas be accepted and the charges dropped. M was sentenced to six months imprisonment for affray, three months imprisonment for assaulting a police officer, one month for being in unlawful possession of a class B drug, two months for being in unlawful possession of a class A drug. These sentences were to run concurrently.

These two defendants were found in possession of what was considered to be large quantities of a class B drug; they were both found with sums of money believed by the complainants to be their proceeds from drug trafficking. In addition, items identified to be related drug trafficking were found in their respective homes, and the drugs found on the white defendant were separately wrapped in packages. The defendants pleaded differently to their drug charges - T pleaded guilty to the charge of 'possession' and not guilty to the 'intent to supply' charge, while M pleaded not guilty to all the charges. M agreed to plead guilty to the two charges of 'possession' in exchange for a dropped charge of 'intent to supply' irrespective of the quantity of the drug, the money, the separate wraps and the drug-related paraphernalia involved.

That the 'intent to supply' charge was dropped in M's case was a result of negotiated plea settlements between the concerned participants. As the Prosecution told the Judge "Your Honour, after consultation with my learned friend, the second charge of intent to supply, we have mutually agreed to drop. The defendant has changed his plea to guilty on the two charges of possession". The dropping of the 'intent to supply' charge meant a reduction in the seriousness of the drug offence allegations, an exemption from adversarial trial and of course a reduction in the likelihood of a harsh sentence. Apparently, an offence is considered serious when an offender is accused of intending to commit the offence. McBarnet (1983, p.114) expresses this point thus:

> Intent or mens rea is an important part of the ideology of criminality
> as the ultimate justification of punishment: it ties in with the
> democratic notion of the rule of law. The common law maxim is
> Actus non facit reum nisi mens sit rea: the deed does not make a
> man guilty unless his mind be guilty.

Factors which are usually construed as prima facie evidence of possession of a controlled drug with intent to supply were in the case involving M disregarded but strongly utilised in pressing a prosecution against T. This finding can be substantiated with Banks' (1977, p.41) view that the prosecutor is not always 'required by law to prosecute individuals against whom there is sufficient evidence of criminal conduct' and that the prosecutor's decision to prosecute is 'based on his own judgement'. For although T pleaded guilty to being in possession of the named drug, the 'intent to supply' charge resulted in a contested trial that lasted for four days. In M's case, the affray charge took precedence because the drug offence allegations were reduced in their seriousness by the dropping of the drug trafficking offence charge. The fact that he received the respective one month and two months custodial sentences for each charge of 'possession' was irrelevant in the sense that the sentences were to run concurrently with the six months custodial sentence for affray.

No doubt, charge alterations or charge manipulation (Bottomley, 1973) between the prosecution and the defence is not an uncommon practice in the court process; it is acknowledged and encouraged by the legal rules (Blumberg, 1969a, 1969b; Thomas, 1979; McBarnet, 1983; Baldwin and McConville, 1977; McConville and Baldwin, 1981; Ashworth, 1994; Davies et al., 1995). From the point of apprehension of an offender to the point that the offender appears before the court, there is always a possibility of plea bargaining and it is not unusual to find that some defendants change their pleas later in the court process. The decision to plead guilty under this condition does not go without considerations (Newman,1969; Chambliss, 1969; Davies et al., 1995). One concession given to defendants in this study in exchange for a guilty plea involved a promise of dropped charges whereby a defendant pleads guilty on the grounds that the more serious charge is dropped. This concession which was apparent in white defendants' cases was not applicable to any of the cases involving their black counterparts (not that it could not have occurred in the cases that were not observed). A promise of a lighter sentence, according to defendants interviewed, is a common consideration usually offered defendants in exchange for a guilty plea. Nevertheless, it is not in all cases that considerations promised are granted, for example, a black defendant who pleaded guilty to being in possession of a controlled drug was 'conned' into revealing information as to his supplier in exchange for immunity from prosecution but the defendant was still charged to the annoyance of his relatives present in court.

The reasons for pressing particular drug offence charges in the routine practices of the complainants could be multifaceted. Police-suspect encounters at the point of arrest and during interrogation play a part in charge decisions (McConville, et al., 1991; Sanders, 1994). McConville and Baldwin (1981) identify verbal and written statements made by suspects and reports of interviews conducted by the police with suspects as somewhat influential in the decisions to prosecute cases. During the drug trials, defendants' verbal or written statements did not play a crucial part in the proceedings as they were occasionally referred to by the prosecution. Perhaps, one reason was that the defendants never agreed to the charges brought against them from the outset and invariably, avoided making statements of an incriminating nature. In some cases, statements were refuted by defendants as incorrect or a misrepresentation of what they actually meant.

Such factors as 'practical and organisational contingencies' which according to Emerson (1991) make up the underlying 'real reasons' behind what he calls the 'official reasons' for making referrals, could influence prosecutorial charge decisions. Emerson (ibid., p.203) describes 'official reasons' for making and sending referrals to receiving agents as those reasons that 'legitimate the requested transfer of authority to the receiving agent by specifying some alleged misconduct or some quality or condition of the person referred as grounds for referral'; they '...are oriented to laws, rules, and official procedures, providing formal, organisationally accountable grounds to qualify a case for handling by the receiving agent'. So far, we have concerned ourselves with those 'official reasons' given by the prosecution for instituting proceedings against a defendant for allegedly committing a drug offence. In the second part of this chapter, we need to look beneath the 'official reasons' in order to identify the complainants' 'real reasons' for their claim. These reasons which are covert are unearthed in the way that the 'official reasons' or grounds for complaints are subjectively defined and interpreted to justify and solidify a drug offence allegation.

The Subjectivity of Evidence

The grounds for a drug offence allegation are not enough to secure a conviction. In other words, the presence of the objective elements, that is, a quantity of drug in a portion or portions, drug-related paraphernalia and proceeds of drug trafficking do not on their own - whether singly or jointly - finalise the creation of a drug offence in a trial until they are further given meanings and interpretations by the prosecution that relate them to a particular drug offence charge. The initiation of a criminal action against a suspect embodies inter alia the significant issue of gathering information to support the prosecution's case against the suspect. Unlike the defence, the prosecution have legal powers to obtain what they consider incriminating evidence against a defendant; they have total access to documentary evidence and can conduct an inquiry into any available evidence (McBarnet, 1983). In substantiating and validating s/he allegations during claims-making, the prosecution draws upon various sources of information on defendants - which even if factual - are often expressed in a language that is informed by knowledge, stereotypical images, beliefs, moral values and so forth. In other words, the prosecution tries to make certain facts understandable to the judge and jury by placing them within a social context.

In doing so, similar situations are constructed differently with race as a significant factor, for although the prosecution's 'goal' in the combative process is to validate his/her impression that a defendant did actually commit a drug offence, information or evidence employed to substantiate assertions do not always seem to incriminate all defendants (Cooney, 1994). The court observations reveal that the prosecution is more likely to generate detailed incriminating information on cases when defendants are black. Furthermore, informational clues on a subject are utilised in a way that portray black and white defendants differently, placing the white defendants at an advantage and their black counterparts at a disadvantage. At this stage where rhetorical persuasion is brought to bear, the pattern that the prosecution process takes is influenced not by how true or false an argument is but by how rational it is to gain acceptance. The prosecution's arguments, derived from information that s/he has on a subject, are portrayed in a way that reflect his/her conception of reality which s/he tries to construct. The differential adoption of justification tactics in black and white defendants' cases seems to coincide with the prosecution's knowledge of British black and white population outside the courtroom, thus, during trials, what s/he knows is demonstrated for his/her own benefit. Here, we witness a scene where the prosecution presents a different context of facts and circumstances about black defendants from which a drug offence can be inferred, and through persuasion try to relate to the judge and jury the plausibility of their case whilst urging them to be reasonable and logical in their thinking.

Those arguments which rest on an interplay of subjective issues focus on the defendants' histories such as their economic, social and personal lives, particularly, those of black defendants who have their history thoroughly investigated and used in evidence against them. In black and white defendants' cases, the prosecution presents to the court an external 'reality' and subtly draws the responding members' attention to existing popular and powerful ideologies about these racial groups of people and the alleged problem. For example, subtle attention is drawn to those popular theories that link race to crime, and stereotypical images of race and drugs become useful in the prosecution's justification strategy. As described below, issues surrounding *drug trafficking* and *immorality* constitute major prosecution arguments.

Drug Trafficking

Possession of a controlled drug with intent to supply, supplying a controlled drug to another and other supplying offences are by law classified as drug trafficking and accordingly, defendants charged with such offence are supposed to be dealt with by the prosecution as drug traffickers. The quantity of drug, the class of drug, to whom the drug was supplied or is to be supplied is irrelevant when establishing a drug trafficking offence, therefore, drug trafficking offence charges deserve a similar level of seriousness in the criminal justice process.

Except for a few number of defendants that appeared before the Crown Court for the straight charge of unlawful possession of a controlled drug, the court process was dominated by drug trafficking cases - which raised the question as to whether or not a defendant did in fact traffic in a controlled drug or intended to do so. Drug trafficking is an act that is treated with a high degree of disapproval in Britain; it is an act that has over the years been publicised in political and official discourse and media coverage as evil and heinous. Although such negative descriptions of drug trafficking are illustrated in practice during the processing of drug trafficking cases by the prosecution, not all the defendants accused of drug trafficking are presented by the prosecution in the image of the 'evil' drug trafficker as is widely portrayed. The clue is found in how the evidence put forward by the prosecution to substantiate their claim about drug trafficking rests upon the construction or de-construction of the drug trafficker stereotype. During trials, the 'agreed upon' evidence - such as the proceeds of drug trafficking and the quantity of drugs - for pressing a drug trafficking offence charge are disparately described by the prosecution according to the race of the defendants. The elements are not given similar meanings in similar black and white defendants' cases, instead, they are interpreted by the prosecution in a manner that seemingly identify with their own use of stereotypical representations of drug trafficking and crime in general.

Proceeds of drug trafficking

In order to prove that a defendant engaged in drug trafficking, it is important for the prosecution to establish inter alia that the defendant was trafficking in drugs for commercial reasons and as such did profit economically from such action. This line of argument is based on legalistic considerations in the sense that the law is determining of such prosecution practice. In the 1986 Drugs Trafficking Offences Act, provisions are made for the confiscation of drug traffickers' assets identified as proceeds of drug trafficking. This Act does not specifically and clearly map out criteria for determining actual proceeds of drug trafficking and in effect, a wide door is opened for the use of legally-provided discretion by the prosecution to identify what they consider to be the proceeds of drug trafficking and to impute meanings to a defendant's alleged involvement in drug trafficking. Consequently, differential interpretations are given to similar items as proceeds of drug trafficking which in turn influence the imputation of meanings to drug trafficking allegations.

The most significant issue that the prosecution raises to determine whether or not a defendant benefited economically from drug trafficking is his/her socio-economic condition. This factor is vital in the prosecution process in that it enables the prosecution to access a defendant's account of the source of his/her assets by weighing the alleged proceeds against the socio-economic status of the defendant. Nevertheless, the utilisation of this factor in evaluating a defendant's accountability is discretionary. Apparently, the majority of the defendants belonged to the lower class: they were mostly unemployed or self-employed (irregular), and the majority of them claimed state benefits. Only a few of the defendants claimed to have regular employment. This fact seems to coincide very much with the ideology that economic deprivation and illicit drug use/drug trafficking among the lower class are intertwined, with the former leading to the latter. Whether or not the defendants committed an alleged drug offences due to their socio-economic condition is another issue altogether. The fact remains that their socio-economic standing in society - depending on the definition given to it by the prosecution - is used by the prosecution to pursue his/her claim - either for or against the defendants. The black defendants make up a group who find their socio-economic circumstances dysfunctional to them in the trial process but functional and valuable to the prosecution who draws upon them to enhance or boost their complaint against black defendants in relation to the issue of proceeds of drug trafficking. In spite of the similarities in the socio-economic conditions of black and white defendants, black defendants' cases are specifically described and highlighted in terms of the significance of a deprived socio-economic context.

The image of the black community as socio-economically deprived and consequently criminally minded is widely acknowledged; it is a belief commonly shared by those in authority. Gus John (1981, p.155) indicates this widespread notion thus:

> the state, the police, the media and race relations experts ascribe to young blacks certain collective qualities e.g alienated, vicious little criminals, muggers, disenchanted, unemployed, unmarried mothers, truants, classroom wreckers etc.

The following brief conversation between a police officer (a prosecution witness) and a court staff exemplifies the shared understanding of the supposed link between 'black deprivation' and 'black criminality'. The conversation which took place during a short adjournment of a drug case involving a black defendant started with a discussion about the weather and progressed into this:

Court staff: I am amazed at the number of black people that appear in this court everyday (that is as defendants).

Police Officer: It is unemployment. They can't help it, can they? Many of them haven't got a job and they don't seem to be interested in getting one anyway.

Court staff: It's a shame, isn't it? They do suffer the recession more but that is no excuse....

The low socio-economic status ascribed to the black population appears to form a solid ideological construction that permeates the prosecution and creates a bedrock upon which is based the prosecution justification process regarding proceeds of drug trafficking. Such arguments do not seem merely situational but are rather consistent with existing ideologies and stereotypical images of black people and deprivation. In addressing the relationship between black defendants' economic conditions, alleged proceeds of drug trafficking and their alleged involvement in drug trafficking, the prosecution's representations have a clear resonance with academic, official and media accounts of black people, deprivation, crime and drug trafficking. Indeed, no consensus exists in the pattern that black and white defendants' material conditions are portrayed in relation to the subject of proceeds. Interrogations aimed at establishing that defendants benefited economically from drug trafficking are 'detailed' and 'emphasised' in cases involving black defendants. So are negative comments and suggestions (embedded in the interrogation) made about the relationship between defendants' economic circumstances and drug trafficking apparently confined to the black defendants. What forms the primary issue here is the prosecution's role in the social construction of an alleged black drug trafficker within the context of socio-economic circumstances.

Unemployment and proceeds of drug trafficking   How the prosecution specifically defines the association of black defendants with proceeds of drug trafficking within the realm of unemployment - unlike their white counterparts - is of interest here. The prosecution's allegation against unemployed black defendants is supported by intricately hammering on the ideological link between 'blackness' and unemployment, and 'black unemployment' and crime. What is subtly presented by the prosecution to the judge and jury is that an unemployed black defendant deals in drugs because s/he is constrained by economic circumstances.

On presenting defendants' possessions to the court as evidence of proceeds of drug trafficking, the question ultimately rests on the source of personal possessions and apparently on the defendants' private lives. In relation to the black defendants, once the source of their personal possessions is located in drug trafficking, the very notion of unemployment being consistent with drug trafficking rears its head. The fact that a black defendant is unemployed is presented by the prosecution as a justifiable argument; in addition, welfare benefit is defined as unable to legitimately provide for the defendant's possessions, the argument being that it is inconceivable for a defendant whose economic dependence is wholly on state welfare to acquire what the prosecution considers to be luxurious possessions unless that defendant is into some sort of crime - in this case, drug trafficking. Punch (1979) has noted that a drug trafficking allegation against blacks people is justified and strengthened with any existence of assets considered as expensive. In my observations, cash (no matter the amount), clothes, jewellery and cars (irrespective of their age) are construed as luxurious assets acquired through no other source but drug trafficking.

Even when the supposed proceeds are 'accounted for' by the defendants, such accounts are disputed and subsequently interpreted to suit the prosecution's version. The picture of an unemployed black defendant created for the judge and jury is one of typical economic deprivation. In the bid to explain logically to the judge and jury that an unemployed black defendant, because of his/her 'poor' economic condition, did resort to drug trafficking in order to make ends meet, the prosecution ensures that the defendant accounts for each and every one of the items presumed to be the proceeds of drug trafficking:

Prosecutor: Mr X you are unemployed and on social security of £54 per fortnight?

Defendant: Yes sir.

Prosecutor: You have four children and I suppose you contribute to their upkeep?

Defendant: Yes sir.

Prosecutor: ....On the day of your arrest, you had £104 in your possession. For someone that is unemployed, where did the money come from?

Defendant: Actually, I had £160 on that day. Part of the money was my social security which I collected the previous day and money that I borrowed from a girlfriend to help decorate my kids' bedroom. I had spent some of the money on wallpaper before I was arrested?

Prosecutor: How much did you spend on wallpaper?

Defendant: About £50.

Prosecutor: ....When you were arrested, you were wearing three pairs of trousers, two jumpers and the police told you that they were quite new and asked you where you got the money to buy them. What did you tell them?

Defendant: I told them that I get money from my relatives and girlfriends and that I share clothes sometimes with friends.

Prosecutor: ....Did you pay for this jumper yourself (referring to one of the jumpers that the defendant wore on the day of his arrest)?

Defendant: Yes sir.

Prosecutor: How much did you pay for it?

Defendant: About £10. I bought it from a street market.

Prosecutor: ....What about your car? How were you able to afford a car and maintain it on £54?

Defendant: I don't have the car now. I paid £280 for it and I bought it when my girlfriend was pregnant to make life easier for her, like take her to the hospital and shop, you know!

Prosecutor: You must have paid to fuel the car?

Defendant: I never drove it anytime I didn't have money for fuel.

Prosecutor: And maintenance?
Defendant: I did a lot of repairs myself.

To add validity and strength to his/her logic about unemployment and crime, the prosecution searches for 'accuracy' in black defendants' evidence. With the advantage that the prosecution have for obtaining evidence, it is easier for them to have access to 'incriminating' information although the extent that the prosecution want to go in the process of collecting what they consider evidence is discretionary. In the above case, the prosecution had some of the defendant's alleged proceeds of drug trafficking valued and presented to the judge and jury, and the defendant was interrogated in relation to that:

Prosecutor: If you are not a drug dealer, from where did you get the money to pay for all the jewellery you were wearing on the evening that you were arrested? You do not expect us to believe that your benefit covered the cost of the jewellery, do you?

Defendant: I got them from America. I bought some and my relatives and friends gave me some.

Prosecutor: That was what you told the police. The jewels are estimated to be worth $600. They are quite expensive gifts, are they not?

Defendant: They were not up to $600 dollars at the time.

Prosecutor: You have told us that you paid for some of the jewels, how much did you pay for them?

Defendant: About $200 (some of which he said was given to him by a girlfriend).

Prosecutor: Can you produce the receipts for the jewels you paid for?

Defendant: I have receipts for some of them (the receipts were presented to the jury).

Prosecutor: You presumably paid $200 dollars for some of the jewels. Why would your relatives and friends give you jewellery worth $400?

Defendant: They were not that value at the time sir. They know I am crazy about jewellery, they form part of my collection.

Prosecutor: In that case you can do anything to have them, like selling drugs.

Defendant: No sir. I am not a drug dealer.

Prosecutor: Mr X do you use drugs?

Defendant: I used to smoke cannabis.

Prosecutor: ....How much did you spend on cannabis a week?

Defendant: Not more than £10.

Prosecutor:	Meaning £20 out of £54 every fortnight. How did you survive on the remaining £34 if you were not dealing in drugs?
Defendant:	I did not smoke cannabis every week sir. I sometimes got from friends.

Whilst unemployment is portrayed as a convenient synthesis of drug trafficking in relation to the black defendants, it is not made a crucial issue in the prosecution of cases involving unemployed white defendants. It appears unimaginable for an unemployed black defendant to own assets through legal means and in contrast, it seems normal for an unemployed white defendant to legitimately have possessions. Questions regarding the source of possessions are in white defendants' cases not emphasised when compared to black defendants' cases. Below is an interrogation of an unemployed white defendant accused of drug trafficking. He was on state benefit, had two children and lived in a council accommodation. It was alleged by the prosecution that the defendant made a profit of £96 from drug trafficking:

Prosecutor:	....When did your girlfriend give you the money (the defendant claimed that he borrowed £100 from his girlfriend)?
Defendant:	Same day I was arrested by the police, in the morning. It's a loan.
Prosecutor:	Why is it taking you a long time to pay back the money that you owe?
Defendant:	I mean to pay her back when I start work soon. She's not in a hurry for the money. She knows I'll pay her back

In the above case, interrogation regarding the alleged proceeds was 'minimal' and did not seem to be aimed at refuting the defendant's story; there was no question about the defendant's economic background. The fact that he was unemployed was in no way related to the supposed proceeds of drug trafficking. This was a common prosecution practice in white defendants' cases that were observed.

In five white defendants' cases, the drug trafficking offence charges brought against them were dropped. Three of the defendants who had never been employed since they left school were associated with money believed by the prosecution to be their proceeds from drug trafficking. The drug trafficking offence charges against these three defendants were dropped on the principal ground that they changed their plea from not guilty to guilty to the less serious charge of 'possession'. Obviously, they must have satisfied the prosecution with their explanation regarding the source of the respective sums of £220, £46 and

£150 found on them on arrest. According to their defence barristers, the monies were accounted for: the £220 was money that the first defendant borrowed from his girlfriend who was self employed; the £46 was part of the second defendant's social security benefit; and the £150 was lent to the third defendant by a close friend. In the fourth case, the unemployed defendant, according to the prosecution was seen trafficking in drugs by the police and when he was searched, drugs and £53.20 were found on him. The money was believed to be his proceeds from drug trafficking. However, the drug trafficking offence charge was dropped and what the prosecution previously believed to be the proceeds of drug trafficking was afterwards not considered as such. When the Judge asked:

> What about the money found on him when he was arrested?

The prosecution replies:

> He accounted for the money your Honour. The defendant said that the money was part of his pocket money from his mother. He lives with his mother and sister. In fact the police went to his residential address to enquire about his belongings and nothing worthwhile belonged to him....Your Honour, he does not seem to have made any profit from drugs.

The defendant in the fifth case was charged with two drug trafficking offences and three charges of 'possession'. It was after a brief submission by the prosecution that a negotiation erupted leading to the dropping of the drug trafficking offence charges:

Defence:	Your Honour, the defendant has pleaded guilty to being in possession of all the mentioned drugs but he has maintained that he never supplied nor intended to supply drugs for financial gain.... He uses drugs but does not sell them.
Judge:	What have you got to say about this Mr B (that is, the prosecution)? Is there any evidence that he sells drugs?
Prosecutor:	(pause) No your Honour. The police found £170 at his residence. He lives with his parents and the money was jointly owned and was meant for domestic use.
Judge:	Did he have money on him at the time of his arrest?
Prosecutor:	Not much. I think it was about £12....The defendant told the police that he only supplied drugs to friends who also gave to

him when he had none and that it was entirely on a social basis. No sale was involved.

Judge: I would like to know about his background?

Prosecutor: ...and he left school without qualification. At the moment, he is unemployed and in receipt of unemployment benefit. He is hoping to get a job soon.

Judge: (interrupted) You do not wish to pursue the charges on supplying?

Prosecutor: No your Honour, I agree with my learned friend that he did not make any financial gain from drugs.

Judge: In that case I will disregard the charges. We do not have any need for a jury. I would like to have a social inquiry report on the defendant.

These cases exemplify Cooney's (1994, pp. 840 and 841) observation that:

> legal officials often cite lack of evidence as a reason for the attrition of criminal cases....That evidence is uncovered is no guarantee that it will be useful or important. A considerable amount of legal strategy revolves around excluding or suppressing information that is available to at least one party.

If we look at how 'trivial' assets are brought to the limelight as proceeds of drug trafficking albeit in relation to black defendants' cases, we may understand how the dominant image of race, poverty and crime has become internalised to be a valuable prosecution evidence. We may also understand how the prosecution claims-making activity subtly reinforces and solidifies this conception:

> A black male was alleged by the prosecution to have made £14.50 from drug trafficking. The prosecution interrogation in relation to this included the following:

Prosecutor: You have told us that you are unemployed and that you only receive £28 unemployment benefit a week?

Defendant: Yes.

Prosecutor: I believe that you spend money on at least food?

Defendant: Yes.

Prosecutor:	You have told the court that you are a heroin addict and that on the day you were arrested, you were buying drugs?
Defendant:	Yes.
Prosecutor:	You had £14.50 in your possession when you were arrested. Am I right?
Defendant:	Yes.
Prosecutor:	And you have also told us that you had £40 on that day and that you gave £25 to the dealer?
Defendant:	Yes.
Prosecutor:	....Could you tell the court how you came to have £40 on the day that you were arrested when you claim £28 unemployment benefit a week?
Defendant:	My grandma gave me some money plus my social security.
Prosecutor:	How much did your grandmother give to you?
Defendant:	(pause) I can't remember.
Prosecutor:	Did she give it to you on the day you were arrested?
Defendant:	No. About two or three days before but I collected my social security on that day.
Prosecutor:	....If you had £40 on you on that day and you paid £25 to the dealer, you should have had £15 on you on arrest but you had £14.50. Why was that?
Defendant:	I paid 50p for a bus ride.
Prosecutor:	From which area did you catch the bus?
Defendant:	From Y road. I walked to that road from where I live to avoid paying more bus fare.
Prosecutor:	....What quantity of heroin do you use in a day?
Defendant:	Half a gram.
Prosecutor:	And how much does half a gram of heroin cost?
Defendant:	About 50 quid street price.
Prosecutor:	You spend £50 on heroin alone. On £28 a week, how could you possibly afford to pay £50 daily on heroin that you must have? I suggest it to you that you sell drugs to make profits in order to meet your habit and that on the day that you were arrested, you were dealing in drugs.
Defendant:	I was there to buy 'gear'(that is, heroin). I don't sell drugs.
Prosecutor:	Then how do you afford to spend £50 on heroin everyday?
Defendant:	I get money from my grandma.
Prosecutor:	Always?
Defendant:	(pause) No. Sometimes.

Prosecutor:	If you are not a drug dealer, how else do you raise money for drugs?
Defendant:	(pause) Theft and burglary (looks were exchanged between the prosecutor, police officers, the Judge and jurors). I don't always pay £50.
Prosecutor:	Oh you steal from people and burgle buildings and homes to raise money to buy drugs. Is that right?
Defendant:	(pause) Yes.

We may understand at this point how the ownership of a 'trivial' amount of money reputed to be the proceeds of drug trafficking can be constructed into the criminalisation of a black defendant. With this method of interrogation, the objective to prove the drug trafficking offence charge resolved in subjectively creating an additional form of criminality as shown in the way that a negative highlight on the defendant's background was produced from the prosecution's incessant questioning. Emphasis was placed on the relationship between the defendant's drug habit and drug-related criminal behaviour rather than the drug trafficking offence charge in order to prove to the judge and jury that after all the defendant was a criminal. The interrogation on this issue continued thus:

Prosecutor:	If you use £50 worth of heroin a day, why did you spend £25 on the drug when you had £39.50?
Defendant:	The 40 quid right! was all I had. I needed some money for food, transportation and other things. All I wanted was a small amount of 'gear' to keep me stable for some hours.
Prosecutor:	I would have thought that a desperate addict would forego such things as food and transportation for drugs. Since £25 worth of heroin would not have sustained you throughout the day, how did you intend paying for the remaining quantity that you needed for that day?
Defendant:	(pause) Thieving.
Prosecutor:	Could you please speak up so that the jury can hear you?
Defendant:	Thieving. I only needed a small amount to keep me stable for some time (the Judge and jurors exchanged looks).
Prosecutor:	How many hours would that quantity have lasted you?
Defendant:	About 12 hours.
Prosecutor:	Enough time for you to steal to raise money for more drugs?
Defendant:	(pause) Yes.

In the process of claims-making by the prosecution, jurors are being persuaded through language manipulation, to relate to the deprived socio-economic status of black people in order to understand the relevance of proceeds of drug trafficking to an unemployed black defendant's case.

Deconstructing self-employment Being self-employed does not exonerate black defendants from the prosecution's scrutinization of their socio-economic standing and the subsequent interpretation of a link between assets and drug trafficking. The prosecution claims-making activity still moves beyond the objective facts of the case into a 'detailed' and critical examination of the significance of material possessions. Again, racial ideologies which establish how black defendants turn to crime, including drug trafficking, in response to their 'poor' economic condition subtly re-emerge as a focus of attention. In the interrogation of self-employed black defendants within the context of socio-economic criteria, the message that the prosecution delivers seems to be the inevitability of endemic marginalisation with the impossibility of an escape from the inner-city web of deprivation amongst the black population. This coincides with an observation by the Indian Workers Association (1987, p.12) that the 'police assume that all blacks are on the dole, and if they are not they ought to be'. Similarly, a black defendant commented on the police conception of black people who do not fit their description of the economically deprived:

> The police have the general impression that all black people are drug dealers, especially if you have a car. They stop you in your car and ask you, where is your Mercedes? Where is your BMW? Because you drive, you are a drug dealer.

Humphrey (1972) has observed that black people who drive sports or unusual cars are subjected to police suspicion and harassment.

Black defendants who claim that they are self-employed and relate their alleged proceeds of drug trafficking to their employment have their claim construed by the prosecution as ill-founded and unimaginable. A negative picture of their employment is painted, doubts and suspicion are cast on self-employment, and in doing so, the defendants are presented as people who do not fit into the image of the economically productive by way of legitimate self-employment, whose means of achieving success through self-employment is unacceptable and deviant. In order to logically and conveniently dispose of the defendants' claim of a relationship between their possessions and self-employment, their economic situation is screened over and over by the prosecution to effect the application of a drug trafficking offence label:

> A self-employed black defendant was alleged by the prosecution to have made a profit from drug trafficking. The alleged proceeds were a car, two separate sums of £700 and £300, jewellery, clothes, gas shares, a building society account of £2,500 and another building society account of £30,000 in a name different from the defendant's. The defendant was living with his girlfriend and their daughter in a council flat.

The following is part of the claims- and counter claims-making activity between the prosecution and the defendant regarding the supposed proceeds:

Prosecutor:	....Mr M, two building society passbooks were found in your flat and you have told us that the one that bears your name belongs to you and that the other belongs to a friend of yours called X....Why was X's passbook in your possession?
Defendant:	He is a very close friend of mine. He left it with me to look after till he comes back from the U.S.
Prosecutor:	He is still not back to collect his passbook. You have not been of assistance to the police regarding the whereabouts of this man?
Defendant:	I have told the police all I know. He travelled to the U.S.
Judge:	Does this mean that this X cannot be located?
Prosecutor:	Your Honour, the police have checked their records, DHSS, Immigration. The name happens to be common and no headway was made....
Prosecutor:	I am made to believe that the account in the name of X belongs to you. You opened an account in a false name in order to store away money from your illegal drug dealing business and that explains the £30,000 in that account.
Defendant:	It is not true.
Prosecutor:	I still suggest it to you that X does not exist.
Defendant:	He does.

During the interrogation, the defendant had earlier related the £2,500 in his building society account to his employment. The prosecution still inquires:

Prosecutor:	....You have not told us how you came about the £2,500 in the account in your name?
Defendant:	It is my savings.
Prosecutor:	Your statement of account shows that you were regularly withdrawing as well as paying in money into that account (the prosecutor read out the statement). The withdrawals and pay ins can only be explained in relation to drug dealing, am I correct?
Defendant:	No.
Prosecutor:	You claim approximately £57 social security benefit per fortnight and you have a family to maintain. From where did you get money to pay into your account amounting to £2,500?
Defendant:	I saved up that money. I told the police that I am an industrial cleaner. They saw an industrial machine in my flat.
Judge:	What is that for?
Defendant:	I use it to clean big company offices your Honour.
Prosecutor:	So you are telling us that you receive social security benefit and work at the same time. You must know that it is illegal to do that (looks were exchanged between the Judge and jurors).
Defendant:	I only do the job sometimes.
Prosecutor:	And how much do you earn from the cleaning job?
Defendant:	When I work, sometimes £100 a week, sometimes more and sometimes less.
Prosecutor:	Surely, you could not have saved £2,500 from that. You have a car, £2,000 worth of jewellery (valued by the prosecution), some expensive clothes (the jewellery, three silk shirts and two suits were presented to the jury as evidence). Mr M, do you not think that your lifestyle is above your means?
Defendant:	I have worked as a mechanic, a full-time trader and a builder. I saved that money over a long period of time. I did not buy my clothes and jewellery all at the same time. My car is a Volkswagen and I have had it for seven years.
Prosecutor:	How much were you earning from these jobs in a week?
Defendant:	As a mechanic, I was earning about £200 a week.
Prosecutor:	What about the other jobs?
Defendant:	I can't remember. It has been a long time.
Prosecutor:	Can you account for the £2,000 worth of jewellery?

Defendant: They don't all belong to me. Some belong to my girlfriend and
                some belong to friends that owe me money.
Judge: Why should your friends owe you money? Did you lend them
                money?
Defendant: Yes. I like jewellery and when they borrow money from me,
                they give me jewellery to keep till they return the money.
Prosecutor: Or is it that they gave you the jewellery in return for the drugs
                you sold to them (with a cynical smile)?

The defendant was asked by the prosecution with the approval of the defence and
the Judge to divide the jewels into three sets - those that belong to him, his
girlfriend and his friends. As the defendant separated them, the court usher listed
them individually. The categorised jewels were shown to the responders after
which they were mixed together. The defendant was again asked to separate them
exactly as he previously did. He did and the separate sets were cross-checked
against the list. The interrogation continues:

Prosecutor: Could you tell the court how you were able to afford the set that
                belongs to you?
Defendant: Most were gifts from friends and relatives. This necklace
                (holding it up and shaking his head in disbelief) I have worn for
                over twenty years without taking it off but the police took it off
                me. These rings (still shaking his head in disbelief), I have had
                for more than fifteen years. I paid for them (he was
                dumbfounded).
Prosecutor: Could you show us the ones that were given to you by your
                relatives and friends? (the defendant did and the jury had a look
                at them). How could your relatives and friends give you such
                expensive jewels? What do they do for a living (police officers
                exchanged looks and sneered)? If you insist that you paid for the
                ones you have shown us, could you produce the receipts?
Defendant: I don't have the receipts any more. It has been a long time since
                I have had them.
Judge: Ms B, you do not expect him to still have the receipts for the
                jewels.
Prosecutor: Two separate bundles of £700 and £300 were found located in
                different areas of your flat. Why was that?
Defendant: I separated them for safety reasons.
Prosecutor: How did those large sums of money come about?

Defendant:	The £300 I withdrew from my account. I borrowed £700 from my baby's mother in Italy.
Judge:	What does he mean by baby's mother? (giggles in the courtroom)
Prosecutor:	Your Honour, I think he is referring to the lady in Rome (in relation to an issue that had earlier formed part of the interrogation). Is that right?
Defendant:	Yes.
Prosecutor:	....(reading out the defendant's bank statement) Your statement shows that you withdrew £300 on (date). After that you made three other withdrawals. Is the £300 found in your flat the money you withdrew on (date)?
Defendant:	I am not sure.
Prosecutor:	When did you withdraw the money?
Defendant:	I can't remember.
Prosecutor:	....Why would the lady in Rome lend you £700?
Defendant:	She is my baby's mother. I am supposed to pay her back the money.
Prosecutor:	She must be rich. Your passport shows that you have been to Rome and you have told us that this lady sponsored the trip. For a lady you are not married to, why would she do that if she does not gain something in return?
Defendant:	We are very good friends and she has a very good job there.
Prosecutor:	I suggest it to you that the lady in Rome is your partner in the drug trafficking business and that explains your trip to Rome and the monies in your flat.
Defendant:	(silence)
Prosecutor:	If you borrowed £700 and withdrew £300 from your building society account, why did you need £1,000?
Defendant:	I wanted to start up a cleaning business?
Prosecutor:	You had £2,500 in your building society account. You did not have to borrow money, did you?
Defendant:	I needed more than that.
Prosecutor:	So you had to buy and sell drugs to raise more money?
Defendant:	I don't buy and sell drugs.
Prosecutor:	....what about the £200 worth of gas shares?
Defendant:	That is an investment....

In the above case, the image of race and deprivation was illustrated on a broader scale in that by questioning the economic position of the defendants' relatives and friends, deprivation appeared to be consolidated in the prosecution's mind as a permanent structural feature amongst black people. Evidently, the defendants' relatives and friends who were in court during the trial were black. In addition to the ascription of a peripheral socio-economic status to the defendant' relatives and friends, criminality was ingeniously placed in the imputation. This case also shows that the fact the defendant received supplementary benefit in addition to money earned from his self-employment made a positive contribution to the prosecution's case for it effected the application of a criminal label to a particular act not directly related to the alleged drug trafficking offence. By presenting the defendant's self-employment as suspicious and further making an issue of the 'illegality' in drawing state benefits whilst obtaining income from some sort of work, another criminal dimension was added to his alleged involvement in drug trafficking. As will be shown, this contrasts very much with the presentation of similar white defendants' cases in the sense that being in receipt of welfare benefit is not an issue addressed by the prosecution thereby exempting the defendants from any criminal definition of such an act. Again, there is an absence of a prosecution inquiry that link economic aspects to drug trafficking in cases of self-employed white defendants which seemingly indicate normality and acceptability of self-employment as a legitimate access to income and wealth amongst white people.

Below is another illustration of the sort of interpretation that the prosecution gives to black defendants' claim of an engagement in self-employed jobs. This is a case that involved a black male defendant whose profit from drug trafficking was said to be £360. In court, the defendant claimed that he was a second-hand car dealer. He was not on supplementary benefit. Part of the prosecution's interrogation of the defendant regarding the £360 is as follows:

Prosecutor: ....What exactly do you do in your job?
Defendant: I fix and sell cars.
Judge: Pardon. What does that mean?
Defendant: I fix up cars and I then sell them.
Prosecutor: You mean you repair cars and after repairing them, you sell them?
Defendant: Yes.
Prosecutor: Is it a legitimate business?

Defendant:	Yes. People bring old worn out cars they don't want and ask me to sell them for them, you know! I then work on the cars and sell and make some profit?
Prosecutor:	Where do you do this business of yours?
Defendant:	I have a garage.
Prosecutor:	Is the garage rented?
Defendant:	Yes.
Prosecutor:	How long have you been in this business?
Defendant:	Three years.
Prosecutor:	How much do you pay in rent?
Defendant:	£200 a month.
Prosecutor:	Tell us, how much profit do you make from this business in a week or a month?
Defendant:	It is not a regular job, you know what I mean? Some weeks, I don't get any business. In a month, if the business goes well, I can make about £800–£1,000 profit.
Prosecutor:	You are not on social security?
Defendant:	I am not.
Prosecutor:	How do you cope financially during those weeks that you do not make any profit from your business?
Defendant:	I use my savings and my girlfriend also assist me.
Prosecutor:	And you can also traffic in drugs, am I correct?
Defendant:	No.
Prosecutor:	Your bank account shows that you have less than £100 and there is no evidence that you withdrew £360 from that account. How would you account for the £360 found in a jacket pocket in your flat?
Defendant:	I use my girlfriend's building society account. I drew £100 from her account. The rest of the money was profit from a car sale.
Prosecutor:	How do you withdraw money from her account?
Defendant:	She gave me her cash card.
Prosecutor:	Do you pay money into her account?
Defendant:	No. I only withdraw.
Prosecutor:	(after going through the defendant's girlfriend's statement of account and asking the defendant who drew what money on what date) On seven different occasions you withdrew money from her account, a total sum of £415?
Defendant:	Maybe I did. She doesn't mind because she knows I will pay her back. I have paid some back.

Prosecutor:	From the profit you made from drug dealing? Mr T am I correct to say that the money in your girlfriend's account actually belongs to you and that you used the money from that account to purchase drugs for sale and each time you made a profit from drug trafficking, you gave it to her to pay into her account?
Defendant:	I grow cannabis right! I don't buy drugs. She is a student and she is on a grant of £1,900. Her father pays £150 into her account every month.
Prosecutor:	....What did you need the £360 for?
Defendant:	To pay my rent on the garage and to buy some tools.
Prosecutor:	You seem to be quick to pay your rent on the garage, yet you are owing five years rent on the property where you live.
Defendant:	Well, the council will always wait for their money but if I don't pay the rent on the garage, the owner will throw me out.
Prosecutor:	....Mr T would you say you are successful in your business?
Defendant:	I wouldn't say it is too bad.
Prosecutor:	Your bank account does not show that. So where does the profit from your business go to?
Defendant:	A lot goes back into my business.
Prosecutor:	Mr T I suggest you were using your garage as a cover for your drug trafficking business. I also suggest that the £360 found at your flat was profit from your illegal drug dealing....

The irony in this case is that what the prosecution viewed as a non-existence of financial security on the part of the defendant did not alleviate the onslaught of an in-depth questioning regarding the defendant's economic circumstances. In the absence of social security benefit, his method of economic survival was questioned. The fact that he had less than £100 in his bank account was treated suspiciously by the prosecution who believed that the defendant had hidden assets. When the defendant stated that he withdrew part of the alleged proceeds from the girlfriend's building society account, the prosecution located the presumed hidden asset in the lady's account and for sometime that issue dominated the debate. Furthermore, a notable degree of criminalisation was attached to the fact that the defendant was in arrears of council rent for a period of five years although owing council rent is not a criminal offence, nevertheless, this issue was used to diminish the defendant's status.

Because the question of guilt seems not to balance upon white defendants' economic condition and lifestyle, they are not made to answer to critically detailed and demanding questions regarding their alleged proceeds of drug trafficking and self-employment:

> In a case involving a white male self-employed defendant, the alleged proceeds of drug trafficking were £725, sums of money paid into his bank account by the defendant, the largest being £5,000. Found on the defendant on arrest was a list of people's names, weights and prices which the prosecution related to names of customers and weights and prices of drugs. The defendant was divorced and was living in a bedsit. He was self-employed and on state benefit. He was an alcoholic. Before the jury was seated, a debate erupted between the prosecution and the defence over what should and should not be presented to the jury as proceeds of drug trafficking. The defence argued that the list should not be mentioned because it had nothing to do with the case. The defence also claimed that there was no evidence to show that the £725 was derived from drug trafficking. The £5,000 was attributed by the defence to the defendant's share of proceeds from his matrimonial home and other payments made into the defendant's bank account were related to his self-employment and a previous business which collapsed when he broke up with his wife. The story was accepted by the prosecution who, however, insisted on using as evidence the list and the £725 to support his claim of drug trafficking. The Judge agreed to this but advised the prosecution not to emphasise the list, adding that the prosecution would be advised if he strayed. The defendant was questioned about the alleged proceeds thus:

Prosecutor: When you were searched by the police, a list was found on you. The list contained names of people, weights and prices, is that right?

Defendant: That is correct.

Prosecutor: Why would you keep such a list?

Defendant:	Some of the names on the list are people that borrowed money from me and others are people that I sold metal powder to.
Prosecutor:	Mr H you wrote down weights and prices against the names on the list, why would you do that?
Defendant:	I sell metal powder and I weigh it before selling. That is what the weights on the list mean. What you call prices are money paid to me for metal powder and money that people owe me.
Prosecutor:	A sum of £250 is included in this list. Was that payment made to you or money borrowed from you?
Defendant:	I think that was money borrowed from me.
Prosecutor:	What about the sum of £535?
Defendant:	I don't have the list so I can't explain all the details on the list. I wouldn't have kept a list if I could remember all that.
Prosecutor:	Why would you lend a person £250?
Defendant:	Why not if I have it and a friend of mine desperately needs it.
Prosecutor:	Do you always lend money to your friends when they ask for it?
Defendant:	Not always. If I have the money, I do. I do a bit of sculpturing and moulding as well as sell metal powder. My friends do favours for me and I don't see why I should not help them if I can.
Prosecutor:	Why did you have the list on you on the day that you were seen supplying drugs to Mr X?
Defendant:	I don't see anything wrong with having a list on me. The list has nothing to do with drug dealing and I never supplied any drug to him.
Prosecutor:	Mr X's first name is included on this list as Ray. He is one of your customers?
Defendant:	I don't call him Ray I call him Raymond (whilst giving evidence, the defendant on one occasion called Mr X Ray but that did not seem to be noticed by the prosecution).
Prosecutor:	Mr H is it not correct to suggest that the names on the list are names of customers that you sell drugs to and that the weights and prices indicate the quantity of drugs sold or to be sold and the monies you have received or yet to receive?
Defendant:	That is not true.
Prosecutor:	....Why was £725 found on you at the time of arrest?
Defendant:	That was payment for a moulding job I did.
Prosecutor:	So you are telling us that the money was not your profit from drug dealing?

Defendant: I don't deal in drugs.

As the above case demonstrates, the process and outcome of the negotiation that took place (similar to the other white defendants' cases already shown) over what assets should be defined as proceeds of drug trafficking reveals that what constitutes evidence of drug trafficking (or even any offence) may vary and that the variation may be determined by the discretion of legal actors, which in turn may result in a difference in what is presented as evidence before a jury and ultimately affects conviction and acquittal decisions. This case also illustrates a difference in emphasis allocated to the issue of proceeds of drug trafficking and the relevance given to socio-economic factors. The prosecution did not question the defendant's economic condition; his self-employment was not made to seem unusual or abnormal neither was any criminal definition given to his employment and the fact that he claimed welfare benefits.

Whilst white defendants are not subjected to a complex form of questioning about their personal possessions and whilst their explanation about how they came to possess what the prosecution term to be the proceeds of drug trafficking do not result in obvious doubts and suspicion in the mind of the prosecution or humiliating and intimidating questioning, black defendants on the other hand, who at first appear to 'account' for their possessions find themselves facing some form of criminalisation by the time an in-depth examination of their lifestyle is over

Quantity of drug and drug trafficking

> "Not long ago, he was acquitted in T Crown Court for the same type of offence....These drug dealers have devised new methods. They now carry small quantities of drugs at each time to avoid being convicted for being in possession with intent to supply" (A court staff referring to a black defendant who was acquitted).

The quantity of drug is another factor that indicates shifts in the imputation of meaning to drug trafficking by the prosecution. There seems to be no clear distinction made between quantities of drugs that should either characterise a suspect as a drug trafficker or a mere possessor of drugs. However, the prosecution finds it more justifiable to refer to the quantity of drug if the amount involved is believed to be large, although such reference is made in ways which are essentially relative in nature. On occasions, certain quantities of drugs described by the prosecution as "large" are interpreted as an indication of drug trafficking and on other occasions, similar amounts are presented differently - in a manner that do not bring the picture of drug trafficking into the scene. As will be shown, this variation in definitions given to similar situations suggests an intrusion of the prosecution's own frame of reference in the perpetuation of the myth surrounding the drug trafficking business.

In the absence of a universal consensus over a relationship between a specified amount of drug and drug trafficking, what tends to be presented is a picture which has the potential of leading to an automatic designation of some defendants and not others, as drug traffickers. During the prosecution claims-making and justification process, this discrepancy which is intrinsically imbued with racial overtones surfaces. There are two racially underlined dimensions in the prosecution's description of the link between drug trafficking and quantity of drugs. For black defendants, the main premise of the 'drug trafficking and quantity of drug' argument is that the amounts of drugs found in the defendants' possession or control could only be explained in terms of drug trafficking. At this end of the spectrum are definitions that describe this group of defendants as the drug trafficking class, the real criminals whose principal reason for being in possession of what is notably described by the prosecution as "substantial" amounts of drugs, is to sell them in order to make a financial gain. No other explanation is portrayed as rational by the prosecution. At the other end of the spectrum, we witness the prosecution seeming to assign or assigning a non-drug trafficking definition to a drug trafficking offence charge brought against white defendants linked to 'large' quantities of drugs. In a significant number of white defendants' cases where the issue of the quantity of drug was raised, the drug trafficking offence charge was dropped. Although the prosecution acknowledged the presence of 'large' amounts of drugs in these cases, alternative explanations were given for their existence. For example:

> A white male defendant charged with 'possession' and
> 'possession with intent to supply' was associated with
> 13.04 grams of a class B drug which was described by
> the prosecution as "a substantial quantity of drug".
> Whilst dropping the drug trafficking offence charge,
> the prosecution stated that "the defendant said that he
> had that amount of drug because he intended sharing it
> with his friends who are known drug users. He said
> that he did not intend making any financial profit".

Claiming drug use or addiction in order to reduce the possibility of a conviction or to avoid a severe penalty, was common amongst defendants who pleaded guilty to unlawful possession of drugs but disputed the drug trafficking allegation. This occurred irrespective of race and the amount of drug involved. For the prosecution, this explanation along with that which portrays a defendant as a non-drug trafficker who merely supplies to friends on a social basis justified dropping drug trafficking offence charges against some white defendants linked to 'large' amounts of drugs, thereby exempting them from a trial-by-jury process. In the case of those white defendants who went through a contested trial for drug trafficking, the quantity of drug even when construed as large did not receive a significant negative attention. The defendants' explanation that the 'large' quantity of drug in question was for their own use did not give rise to the type of interrogation aimed at creating the image of an 'evil' drug trafficker. The case of a white female defendant charged with (1) unlawful possession of 14.6 grams of cannabis and (2) unlawful possession of 14.6 grams of cannabis with intent to supply, provides an illustration of this type. In trying to refute the defendant's explanation that the 14.6 grams of cannabis was not meant for sale, the prosecutor asks:

Prosecutor: In your statement made at the police station, you said that the 14.6 grams of cannabis found in your flat was for your own personal use?

Defendant: Yes.

Prosecutor: Did you intend using that amount of drug in one day?

Defendant: No. That could have lasted me about two weeks unless I gave some to friends.

Prosecutor: Would those friends have paid you?

Defendant: No. I wouldn't have paid them if they gave me some.

Prosecutor: Why would you buy two weeks supply?

Defendant: I don't like running out. I buy enough to last me till I get my giro.

Most negative accounts on drugs tend to concentrate on trafficking deals and therefore the spotlight is taken off the drug user or addict. Whilst the drug user/addict is viewed primarily as a sick wo/man and presented as an object of pity who needs societal help (Black, 1991; Dorn and South, 1985), the drug trafficker is considered morally culpable; whilst law enforcement strategies are directed towards penalising the trafficker, preventative and rehabilitative measures move towards helping the drug user/addict (Home Office, 1985). Drug traffickers are considered a threat to society; they are always on the attack. Because there is a lesser degree of seriousness ascribed to illicit drug use (Young, 1971; Dorn et al., 1992), defendants find it a favourable explanation to give in contradiction to any allegation of possessing drugs for the principal purpose of drug trafficking. The 'personal use' or 'sharing with friends on a social basis' explanation does not always receive a 'minimal' form of questioning as illustrated in the case below. Black defendants who relate the 'same' explanations to the supposed large quantity of drugs found in their possession or control are, however, faced with the image of an indisputable drug trafficker:

> A black male defendant was charged for being in possession of 6.2 grams of cocaine with intent to supply. One of the arguments raised by the prosecution to consolidate the drug trafficking allegation against the defendant was that the quantity of drug involved was large. In relation to this issue, part of the claims-making activity follows thus:

Prosecutor:	Mr L do you still use cocaine?
Defendant:	(pause) No.
Prosecutor:	When did you stop using cocaine?
Defendant:	When. About six months ago.
Prosecutor:	After you had been arrested and charged for this offence?
Defendant:	Yes. I tried several times to give it up.
Prosecutor:	And that was not possible, you had to have 6.2 grams of cocaine in your home for your own personal use?
Defendant:	(silence)
Prosecutor:	Mr L do you really want us to believe that amount of drugs was for your own consumption and not for sale?
Defendant:	It was not for sale. It was for my own use. I have told you that.
Prosecutor:	6.2 grams?
Defendant:	Yes.
Prosecutor:	....For how long were you using cocaine?
Defendant:	Up to six years
Prosecutor:	I believe that you were using it everyday?
Defendant:	Yes.
Prosecutor:	How much were you using in a day?
Defendant:	A quarter of a gram.

Prosecutor:	If you used a quarter of a gram of cocaine a day, why did you have 6.2 grams in your home on the day that you were arrested?
Defendant:	I needed it, that was why I had it.
Prosecutor:	You mean you needed 6.2 grams of the drug on that day?
Defendant:	No. I only used a quarter a day.
Prosecutor:	And what did you intend doing with the rest, sell it?
Defendant:	No. It was all for my use. I shared with my friends sometimes.
Prosecutor:	Did these friends you supplied to pay you for the drugs?
Defendant:	No. They are my friends, you know! We shared.
Prosecutor:	Considering the price of the drug, why would you freely give it away?
Defendant:	I never said I gave all I bought to my friends. I didn't say that. I bought for my own use and sometimes gave to my friends.
Prosecutor:	Did you intend sharing the 6.2 grams with your friends?
Defendant:	Perhaps.
Prosecutor:	That does not explain why a person that uses a quarter of a gram of cocaine a day should have 6.2 grams, does it Mr L? I suggest you had the drugs for commercial reasons....

The prosecution does not place black defendants within the ranks of helpless drug users/addicts - in a way that could advantage them - which could stem from existing beliefs that black people are noted for drug trafficking. As already noted, the media have played a crucial role in the representation of black localities as drug trafficking areas (especially in relation to cocaine and crack) with black people as the trafficker, and attention has been drawn to drug-related violence that takes place in these areas. Although drug-related problems may be adversely experienced within the black community (Dorn and South, 1985), the image of the problem drug user who falls victim to the 'cruel' drug trafficker does not incorporate black defendants, accused of drug trafficking, who claim drug use/addiction. The problem drug users, as studies on drug abuse (particularly 'hard' drugs such as heroin) have served to highlight, are white - who make up the highest percentage of drug users known to helping drug agencies (Dorn and South, 1985; Dorn and South, 1987; Mirza et al.,1991b). In their study on *Drug Misuse in a South London Borough*, Mirza et al.(1991, p.120) note that 'whereas 85 percent of crack users known to helping agencies were white, 95 percent of those known to the police were black'.

In the courtroom, it therefore appears more logical for an alleged white drug trafficker to claim drug use or addiction even when the amount of drug involved is described as "large". On the contrary, the language that the prosecution uses when presenting a case concerning a black drug user or addict aims at overshadowing the drug use/addiction explanation offered for being in possession of a quantity of drug. In fact, the larger the amount of drug involved, the more justifiable it is for the prosecution to apply the drug trafficker label.

Drug-related paraphernalia and drug trafficking

Drug paraphernalia related to the production and distribution of drugs constitute a further instrument that the prosecution uses to justify his/her assertion about drug trafficking. Items such as a set of weighing-scales, cling film, tin foil, bicarbonate of soda, vitamin C, baking powder are identified by the prosecution as drug-related paraphernalia associated with drug trafficking. A radio pager is another item that would be classified under drug trafficking paraphernalia in as much as it is believed by the prosecution to have a direct link to the drug trafficking business. A set of weighing-scales was associated with one black and one white defendant; the presence of a radio pager was evident in two black defendants' cases although it was in one of these cases that its supposed link to drug trafficking was made an issue in the sense that all the messages received on the pager were questioned and subsequently related to drug trafficking. The other noted drug trafficking items were most commonly identified with defendants.

Each defendant refuted the prosecution's allegation about drug trafficking paraphernalia. Except for a set of weighing-scales for which there occurred a disparity in the explanations given by the two defendants regarding its presence, domestic use was a common explanation given by the defendants for having the alleged drug-related items; in very few cases, personal use was another reason cited. In some cases, the alleged drug-related items are clearly or intricately portrayed by the prosecution to be for domestic use or personal use. In others, the 'same' items are exclusively defined as drug trafficking accessories. This finding coincides with Holzner's (1972, p.7) view that:

> one can incorporate the same given actuality into a variety of possible value perspectives....The value perspectives may incorporate the same actuality into different contexts and thus give it quite different specific meanings, even though there is no doubt that it is the same actuality.

Despite the differential imputation of meanings to identical objects by the prosecution, one factor remains specific - race. It seems clear that the significance in the disparate definitions given to the 'same' items remains in the perpetuation of the notion of a racial difference located within the context of culture. Counter claims made by black defendants, relating alleged drug-related items to domestic use, trigger off disbelief on the part of the prosecution. The interrogation of a black male defendant associated with a tin of baking powder, identified as a drug trafficking item, illuminates this point:

Prosecutor:	....I suggest you used baking powder to mix with heroin to produce a larger quantity to sell?
Defendant:	That is untrue.
Prosecutor:	And that explains why a tin of baking powder was found by the police in one of your kitchen cupboards.
Defendant:	(in temper) Untrue.
Prosecutor:	If you say that the tin of baking powder found in your kitchen was not for the purpose of drug dealing, why would you have it?
Defendant:	My Mrs must have kept it there.
Prosecutor:	What did she need it for?
Defendant:	It was in the kitchen. For cooking I suppose. She does the cooking.
Prosecutor:	Do you know exactly what she used it for?
Defendant:	I don't know.
Prosecutor:	Have you ever seen her using baking powder?
Defendant:	Maybe, maybe not. I don't nose around to see what she uses when cooking.
Prosecutor:	Did you know that a tin of baking powder was in that cupboard?
Defendant:	I didn't have any need for it so I can't remember noticing it.
Prosecutor:	You used that cupboard, did you not?
Defendant:	Yes. It's my home in't.
Prosecutor:	Mr C I do suggest you knew perfectly well that tin of baking powder was in that cupboard and you used it to adulterate heroin to produce a larger saleable quantity.
Defendant:	I don't know what you are talking about.
Prosecutor:	That your common-law wife used it for domestic purposes is a story you have made up to hide your drug dealing activities....

In this case and others, the black defendants find themselves at complete variance with the prosecution's perception of the purpose of what the defendants considered as household items, a situation not experienced by their white counterparts. Whilst there is a reluctance on the side of the prosecution to view certain supposed drug-related paraphernalia in terms of their domestic value in black defendants' cases, the 'same' items appear, in contrast, to be recognised as acceptable culinary apparatus in English households. This is reflected in the minimal attention focused on the relationship between white defendants and drug trafficking on the basis of the presence of drug-related paraphernalia.

I have previously cited five cases where five white defendants had the drug trafficking offence charges brought against them dropped by the prosecution. In four of those cases, the defendants were linked to drug-related paraphernalia namely tin foil, cling film, bicarbonate of soda and baking powder. However, the prosecution, the defence and the Judge shared a common understanding of the acceptability of these items as domestic items rather than drug trafficking objects. For instance, in one of the five cases, the Judge and the defence agreed with the prosecution's assertion that "...the tins of baking powder and bicarbonate of soda that the police found in the   defendant's home were claimed by his mother to be purely for domestic use". Other white defendants' cases show that a brief interrogation like the following finalises the claims - and counter claims-making activities between the prosecution and the defendant regarding drug trafficking and drug-related paraphernalia:

Prosecutor: The police found a quantity of cling film and tin foil in your flat which we suggest was used to wrap drugs prior to their sale?

Defendant: (smiling) It's not true. Everybody has got cling film and tin foil in their homes. They are for cooking in't?

The above illustrations have shown how the justification process is meant to work in the prosecution's favour to the disadvantage of black defendants. The discrepancy in definitions of, and emphasis placed on, objects termed as drug-related, appears to be a product of cultural variations; it is symptomatic of the prosecution's affirmation about the cultural difference between British black and white population. And as was made to appear, it is from this cultural framework that the link between race and drug trafficking derive part of its strength. By portraying the 'domestic use' explanation for a 'domestic' item as un-cultural for black defendants and cultural for their white counterparts, a logical understanding is anticipated to arise in the minds of the judge and jury as the prosecution gradually forms the picture of race and drug trafficking.

Separate wraps of drugs and drug trafficking

Splitting a quantity of drug into separately wrapped portions is an act construed by the prosecution as being fully cognisant with drug trafficking. It is an issue raised by the police during cross-examination to oppose the defence's claim that alleging drug trafficking on the individual or collective grounds of quantity of drugs, drug-related paraphernalia and proceeds of drug trafficking is hypothetically-based and therefore unwarranted. This logic surfaces regardless of the racial background of the defendants. The amount of drug involved is of no relevance in the pursuance of this argument, instead, the more the number of separately wrapped drugs involved, the more convincing the prosecution expects the drug trafficking claim to be. The prosecution's confidence is premised on the conception of why an individual would have a quantity of drug in separately packaged portions. Nevertheless, counter claims are made by the defendants regarding this issue.

The plea status of defendants influences the degree of attention that the prosecution focuses on this piece of evidence. In cases where defendants pleaded not guilty to charges of possession and drug trafficking, it appears rather problematic for the prosecution in the trial-by-jury process to 'rationally' peddle the 'separately wrapped drugs' claim to the court, and this is because the prosecution faces a twin responsibility of establishing that a defendant actually had the separate wraps of drugs in his/her possession or control and that s/he had them for the purpose of drug trafficking. Defendants who agree to being in possession of separately wrapped drugs but refute the drug trafficking allegation make it convenient for the prosecution to locate the act of having separate packages of drugs in drug trafficking in the sense that a way is paved for such questions as "why was the drug in separate packages" to arise. This sort of question is generated by 'the drug was for my own use' type of explanation that is given by defendants for having drugs in their possession, and from there progresses into a pattern of interrogation that provides two different images of black and white defendants even though the prosecution's general form of argument relies on the belief that drugs meant for personal use would not be split into separately wrapped portions. The two cases below illustrate how differential treatment by race is created from the disparate emphasis that is placed on the question of separate wraps of drugs in the prosecution's claim about drug trafficking.

In the first case concerning a black defendant, four wraps of cocaine were involved; in the second case, it

was seven wraps of cannabis and the defendant
involved was white. In the black defendant's case, the
following shows part of the competing claims
regarding the issue of 'separate wraps':

Prosecutor:	....If the drug found in your flat was for your own use as you try to make us believe, why was it split into separate wraps?
Defendant:	I bought them like that.
Prosecutor:	You mean you purchased the drug in the state it was found hidden away in your jacket pocket, in four wraps?
Defendant:	Yes.
Prosecutor:	You are not telling us the truth Mr E, are you?
Defendant:	I am.
Prosecutor:	Why did you not buy the drug in one portion? Why did it have to be in four separately wrapped portions?
Defendant:	That was all the dealer had at the time
Prosecutor:	But it is possible to buy the same quantity of drug in one lump?
Defendant:	Yes.
Prosecutor:	Mr E it is hard to believe that you were not dealing in drugs. The drug that we are talking about has only a purity of 36%. Am I right to say that you had adulterated cocaine with another substance and then separated it into four wraps ready to be sold for other people's consumption?
Defendant:	They were in wraps when I bought them.
Prosecutor:	Did you know that the wraps contained a substance that was highly impure?
Defendant:	You can't buy drugs with 100% purity on the streets.
Prosecutor:	But you wouldn't buy drugs with that little purity for your own consumption, would you?
Defendant:	I was supposed to use it.
Prosecutor:	Have you ever bought drugs in one lump?
Defendant:	Yes.
Prosecutor:	And never on one occasion have you split drugs into separate quantities for the purpose of selling them?
Defendant:	No.
Prosecutor:	Tell me, did you always purchase drugs from one source?
Defendant:	Not always.
Prosecutor:	What is the name of the dealer that you claim you bought the four wraps of cocaine from?

Defendant:	I know him as Jigsy.
Prosecutor:	The dealer that you claim sold you the four separate wraps of drugs does not exist.
Defendant:	He does exist.
Prosecutor:	I suggest that you are the dealer and that you produced the four wraps from cocaine that you had adulterated with another substance....

And in the white defendant's case:

Prosecutor:	...and that you had the drugs in several separate wraps does suggest that you had the intention of selling them?
Defendant:	They were not for sale.
Prosecutor:	Could you then tell the court why the drugs found on you were in seven separate wraps?
Defendant:	They are sold in wraps.
Prosecutor:	Why did you buy seven wraps? You intended to sell them to make a profit, did you not?
Defendant:	No. That is not correct.

The general image that emerges from the subject of 'separate wraps' and its alleged relationship with drug trafficking moves in the direction of making inferences consistent with a definition of drug trafficking in terms of race. The disparate portrayals of black and white defendants by the prosecutor in relation to this issue seems to draw legitimacy from the overall public concerns over drug trafficking which through saturation media coverage and other sources, has been linked to the black community. Evident in the case of the black defendant illustrated above is the image of the 'evil' drug trafficker who exploits and sells deadly substances to helpless and innocent drug users for financial gains. White defendants accused of having separate wraps of drugs for the purpose of drug trafficking receive little derogatory attention in comparison to their black counterparts. It should also be noted that in the aforementioned five white defendants' cases where drug trafficking offence charges against them were dropped, each of the defendants involved was associated with 'several' separate packages of drugs. Justifying their action in dropping the charges, the prosecution merely stated that the defendants had the drugs for their own use or to share with friends, and apparently put silence to the significance that the prosecution attach to the presence of separate wraps of drugs in contested trials. Clearly, significance lies in the use of this information and not in its existence.

Immorality

By immorality I refer not to a drug offence charge per se but to other behavioural patterns construed by the prosecution in the claims-making process to be at variance with the typical standards of an ideal, traditional English lifestyle. My interest lies in those attitudes which are not officially labelled criminal by the prosecution but which are considered un-English or perceived to be outside the realms of a normal English way of life and viewed on occasions in relation to criminality. Such behaviour serves to justify and maximise moral judgements as reflected in the prosecution process. Undoubtedly, the prosecution's own conception of what character is moral or immoral, normal or abnormal is an expression of their own morals and values which reflect the dominant societal values and moral standards. As Banks (1977, p.41) states:

> The typical prosecutor is generally from a middle-class background and may be easily influenced by simple factors such as the dress, speech and manners of an offender....A certain manner of dress or speech, common in another culture, may be perceived as an indication of moral unworthiness. The prosecutor may also believe that a neatly dressed, humble person is merely a victim of circumstances. In light of these considerations, it is not at all surprising to find oversentencing and undersentencing to be an everyday occurrence in our criminal justice system.

The intention in this section is to show how the prosecution represent immorality in the process of claims-making, how in that process, an alleged drug offence by a defendant is subjectively judged within the context of the defendant's moral standards, and how defendants' morals are evaluated in a manner that highlights behaviours in some cases as a threat to the moral order, and in others, are ignored or looked upon as harmless. In the immorality-construction process, it is in the subtle portrayal of the need to maintain a common set of morals by dealing with the society's unacceptable tendencies and enhancing the typical English moral standards that the prosecution creates an alien image of black defendants before the judge and jury. It is underneath the guise of maintaining public morality that there emerges a gradual reproduction and stabilisation of the ideology of cultural inferiority and the prevalence of ethnocentricity. Myths and stereotypes are gently revealed and used by the prosecution in the name of supporting and upholding English morals and values to advance rather than undermine a long lasting ideological link between 'blackness' and savagery, and at the same time push the debate on the drug offence in their favour.

Each of the themes to be described may be understood if looked at within a cultural framework that developed historically, a cultural structure that gained substance from slavery. Without delving into this issue, we should understand that generations after generations have learnt about black people through stereotypes that generated from culturally-transmitted conceptions of race. Such stereotypes, portrayed within the context of culture, are instrumental in the prosecution's judgement about immorality.

The image of sexuality

> No aspect of the unfavourable negro image had wider or deeper roots than the allegations of insatiable sexual appetite (Barker, 1978, p.121).

The widespread conception of black people as constituting a branch of humanity with unusual powerful sexuality has undergone a gradual construction process which found its origin in the sixteenth century encounters between the English and Africans on the coast of Africa, and in the slave societies of the West Indies (Walvin, 1973). Those periods of slavery saw sexuality as a black quality and a characteristic symptomatic of an incurable black immorality (Barker, 1978). In many ways, black sexuality was conceived in both cultural and biological terms. It was African nakedness that gave importance to the concept of black sexuality in the minds of the English and the Europeans as a whole, for it was a conduct visualised as an indication of sexual abnormality and cultural inferiority. This was followed by a biological interpretation of sexual relationships between black males and females in which the black race was described as libidinous, naturally promiscuous with uncontrollable sexual urges, and whose response to sexual desires is inevitably animalistic in nature (Caplan, 1987; Walvin, 1973; Barker, 1978). Polygamous relationships in both Africa and the West Indies, and alleged public prostitution in Africa received explanations that related them to Africans' craving for sexual needs.

The English description of blacks as sexually immoral, as having a peculiar sexual morality far too inferior to the English sexual morals (Caplan, 1987) during those periods of slavery did not disappear with the abolition of slavery. Like other mythical beliefs about the black race, the myth of black sexuality has since undergone reproductions in different contexts. In 1953, a Mr Craddock made a statement in the House of Commons regarding the sexual behaviour of Africans. In stating that '...the attitude of the African towards women and sexual matters is entirely different from the attitude of the general run of Europeans...', he assumed the racial superiority of Europeans and the inferiority of the black race (Miles and Phizacklea, 1984, p.1). Hill (1967) has drawn attention to black sexuality by making reference to the popular belief which holds that black men are more strongly sexed than white men. Recent years have reproduced the myth of black sexuality although the outlook has taken a slightly different turn in the sense that black sexuality is looked upon not only in its moral context but also in terms of its relationship to crime. Gilroy (1987b) draws attention to images of race and sexuality, indicating the association between black people and vice offences.

As the myth of black sexuality has permeated the British society, it is not surprising that it is one of the images that gains significance in the debate within the courtroom arena. The courtroom itself is a site in which the need to maintain English morals and values is revealed. Apparently, sexuality remains one amidst a variety of themes that the prosecution dwells on in order to prejuce the mind of the judge and jury against a defendant. Apparently, this justification stratagem is confined to black defendants. In those black defendants' cases where reference is made to sexuality, the prosecution portrays and condemns such behaviour as inappropriate and as a negation of English morality. The following case will illustrate this point.

> This is the case of a black male defendant alleged by the prosecution to have made a profit of £104 from drug trafficking. Whilst being interrogated by the prosecution about the money, the defendant claimed that part of it was money that he borrowed from a girlfriend. In response, the prosecution's questions include the following:

Prosecutor:	....Is the girlfriend you are talking about the mother of your children?
Defendant:	No sir (looks were exchanged between the Judge and jurors).
Prosecutor:	Do your children live together?
Defendant:	Yes sir.
Prosecutor:	With their mother?
Defendant:	Yes sir.
Prosecutor:	Your children's mother is your girlfriend. Am I right? (the Judge and Jurors exchanged looks)
Defendant:	(pause) Yes.

Prosecutor:	You told the police that you have many girlfriends. Is that right? (the Judge and Jurors exchanged looks)
Defendant:	I did not tell them that. I told them I have other girlfriends.

The defendant also told the police and the court that his girlfriends (and relatives) assist him financially. In relation to this, the prosecution asks:

Prosecutor:	Do these girlfriends of yours give you money whenever you ask for it?
Defendant:	No sir. Sometimes they lend me money or give it to me and I don't have to pay back.
Prosecutor:	Why would they give you money without asking for it back?
Defendant:	They are my girlfriends.
Prosecutor:	You told the police that you get your money from girlfriends who pay you after gratifying them sexually (the Judge smiled cynically and exchanged looks with jurors).
Defendant:	No sir. I didn't say it like that. There must have been a mistake.
Prosecutor:	That was exactly what you told the police (the prosecutor read out the written statement of the interview that the police had with the defendant). You prostitute for money. Am I right?
Defendant:	I don't think I said that.
Judge:	The interview was recorded, was it not? Perhaps the tape should be played since the defendant has some doubt in his mind.

After about two hours of adjournment, the tape on which the police interview with the defendant was recorded was played. On the disputed issue of whether or not the defendant told the police that his girlfriends pay him "after gratifying them sexually", the recorded interview says:

Police:	Why do these girls give you money?
Defendant:	They are my girlfriends and they like me.
Police:	They give you money because they like you. Is that enough reason for them to give you money?
Defendant:	Yes sir. They like me because I satisfy them in bed.
Police:	(laugh) Did you say you satisfy them in bed? Is that why they give you money?
Defendant:	They give me money because they like me....

A black female witness gave evidence claiming that she had given money to the defendant on occasions. The prosecution asked her if she had had sex with the defendant, how many times she had sex with him and if she paid him for sex.

We have seen the extent to which the image of sexuality dominated the discourse in the courtroom drama in this case. This image found importance in the prosecution claims-making and justification process, and was further accorded strength by the Judge's demand that the recorded interview that the police had with the defendant be played in order to clarify the issue of sexuality. It was worth adjourning the trial for about two hours because a tape recorder was not readily available. Evident in the prosecution's interrogation of the defendant are familiar stereotypical images of black sexuality, with added credence to this representation demonstrated in the questions regarding the sexual relationship between the female witness and the defendant. Promiscuity on the part of the defendant was revealed and so was the fact that the defendant had children outside wedlock. Reflected in these demonstrations is the popular belief noted by, for example, Weeks (1985) and Chigwada (1991) that the black family lack the moral security and stability which an 'ideal' family life provides due to the sexual promiscuity common in black communities. Along the line in the claims-making process, a criminal definition was given to the defendant's promiscuous relationship with women whom he claimed gave him financial assistance. By indicating prostitution, the prosecution's construction of sexuality in this case advanced from merely being an immoral conduct to being both immoral and criminal behaviour.

Sexual immorality is not a status that the prosecution associate with white defendants, which does not mean that the white defendants in the cases observed had impeccable sexual morals judging from the prosecution's assessment of immorality. There were some who had children outside marriage, were promiscuous, divorced and received financial assistance from female partners. None of these facts, which were provided by the defendants themselves whilst under examination, is raised or used by the prosecution to depict inappropriate behaviour in any white defendant's case; the interrogation poses no challenge to the defendants' sexual moral standards. That sexuality is an image revealed in the courtroom and confined to the black defendants suggests a deeply rooted acceptability of this long standing conception of the black race as sexually immoral - and the English as the epitome of sexual morality.

The violent and the non-violent

Violence is represented in a discursive form in the prosecution's discourse and forms part of a conduct that the prosecution believes to deviate from the 'agreed upon' norms that they themselves supposedly subscribe to. Such qualities perceived by the prosecution as 'unconventional' and 'odd' at some point in the claims-making process take the spotlight off the drug offence allegation and apparently dominate the courtroom drama. However, the prosecution's intricate reference to the violation of English moral standards and values in this aspect is conceived in terms of racial or cultural differences. The racialisation of behaviour, defined as violent and disruptive, in the courtroom is not unfamiliar for the prosecution's presentation of such behaviour as being incompatible with normal English lifestyle remains compatible with stereotypical images and ideologies provided by historical (Walvin, 1973) and criminological studies (Gilroy, 1987b; Hall et al., 1978), the media (Hall et al., 1978), politicians (Benyon and Solomos, 1987; Solomos, 1988a) and so forth in relation to race and violence.

So another view that emerges from the prosecution's claim about alleged black drug offenders lies in the overall idea that black people are notably aggressive in their actions. Those black defendants who are believed to conform to the stereotyped notions of how black people behave in terms of aggression, fall prey to the prosecution's demonstration of black incompatibility with the civilised English lifestyle. Resisting arrest in a violent manner or putting up a struggle with the police exemplifies alleged hostile actions that amalgamate an alleged drug offence with further aspects of black law-breaking:

> In this case, two police officers gave account of 'what happened' leading to the arrest of a black male defendant. The police officers were on general patrol at about 1.15 am on a council estate when they saw the defendant and a rastafarian walking towards them. The defendant, they claimed, was talking loudly. The defendant and the rastafarian were stopped the police officers and subjected to questioning. On being examined by the prosecution, the police officers described the defendant as noisy, abusive and violent. In the words of one of the police officers, the defendant "acted so violently" during their encounter with him.

During cross-examination by the prosecution, the defendant refuted the allegations of violence and hostility. The claims-making process is exemplified below:

Prosecutor: ....You agree that you were talking loudly?

Defendant: I was not talking loud. I couldn't have been because I knew that it was late.

Prosecutor: You were talking at the top of your voice and one of the officers asked you to lower your voice, did he not and you replied "I haven't fucking done anything"?

Defendant: One asked me to lower my voice but I didn't say that. I must have said something similar but I am sure I didn't use the word "fucking".

Prosecutor: You signed the written statement of the interview you had with the police at the police station, did you not? (the prosecutor read it out. The word "fucking" was abbreviated thus: "F").

Defendant: The police must have added the "F" to suit themselves.

Prosecutor: Two officers could not have been lying about you talking very loudly when people were trying to get some sleep and being abusive when you were asked to lower your voice. They were on duty keeping the peace. Why would they tell lies about your behaviour on that morning?

Defendant: It is not impossible, after all they are mates.

Prosecutor: PC X saw an outline of what was later found to be a plastic bag containing cannabis in your breast pocket. In his suspicion, he did what he had every right to do. He put his hand in your breast pocket to bring out the contents and you violently grabbed his hand and dragged him towards the railing. Why did you do that? Why did you struggle with him if you did not intend getting rid of the plastic bag?

Defendant: Nothing of that sort happened. If I dragged the officer, why didn't they charge me with assault? A little touch on a police officer is assault. Why was I not charged for assault if I dragged him and struggled with him? I know the police and what they can do. I have been charged before for assaulting some police officers and I was acquitted for lack of evidence. Since then I am always careful how I deal with them.

Prosecutor: ....And why would you want to go to his flat (in reference to the defendant's statement that himself and the rastafarian were

	going to the latter's flat)? You wanted to use his flat for cannabis use.
Defendant:	I don't smoke weed. I wanted to go to his flat to listen to some reggae music.
Prosecutor:	So you were going to listen to reggae music at that time of the morning?
Defendant:	I don't see anything wrong with listening to music at any time as long as you don't disturb anybody. You see on that day I didn't want any trouble....
Prosecutor:	If you did not want any trouble, why did you not go straight home? Why did you decide to go with the rastafarian to his flat at approximately 1 am?

Although such alleged actions were not incorporated in the official reason/s for prosecuting black defendants, the above case shows how accusations of violence are, nevertheless, lifted into visibility by the prosecution in a form that present black defendants as representing a threat to law and order. In such cases where a conflict between a black defendant and the police is alleged, the picture that is displayed is that of a disruptive, ill-mannered black wo/man. As indicated, antagonising the police is an expression of an attack on the state, a violation of national interest, a symbol of dangerousness to society and the prominence of non-adherence to the rule of law - which symbolises the unity of societal members. Violence is despised by law enforcers, the state and society; it is seen as endangering social stability and embodying a basic violation of society. As Sarrat (1993, p.21) argues, violence 'speaks loudly, arouses indignation, and, as a result, its representation threatens to overwhelm reason'. The prosecution portrays the police as representing law and order, and black defendants as typifying a danger and disruption to society.

Violence is not related to white defendants by the prosecution even though police accounts of 'what happened' during their encounter with white defendants indicate the occurrence of a scuffle between them. Refusing to be searched, attempting to abscond and obstructing the police are instances of reactions that the police claimed they received from white defendants. Another display of hostility is shown in allegations by the police that white defendants used abusive language during their encounter with them. Statements such as "fuck off", "fucking bastard" and "piss off" exemplify such abusive language. The white defendants involved denied these allegations whilst under examination. And the subsequent interrogation by the prosecution regarding the drug offence with which the defendants are charged does not give significance to the alleged conflict between the police and the defendants. Neither is the alleged use of abusive language the defendants made an issue by the prosecution. In fact some of the alleged abusive statements caused giggles in the courtroom. The significance of the subtlety that goes with what would be classified as immoral behaviour by white defendants appears to lie in the portrayed impression of the English as polite and well-mannered. Violence is widely represented as un-English and so is criminality (Gilroy, 1987b). As it was made to look in the prosecution's response, those white defendants who violated the English moral standards merely acted out of character; they form part of the few bad apples for immorality is not a quality linked with Englishness.

Purity and filthiness

> Let us remember that 95 per cent of them (i.e Africans) are primitive people. One of the reasons why they are not generally accepted into hotels is because their sanitary habits are not all that could be desired.... (A statement made by a Mr Craddock in 1953 cited in Miles and Phizacklea, 1981, p.1).

'Dirtiness' is yet another stereotypical image that is fused with race in the prosecution justification process regarding an alleged drug offence. 'Filthy', 'unclean', 'smelly' are qualities that have for generations been ascribed to black people (Walvin, 1973; Hill, 1967; File and Power, 1981). Gordon (1983) acknowledges the existence of stereotypes that give a descriptive picture of black people as un-hygienic. Chiqwada (1989) cites a case of a black woman who having spent a night in police custody had a police officer look up her skirt and say 'what a sight this is before breakfast'. It is hardly surprising that in the process of claims-making, the prosecution and the police fit black defendants into the images of race and uncleanliness - for example, in relation to their homes or their personal habits. The following dialogue between a prosecutor and a black defendant exemplifies the point on personal hygiene and habits. The defendant was charged for being in possession of cannabis and part of the overall prosecution argument in this case was that the defendant did smoke cannabis:

Prosecutor:	....You were told by the police that you must have smoked cannabis because your breath smelt sweet?
Defendant:	They never told me that. I am hearing it for the first time in this court....
Prosecutor:	Why then did your breath smell sweet?

Defendant: (pause) That comment by the police is an insult. What they mean is that I am dirty. I brush and keep my teeth clean, so I don't see why my breath should not smell sweet.

Prosecutor: If you are that clean, how come the police said that your armpits smelt like death and that you were wiping your nose on your shirt?

Defendant: (long pause) That could have been after being detained for a long time.

Defence: Your Honour, the defendant has said that he drank ribena not long before his arrest. That, I believe is the reason for the sweet breath (the Judge agreed with the defence).

The prosecution's reference to the defendant's sweet breath was undoubtedly in relation to cannabis smoking and not to lack of personal hygiene. This point was misunderstood by the defendant who imputed a different meaning to the prosecution's question as to why his breath smelt sweet. However, with the defendant's answer to a question which he misinterpreted came the image of filth. The prosecution took advantage of the defendant's misconception to slot in an observation that was already there waiting to be put into perspective at any available opportunity. What the home of black defendants look like in terms of hygiene is mentioned in the courtroom irrespective of its irrelevance to the drug offence trial. For example, whilst giving evidence regarding the search of a black defendant's home for drugs and similar evidence of a drug offence, two of the police officers involved in the search described the defendant's home as "unkempt" and "untidy".

The court observations show no indications of this sort of immoral image in any white defendant's case. Whether this means that all the white defendants were remarkably clean in appearance, had spotless homes and conformed to the prosecution's notions of prevailing standards of habits is beyond this analysis. In any case, the observation merely shows that the attribute - filth - is restricted to black defendants by the prosecution. As this suggests, the direct and indirect references to black defendants and filth, in the courtroom drama typifies a broader form of stereotype which leaves no room for individual variation but looks at the black race as a whole through the mirror which such imagery provides. Presenting black defendants in such an image may be one of the stratagems used by the prosecution to add substance to their claim about an alleged drug offence, however, one point is certain: it contributes to the perpetuation of the 'niggers are dirty and they stink' sort of conception.

In the next chapter, the prosecution's overall claims and justifications surrounding allegations of drug offence are challenged by the defence who proceeds by invoking mechanisms different from those adopted by the prosecution. The defence process reveals the vital role of race in the noticeable demarcations which exist in the interpretations and descriptions given to the 'same' subject of inquiry by the defence.

5 Defending the Defendant

In the preceding chapter it has been shown that at various stages in the court process, negotiation and bargaining take place between the defence, the prosecution and the judge. As this chapter and the next will further reveal, what these legal actors negotiate are images of being white as well as those of being black. Being black, as interpreted in court proceedings around drug cases, means having to negotiate, as a matter of legal fact finding, the issue of deprivation and particular imageries about black people which can ultimately be detrimental to black defendants in the court process. The defence, as has been shown, influence the inadmissibility of certain incriminating evidence - albeit in white defendants' cases. Also indicated is the role of the defence in negotiated plea settlements which resulted in the dropping of drug trafficking charges initially brought against white defendants so that these cases were not processed by means of a jury trial and, therefore, the defendants involved faced a less likelihood of receiving a custodial sentence.

Studies have shown how the defence, in situations such as plea bargaining, operate interdependently and closely with the opposing group - the prosecution (Baldwin and McConville, 1977; McConville et al., 1991). Defence lawyers have been known to act as double agents who work for both the court organization and the defendants, but whose practices seem to be more committed to the benefit of the court (Brown, 1991). They are on-going participants in the criminal process; they are part of the system, part of a court organisation that could function to the disadvantage of defendants (Brown, 1991). As Brown (1991, p.96) notes:

> Perhaps the solicitor, rather than representing the defendant in the
> true sense, is also part of the process of the "mobilisation of allies"....

In pleas of mitigation for instance, it is not unusual to find that defence lawyers do not make recommendations on behalf of their clients for different reasons such as the fear of risking their credibility for the sake of a case that is obviously hopeless (Brown, 1991). Where recommendations are made, defence lawyers know what mitigating arguments to present to raise questions about the prosecution's case. Statements which reveal clients' willingness to respond to authority, clients' regret for what they have done, motives which could be condoned by magistrates and so forth are illustrative of 'control indicators and mitigating factors sought by magistrates, and once more reflects the knowledge of solicitors of their court' (ibid., p.92).

At such stages as plea of mitigation in the defence claims-making process, accounts of drug offence cases involving black and white defendants are provided in a context that the defence believes would gain the approval of the judge or magistrate - even though the arguments often raised portray black and white defendants in two different light. In contested trials, the fundamental defence is to offer a plausible version contrary to the prosecution's account in order to exonerate the defendant, however, in the justification process, the defence usually takes different routes depending on the race of the defendant. Extra-legal devices are employed by the defence with the result that a variation in the presentation of black and white defendants' cases is displayed. 'Fact finding' portrays the wider context of criminality rather than the particular incident and this is because the infiltration of subjectivity in the course of the defence justification process appears to stem from the defence's perception of racial or cultural contexts. What is demonstrated is the defence's awareness of popular images and perceptions of drug offenders and criminals, dominant societal morals and values and so forth. An analysis of such devices reveals cognitive frameworks within which to fit the different arguments that the defence raise in the claims-making process. The defence's stocks of knowledge form his/her frame of reference and tunnel his/her utilisation of an approach which selects disparate stratagems to 'suit' cases concerning black and white defendants. Apparently, arguments raised in white defendants' cases are saturated with bodies of knowledge that the defence believes would introduce familiar cues to guide the process to the advantage of white defendants; likewise, issues addressed in black defendants' cases are imbued with stocks of knowledge that are believed would be understood by the judge and jury and positively assist them in their evaluation of this group of cases. In accordance with his/her knowledge and perspectives, the defence presents and emphasises the varied arguments relating to drug cases concerning these two groups of defendants.

The techniques employed by the defence may differ according to the racial background of defendants but they are meant to serve the same basic purpose of securing an acquittal and/or attract a lenient sentence. Some of the tactics utilised by the defence are located within a racial context that suggests racism on the part of the prosecution witnesses - the police. Some tactics do not, but upon close examination, rely upon the defence's common-sense notions of race. Redefining those elements that ground the prosecution's allegation of drug trafficking is one stratagem that the defence employs in the justification process during which the defence re-interprets the prosecution's assessment of defendants' possessions, quantity of drugs and so forth in order to de-construct the drug trafficking allegation. This stratagem finds more relevance in white defendants' cases. Imputing negative meanings to the actions of police officers leading to the arrest of defendants, is another defence stratagem whereby the defence attributes the basis for the police arrest of a defendant to unreasonable suspicion. In black defendants' cases, where this technique is emphasised, a racist meaning is imputed and wider issues of police racism become relevant features of the defence's claims. A third defence stratagem also focuses on allegations of police misconduct - albeit in black defendants' cases. In using this stratagem, the defence deviates from the drug offence allegation and instead makes an issue out of alleged police use of violence and racist language in their encounter with black defendants.

The question is: could the significant utilisation of disparate extra-legal devices in black and white defendants' cases provide the responders with cues that ultimately work in favour or disfavour of the respective groups of defendants? In the absence of a jury, a case involving two black defendants shows how the defence imputation tactics of arrest based on unreasonable police suspicion clearly worked to the ultimate advantage of the defendants (see Chapter six). In jury trials where the claims-making process entails the utilisation of a tremendous amount of different information, there is the possibility that certain forms of argument that the defence apply to black defendants' cases will make no positive contribution to the overall outcome of their case. In other ways, the defence's disparate methods of representation may ultimately disadvantage black defendants - unlike their white counterparts. This is reflected in the observation that the defence and the prosecution seem to share a common understanding over certain issues about black and white people, and in the defence claims-making and justification process, it appears that, on the basis of this common knowledge, the defence portrays particular arguments in ways that depict an agreement with the prosecution's perspectives - to the possible detriment of black defendants.

The Redefinition of Elements

The defence attempts to substitute the 'agreed upon' criteria for pressing a drug trafficking offence charge with meanings that are not compatible with those ascribed to them by the prosecution. The 'agreed upon' criteria are those elements that ground the prosecution's allegation of drug trafficking. The defence, as part of the court system, acknowledges the official relevance of these elements to charges of a drug trafficking offence and is aware that the objects are commonly known as forming a vital part of the claims-making activity in relation to drug trafficking allegations. In fact, the absence of any one of the elements in a drug trafficking offence charge is used to justify the defence's opposing claim, in any case, the defence's supposed responsibility is to challenge any drug trafficking allegation against a defendant even if all the elements underlie the allegation.

To understand the form that the redefinition takes, it should be borne in mind that the introduction of definitions that fall outside the common agreement on the consistency of the elements with drug trafficking may be influenced by how the defence comprehends the elements within the context of his/her own complex of beliefs and knowledge. Therefore, if the defence's understanding and knowledge of those elements differ according to race, the occurrence of a discrepancy is foreseeable in the pattern by which the elements are redefined in cases concerning black and white defendants - which means that the 'same' objects specifying legal proof could be given alternative representations by the defence. Although the defence, in black and white defendants' cases, define those elements in a direction that establishes his/her counter claim, the extent to which this strategy is used seemingly depends on whether the defence believes that it has success potentials. So that as far as *specific* elements - that is proceeds of drug trafficking and quantity of drug - are concerned, they are redefined in different patterns in black and white defendants' cases inasmuch as they elements are often viewed by the defence in a manner that does not deny the implicit racial connotation embedded in the prosecution's definition of them in cases concerning black and white defendants, showing that even though the defence and the prosecution make up different subgroups, they can share similar knowledge of certain issues. The ascription of meanings to the 'same' objects could become a collective definition to which these groups of legal officials observe. The defence may therefore fail to act as an adversary, challenging the damaging prosecution evaluation of certain elements that precipitate a drug trafficking offence charge and instead put forward a response that is suggestive of a reluctance to undermine the prosecution's line of argument.

Both the prosecution and the defence acknowledge the particular contribution of race in the adversarial process. As has been shown, the prosecution's definition of those elements that ground drug trafficking allegations against black defendants reflects the widespread belief in the overall link between race, deprivation and drug trafficking. In the course of redefining the two prosecution grounds for complaints, the defence's pattern of representation indicates a recognition of the relevance of this ideological link. Consequently, 'minimal' effort is made by the defence in black defendants' cases to refute any prosecution argument that reflects particular imageries of race. It can be argued that the 'minimal' challenge put forward by the defence to redefine the prosecution's own definitions of those elements is symptomatic of the defence's belief in those racial imageries that subtly guide the prosecution's joint interpretations of the elements and drug trafficking in black defendants' cases. And this then could be related to fear on the part of the defence that any display of intense conflict would create pitfalls that the prosecution could take full advantage of to emphasise such racial imageries - to the detriment of black defendants.

Redefining Proceeds of Drug Trafficking

The presence of 'large' sums of money or 'valuable' possessions as perceived by the prosecution to be the proceeds of drug trafficking seems to pose a threat to the defence - but only when the defendants involved are black. Such a perceived threat reveals itself in the observation that the defence and the prosecution appear to have far less in opposition to each other owing to what appears to be a common share of understanding between these groups of legal actors of what amount of money constitutes a large sum or what possessions would be classified as luxurious for a black defendant, particularly when s/he is unemployed or self-employed. For example:

> In an informal discussion with a black defendant's mother, she expressed a feeling that provides an example of this type of shared conception between the defence and the prosecution. The lady was upset that an important defence witness was not forthcoming. The witness (the defendant's girlfriend) was supposed to testify that part of the defendant's alleged proceeds of drug trafficking, that is, £210, was given to him by her. According to the lady, the defence barrister said that without the witness, the jury would find it difficult to disbelieve the prosecution's claim that the money was made from drug trafficking considering the amount. The defendant was self-employed.

In cases where the prosecution portrays a black defendant's possessions as 'too much' or 'valuable' indicating evidence of drug trafficking, there appears to be a limited attempt by the defence to extensively argue against the prosecution's claim that the presence of the items is indicative of drug trafficking. Part of that reluctance on occasions is alleviated by the presence and testimony of relatives and friends referred to by the defendants as the source of their possessions. And on the basis of the evidence of such defence witnesses, the defence's counter-claim in connection with this issue becomes relatively significant. Otherwise, the defence makes 'minimal' efforts to re-interpret the prosecution's assessment of black defendants' possessions in relation to drug trafficking. This is particularly shown in the cross-examination of police officers during which the link between assets and drug trafficking does not constitute an issue that the defence addresses in a form that demonstrates its central position in the overall case. The counter-claim is, in other words, barely adversarial in the manner in which it is presented. Unlike the subjection of black defendants to intensive interrogation by the prosecution, the defence utilises a contrasting stratagem which simplifies the defence's interrogation. An example of this pattern of defence is provided below:

> A black male defendant stopped by the police for committing a motoring offence had his car searched and a piece of cannabis cigarette was found. On him was found £260 which he told the police was money paid back to him by a friend he lent it to. His home was searched by the police and crack cocaine was found. The police claimed that the £260 was his proceeds from drug trafficking. The defendant had £1,195 in his bank account which the prosecution also alleged to be his proceeds from drug trafficking. According to the defendant, the money in his bank account was his savings from a job that he held for twenty years. In the course of cross-examining one of the police officers, the defence addresses this issue thus:

Defence: ....Why did you conduct a search of his home? You had arrested him for committing a motoring offence and for having a piece of cannabis cigarette in his car ashtray. He never denied any of these offences. Why then did you decide to search his bedsit?

Police Officer: Your client had £260 on him. We were not satisfied with the explanation he gave about the source of the money.

Defence:	So you decided to search his bedsit? What did you hope to find? drugs? more cannabis?
Police Officer:	We did find drugs, a more dangerous drug, crack cocaine.
Defence:	You assumed that Mr G was a drug dealer because you found money on him, is that what you are telling us officer?
Police Officer:	Initially, we believed he made the money through illegal means but we later believed it to be the proceeds of drug dealing when we found the drug in his home.

It is also common in black defendants' cases for the defence in his/her closing argument to merely assert that the prosecution's evidence in connection with proceeds of drug trafficking is hypothetically-based. At this stage, the defence basically reproduces the defendants' own accounts regarding the source of their possessions with little or no emphasis added. For instance:

> Members of the jury....The defendant has told you how he came about the money in his bank account. He has told you that the money is his savings from his previous employment of twenty years. He has also told you about the £260. You have heard him say that he lent £260 to a friend of his about a year ago and had collected the money from this friend four days prior to his arrest....The prosecution have no concrete evidence to suggest that the monies are the defendant's profits from drug dealing. Their evidence is based on mere assumption.

A claim of self-employment is a piece of information that does not provide a valuable defence to challenge the asset-drug trafficking subject in black defendants' cases. To the defence, the defendants' claim of self-employment simply forms one of those descriptions about themselves provided to the court during examination, but to the prosecution it constitutes a valuable piece of evidence that is used to undermine the defendants' character.

In white defendants' cases, the defence's counter claim in relation to proceeds of drug trafficking does not only rest upon a contrasting interpretation to that of the prosecution's regarding this element but also introduces a pattern of cross-examination and a form of argument that make this redefinition device a central focus, whereby perspectives are communicated to the judge and jury in a manner that indicates a determination to make certain that the responders' interpretation of this element differs from that expected of them by the prosecution. Money constitutes the only alleged proceeds of drug trafficking linked to white defendants with none being associated with an amount of money larger than £1,000. A reasonable number of them had their drug trafficking offence charges dropped as already stated. In the remaining cases, the attempt to disassociate their alleged proceeds of drug trafficking from drug trafficking, irrespective of the sum of money involved, entails directing searching questions at police officers which tend to add favourable emphasis to the defendants' own account of the source of their money. Aside describing the prosecution's evidence in this context as hypothetical in nature, the defence demonstrates the logicality in his/her claim by placing the argument within the popularly portrayed conception and knowledge that do not identify white people with drug trafficking but a group of people who could earn money through legitimate means as the following example illustrates:

> A white male defendant was stopped in his car by the police on the basis of information that they received that the defendant was a drug trafficker. The police claimed to have found wraps of drugs on the defendant. According to the defendant, the drugs were planted on him by the police. The police also found on him £115 alleged by the prosecution to be his proceeds from drug trafficking and a paper containing a list of names alleged by the prosecution to be the names of his customers. Further police investigation revealed that the defendant had £845 in his bank account which was also classed as his profit from drug trafficking. In relation to the alleged proceeds, the defence interrogation of the police officers involved takes this form:

Defence: ....Officer, you have told the court that you and your colleagues believed the £115 found on Mr S at the time of his arrest to be his profit from drug dealing?

Police Officer: Yes.

Defence: What made you so sure?

Police Officer: He had the money as well as the drugs on him when he was searched.

Defence:	Officer, did the defendant tell you that he was a self-employed interior decorator?
Police Officer:	Yes he did.
Defence:	Did he tell you that the £115 was part-payment for an interior decorating job he did?
Police Officer:	No. When we asked him where he got the money from, he simply said that it belonged to him.
Defence:	And he also told you that the money was not made from drug dealing?
Police Officer:	We got information that he was a drug dealer. We couldn't have believed otherwise when we found the drug, the money and the list.
Defence:	....Did it ever occur to you that the money could have come from a legitimate source and not drug dealing?
Police Officer:	We didn't have any reason to think so.
Defence:	You also did not have any reason not to think so. It is possible that the money had nothing whatsoever to do with drug dealing, is it not?
Police Officer:	I find that hard to believe. He did not account for the money.
Defence:	So because he did not specifically state that the money was earned from a self-employed job, you assumed that it was made from drug dealing, just as you assumed that the £845 in his bank account was his profit from drug dealing?
Police Officer:	It was not an assumption.
Defence:	Mr S did account for the money in his bank account, did he not?
Police Officer:	He said it was his savings but we believed that to be money that he made from drug dealing.
Defence:	If the defendant told you that he held a self-employed job, why did you not believe the money to be his savings from the job?
Police Officer:	Not with the information we received that he was dealing in drugs. When he was found with several wraps of drugs, we had every reason to believe that he was making a profit from drug dealing.
Defence:	Your belief does not prove that the monies are proceeds of drug dealing....

The defence may be faced with difficulty in justifying black defendants' alleged proceeds of drug trafficking when the items are defined by the prosecution as exorbitant and when the defendants concerned are unemployed or self employed. For white defendants in similar economic positions, it seems easy for the defence to justify this issue, regardless of the value of the alleged proceeds, through a more intense and critical interrogation and argument during cross-examination and closing statement. There are occasions when a seemingly favourable line of logic geared towards destabilising the prosecution's asset-drug trafficking link arise in black defendants' cases. In such cases, the form of justification that is used gains substance from certain information available to the defence which portrays an economically deprived image of the defendant. Any 'fact' about a black defendant that the defence believes to depict economic marginalisation or poverty is magnified by the defence to disprove the prosecution's asset-drug trafficking allegation. Information such as the non-ownership of, or the presence of a 'small' amount of money in, a bank or building society account; living in council accommodation (often a bedsit); the ownership of an old car visualised as worthless; and the presence of a 'small' sum of money alleged to be the proceeds of drug trafficking are individually or collectively used by the defence to discredit the police and prosecution evidence - by suggesting that the defendant's lifestyle does not typify a form of socio-economic lifestyle that would be led by a commercially oriented drug trafficker. The following interrogation of a police officer in relation to £14.50 alleged to be the proceeds of drug trafficking in a black defendant's case (see Chapter four) will demonstrate the significance of economic deprivation in the representation of black defendants:

Defence: ....The money that the defendant had on him at the time of his arrest was £14.50, am I right officer?

Police Officer: Yes, that was never denied.

Defence: If the defendant and not one of the other men, was the drug dealer and he made a profit of £14.50, he was not very successful, was he?

Police Officer: We intervened and stopped the transaction.

Defence: ....You visited the defendant's bedsit after he had been arrested, did you not?

Police Officer: Yes.

Defence: You could not identify any valuable possessions in his bedsit to suggest that he was dealing in drugs. Officer, I would have thought that a drug dealer would lead a life of comfort if not luxury.

Similar information is represented in the statement of the defence in the closing argument. For example:

> ....The defendant whom the prosecution claim is a drug dealer
> has got only £35 in his bank account.

Whilst allegations of drug trafficking on grounds of what is perceived as huge proceeds from drug trafficking appears to pose an obstacle to the defence of black defendants, any evidence of economic deprivation is, on the contrary, confidently used to demonstrate their innocence. This may imply that the defence implicitly agrees with the ideology that links race to deprivation - a belief that has for decades been widely publicised and in the courtroom reinforced by the prosecution. Accordingly, the defence may acknowledge the logic behind the prosecution's assertion that a black defendant with 'exorbitant' possessions and no regular employment procured those assets through drug trafficking. Whatever the real reasons that underlie the way that the defence addresses the proceeds of drug trafficking issue in jury trials of black defendants, the defence justification process at other stages in the court process reveals an awareness of the ideological link between race, deprivation and crime. As is reflected in pleas of mitigation, the legacy of this ideological link permeates the thinking of the defence, particularly, at the magistrates' court where the pleas seem to clearly demonstrate the ideological position of the defence with regard to the images of race and drug offence or crime. It happens that at this stage, the defence echoes sentiments similar to the prosecution's logic in jury trials regarding black defendants whose alleged proceeds of drug trafficking are portrayed within the realm of socio-economic deprivation. Unlike their white counterparts, it is common in pleas of mitigation for black defendants to be constructed as the underclass or the economically marginalised in spite of the similar socio-economic positions that black and white defendants occupied. At the magistrates' court where the majority of guilty pleas were in connection with straight possession of a controlled drug, the defendants (black and white) involved were mostly unemployed inhabitants of council accommodation in inner-city areas. However, the image of a defendant who committed a drug offence, often illicit drug use, because s/he suffers from a complex of multiple economic deprivation is portrayed in pleas of mitigation concerning black defendants. A black male defendant had pleaded guilty to possession of what was described as "a small amount" of cannabis and theft. In a plea for a lighter sentence, his defence lawyer states:

The defendant is unemployed and has in fact not worked for two years. He lives on his own in a council flat....He co-operated with the police when he was arrested for theft....The reason he took the lady's purse, sir, was because he was in desperate need for money. It was when he was taken to the police station and searched that the drug was found. Sir, he very much regrets committing these crimes. He agrees that he did not behave in a right manner. He only wanted to use the drug to fight stress. At present, the defendant is going through a difficult financial situation. He is on social security benefit but has not received any for two weeks....He has not had electricity for three days because he can't afford to pay for it. He uses a slot machine - type electricity meter, sir. As a matter of fact sir, the defendant has not eaten for sometime as he has no money to pay for food. He has a two year old daughter and he contributes to her upkeep. He is finding it extremely difficult to cope...

A white defendant in similar economic condition pleaded guilty to possession of one gram of cannabis and two charges of handling stolen property. In plea of mitigation, his lawyer explains his crime and circumstances thus:

Sir, I know that the defendant has breached his probation by committing these crimes but sir, I suggest that whatever punishment you have in mind be in the form of supervision. The defendant not only pleaded guilty to these charges, he has also felt awfully sorry having realised that what he did was wrong....There has been a great improvement in his life. He has made several attempts to secure paid employment. When that failed, he tried self-employment. He got into painting and decorating but that collapsed due to financial problems. He is now unemployed and receives social security benefit. He lives alone in a bedsit. He was previously living with his mother....The move from his mother's is a major step for him to gain his independence and shoulder his responsibilities....

The magistrate fined the black defendant ten pounds for the 'possession' offence and twenty pounds for theft. After stating that the white defendant had been of good behaviour, the magistrate in his case gave him a two-year conditional discharge. As the first illustration above shows, the widespread conception of a relationship between race, economic deprivation and crime is typified by the utilisation of unemployment and poverty as justification for the black defendant's involvement in illicit drug use and theft. Apparently, the defence in a own subtle way assists in the reproduction of the belief that holds that the black population suffer adverse socio-economic deprivation which makes them more likely to engage in criminal activities. The white defendant's economic circumstances, although stated, are not related to the crimes he committed; he is instead portrayed as a man who had made genuine efforts to better his life. Also implicit in the above pleas, as well as others, is a construction of the defendants' criminal behaviour as being 'out of place', as indicating a disagreement with the mainstream societal norms - which the defence, like the prosecution, supposedly adhere to.

Quantity of Drug: A Redefinition

Whilst societal reaction to drug trafficking moves in the direction of complete disapproval, drug use or addiction is tolerated. These opposing reactions are also shown in the variations in the sentences that the two categories attract. In drug cases where defendants do not refute the allegation of unlawful possession of a controlled drug but disagree with the prosecution that the drugs in question are for the purpose of drug trafficking, it remains normal practice for the defence, in order to exonerate the defendants from drug trafficking allegations, to claim that the defendants had the drugs because they were drug users and that the drugs were meant for their own personal use or that they intended sharing the drugs with their friends on a social basis. Irrespective of the quantity of drugs involved, this excuse finds significance in white defendants' cases contributing to the dropped drug trafficking offence charges in a reasonable percentage of the defendants' cases. The defence and the prosecution shared a common agreement on those reasons behind the presence of the drugs in those white defendants' cases - an observation not witnessed in cases concerning black defendants with similar charges, plea status and explanations for being in unlawful possession of a controlled drug. During contested trials, the defence always uphold the 'drug is for personal use' sort of explanation in all cases of this type. That the drugs involved are often in separate wraps is not treated as a separate issue but is incorporated into the stated justifications put forward by the defence for the existence of a quantity of drug.

A variation which is racially based appears in the way that those justifications are fed the court by the defence and that discrepancy is influenced by the quantity of drug involved. When black defendants are involved with an amount of drug labelled by the prosecution as "substantial", it appears problematic for the defence to present them, in a challenging fashion, as drug users. Such cases attract a 'limited' display of challenge in the redefinition process. It was only in one black defendant's case that an amount of drug described as "small" by the defence was used as a justifiable evidence to dispute a drug trafficking allegation. In that case, the quantity of drug involved was 475 milligrams. That 'large' or even larger amounts of drugs are associated with white defendants do not seem to pose a threat to the defence, for at this stage of the claims-making and justification process, the defence does not hesitate to assign to this group of defendants the image of a harmless and innocent drug user. Justifying black defendants' possession or control of drugs in terms of drug use is not similarly demonstrated: emphasis is barely placed on the drug use explanation during examination, cross-examination and closing argument. In cross-examining police officers, for instance, the defence effects what seems to be a simple non-probing interrogation that sometimes receives a more challenging response from police officers. For example:

Defence: ...but the defendant did tell you on arrest that the drug (that is, 8.5 grams of cocaine) was for his own personal use?

Police Officer: It is common for drug pushers to give that excuse once they are apprehended. Your client had an amount of drug that we believed was not meant for his own use.

An example of how the defence presents the drug use argument in white defendants' cases during cross-examination of police officers is shown below:

Defence: ....Officer you were aware of the fact that the defendant was a cannabis user, were you not?

Police Officer: He said so. It still doesn't mean that he did not intend selling the drugs that were found in his possession.

Defence: ....Mr Q never denied any intentions to supply the drugs. In fact, he bought the drugs for his own use and that of his girlfriend. He was only going to share the drugs with his girlfriend. There was no intention of supplying her with drugs on a commercial basis. He explained this to you officer, did he not?

Police Officer: Yes but we are not talking about a small quantity of drug....

Defence: It is hardly surprising that he had that amount of cannabis. He was a heavy cannabis user and so was his girlfriend. Both of them could have used up 18.8 grams within a week....

The variations that occur in the style of representation of the 'drug use' argument in contested trials involving black and white defendants with supposedly large quantities of drugs could be attributed to different factors. There is the possibility of fear on the part of the defence that attempting to put across to the court that a black defendant had a 'large' quantity of drug for personal consumption or to be shared with friends on a social basis would sound illogical considering the widespread stereotypical image of black people as drug traffickers - which the defence possibly believe the judge and jury subscribe to. Apparently, the defence feels that the existence of 'substantial' amounts of drugs in black defendants' cases is likely to negatively influence the outcome of their case. Such fear is clearly expressed in one case involving a black defendant. Prior to the trial of this case, the defence suggested that the defendant pleaded guilty to the drug trafficking offence charge brought against him. One of the reasons he gave for his suggestion was the likelihood of the jury not to believe that he had such an amount of drug (6.2 grams of a class A drug) for his own personal use. The defence added that if the defendant pleaded guilty to the charge, his plea of mitigation would be that the defendant meant to share the drug with his friends on a non-commercial basis. In any case, the defendant refused to plead guilty and went through a contested trial.

Alternatively, such reluctance to bring the 'drug use' explanation into the limelight could be related to the observation that the defence may, on the basis of his/her stocks of knowledge, have disparate conceptions of what quantity of drug is 'large' or 'small' and what quantity of drug is for personal consumption or for drug trafficking, and such knowledge and conceptions may determine his/her pattern of argument in black and white defendants' cases. The defence may adhere to the popular belief that black people are more likely to be drug traffickers and accordingly, the defence may believe that the presence of an amount of drug defined as "substantial", in a black defendant's case, is less likely to be for personal use alone. In the magistrates' court, the defence in different ways shows an awareness of the drug user and drug trafficker imageries and stereotypes. In pleas of mitigation and bail applications, the existence of such awareness is revealed. In the only case where a white defendant was refused bail, the defendant had a black co-defendant. The defendants had drug trafficking offence charges brought against them and the quantity of drug involved was described as "large" by the prosecution. In a plea for bail, the defence lawyer for the white defendant states:

> ....The drugs found in his home were not his sir. He was a customer, not a supplier. The defendant has a severe drug problem....He is planning to go for detoxification....

Whilst the black defendant's lawyer argues:

> Sir, the crime was not committed at the defendant's residence...there were five people inside the property at the time. They were all arrested and three were later released.

The magistrate interrupts:

> The others could have been customers.

The lawyer continues:

> ....The defendant has previous convictions but he has not committed any offence since he came out of prison in (year)....He is not a drug addict sir.

The magistrate replies:

> Then he is a wholesaler or retailer. If he is not an addict, he is a dealer.

In reply to this comment by the magistrate, the defence stated that the black defendant was an occasional drug user and happened to be at the wrong place at the wrong time. However, both defendants were remanded in custody by the magistrate.

Whatever the reason for its occurrence, we find, a claims-making process which shows a discrepancy in the presentation of black and white defendants who associate themselves with drug use rather than drug trafficking. Whilst drug use is commonly related to white defendants, it is not presented as a valuable justification in black defendants' cases; it is not an act that the defence clearly defines in a form that moves towards exonerating black defendants from drug trafficking allegations, subtly indicating the defence's awareness of the popular identification of race with drug trafficking.

Imputation Tactics

This section demonstrates how the defence's language whilst interrogating police officers represent the imputation of meanings to police officers' actions and statements. Imputation is a device used by the defence to morally assess the behaviour of police officers with the fundamental intention of challenging the prosecution's drug offence allegation. This stratagem is employed by assigning contrasting meanings and motives to the actions of police officers leading to the arrest of defendants and what the defence seeks to achieve is to make the judge and jury visualise the overall police conduct, that is, the arrest and subsequent drug offence allegations, as behaviour that is in accordance with speculations, stereotypes and so forth, rather than 'accurate' evidence. Through this method of imputation, police officers are accorded qualities with a view to morally degrade them.

The ascription of motives and meanings to events leading to police arrest of a defendant is evident in the defence of black and white defendants although revealed in unrelated forms - even when similar events led to the arrests. In the first instance, there is a prominent utilisation of the imputational tactics in the cross-examination of police officers involved in black defendants' cases. In those cases, the imputation strategy adopts a mode of interrogation practice similar to the widespread representation of the problem of race and policing. In political and official discourse, criminological studies and media publications, it has been observed that the police, in their operations and practices, discriminate against black people and that the police view black people as suspects and potential criminals. Such information, which is portrayed by the defence as common knowledge, provides him/her with the additional tool to strengthen his/her claim. The meaning that the defence subtly attach to such police actions in relation to the arrest of a black defendant corresponds to the widely provided information.

In the interrogation of police officers, the defence raises such questions as "why did you decide to observe the defendant". The police answer to this type of question often reveals that their action stems from their perception of certain behaviour as suspicious. Police evidence also show that some defendants were arrested after being suspiciously identified by the police as some form of deviant due to their appearance and manner of speech (Sacks, 1972). That police arrest of a black defendant had its root in suspicion gives rise to a response whereby racial discrimination on the part of the police is implied in the defence imputation strategy. In the case below, the defence presents police actions leading to the arrest of a black defendant as conduct that was influenced by their assumed typicality of the social characteristics of people who are into drugs:

> The police were on observation duty in an inner-city area of South London and in the process observed a flat where the defendant was later arrested. The following is part of the defence's interrogation of one of the police officers regarding their observation:

Defence: Why did you pick on that particular flat to observe?

Police Officer: Because of the number of people that went in and out of the flat within the space of one hour.

Defence: How many people did you see going in and out of the flat within that time?

Police Officer: About six

Defence: About six. Can you describe them?

Police Officer: They were all black. I noticed a rastafarian go in with another male. I also noticed two ladies. The others were males and they arrived singly.

Defence: Is there anything unusual about six black people going in and out of a flat within an hour?

Police Officer: I think it is unusual.

Defence: Why?

Police Officer: I don't know. I just think it is unusual.

Defence: What did you think was going on in that flat when you saw the rastafarian and the other black people go into the flat, drug dealing?

Police Officer: We were not sure although we suspected that.

Defence: You suspected that drug dealing was going on in the flat. Why was that?

Police Officer: Like I said, I found their movement unusual.

Defence: Officer, did you suspect that a drug transaction was taking place in the flat because of the number of people you said you saw go in and out of the flat within the space of one hour, or was it because you saw six black people including a rastafarian go into the flat within that period of time?

Police Officer: Our attention was drawn to the flat because of the number of people that went in and out of the flat within a short time.

In the above case and others where a black defendant's arrest was aroused by police suspicion, the defence, by insinuation, attribute to such suspicion and arrests motives that are premised on racist ideologies. For the white defendants whose arrests emerged from police suspicion, the defence justification process introduces this issue in a different form. Either the defence simply presents the police interpretation of the white defendant's behaviour prior to arrest as a false judgement based on assumption, or, the defence imputes motives that link the police arrest of the defendant to previous unpleasant encounters between the defendant and the arresting police officers:

Example 1:

Defence: So officer, because you thought that the two men were acting suspiciously, you quickly assumed that a drug deal went on between them when, as you claim, you saw them exchange hands?

Example 2:

Defence: What drew your attention to the defendant?
Police Officer: His movement with the other man.
Defence: That is untrue. You have had two previous contacts with the defendant. You are one of the officers that arrested him for being in possession of £10 worth of heroin. He was charged for being in possession with intent to supply. He was remanded in custody for six weeks. The intent to supply charge was later dropped. Shortly after leaving custody, you and some other officers raided his flat. The door to his flat was smashed and his flat was searched but no drug was found.
Police Officer: I have had contact with him once and on that occasion, I only assisted in his arrest but that had nothing to do with his arrest on (Date).

Police evidence show that certain behaviours are termed as typifying features of some sort of deviant behaviour and those features are used by the police in constructing a typifying portrayal of defendants in a criminal context.

But even though similar behavioural patterns of black and white defendants aroused police suspicion resulting in the defendants' arrest, a racial variation occurs in the application of meanings by the defence to such police action. Police suspicion of black defendants are given meanings that reflect beliefs which hold that the police target the black community for reasons which are racially determined. In an intricate manner, the defence portrays the police force as an organisation within which there exists a strong conception of black people as criminals. As the competing claims further imply, the decision to target, and discriminate against, black people had been made by the police prior to their contact with them. This is imputed in another form. There were black defendants whose alleged drug offence was committed in collusion with whites but the latter were either not arrested at all, or not prosecuted after arrest. The defence questions the exemption of those white people from arrest or prosecution, and in response, the police indicate that the whites were drug users and buyers whilst the black defendants were the drug traffickers. For example:

Defence: ....If the estate is a busy estate as you have just told us, what made you notice the defendant?

Police Officer: He was just standing in the forecourt looking around like he was waiting for someone.

Defence: ....So what got into your mind when you saw this black male standing outside was that he was up to something and when the two white males joined him, you suspected that he was a drug dealer, is that correct?

Police Officer: We suspected that something was going on but we didn't know what it was until we started observing them in the block of flats.

Defence: ....Why did you not arrest the two white males?

Police Officer: They escaped. One jumped off the second floor balcony. There were only two of us and we couldn't manage on our own.

Defence: I agree that there were only two of you but you were there on observation. When you saw a drug deal going on between three men, you must have thought that it could be difficult for two officers to handle the three men. You had time, officer, to radio for help and all three would have been arrested. Why did you not radio for help whilst you had the time?

Police Officer: We thought that they would co-operate. We didn't expect to have any problem with them.

Defence:	But they did not co-operate, did they? They started running as soon as they saw you. Why did you and your colleague concentrate on arresting the defendant?
Police Officer:	Because he was the dealer.
Defence:	....You have told the court that you heard the two white males say to the defendant that they had money?
Police Officer:	Yes.
Defence:	....What you heard was a male voice state that he had money but you are not sure which of the three actually spoke the words.
Police Officer:	They must have been spoken by one of the other men. I know that they were customers.
Defence:	....Did you make any attempt to locate the two men?
Police Officer:	We searched the area when reinforcements arrived but we did not find them.
Defence:	....You have already told us that you and your colleague started suspecting the defendant as soon as you saw him standing in the forecourt. Am I right to say, officer, that from the moment you saw the three men involved in a drug deal, you assumed that the defendant was the dealer. In actual fact, you allowed the real dealer to escape?

In the above case, the defence portrays black people as a member group who are vulnerable to situations that attract police attention, whose behaviour is more open to the imposition of a criminal label. The defence also portray drug trafficking as a crime that is commonly confined to black people by the police. For not arresting the two white men, the police officers are subtly accused of adopting differential police strategies to the disadvantage of the black male.

Police discriminatory practices are also insinuated in another line of argument pursued in the defence of black defendants. The argument unveils the defence's familiarity with the widely provided information that black localities are popularly perceived as high crime areas and thus remain prime targets of saturation policing. The claims-making and justification process also reveal the defence's awareness of the knowledge that areas with a sizeable population of black people remain one of the most visible targets of police drug raid activities. In black defendants' cases, the defence questions the presence of police officers in particular areas - usually a street or an estate in deprived inner-city areas. In response, the police attribute their presence and surveillance practices in those geographical areas to the notoriety of the areas for drug offences, particularly, drug trafficking:

Defence: ....Why were you on observation in that area?

Police Officer: The area is noted for drug dealing.

Defence: ....How long had you been on observation before you noticed the defendant?

Police Officer: About a quarter of an hour.

Defence: How long would you say the defendant had stood on the street before you saw him hand over what you considered to be drugs to the first man?

Police Officer: About ten minutes.

Defence: ....According to you, the area is noted for drug dealing. Apparently, you were looking for such crime?

Police Officer: Yes.

Defence: We have been told that you decided to observe the defendant because you saw the act of standing on the street in suspicious terms?

Police Officer: I thought his behaviour was suspicious. He was standing there and looking around.

Defence: If you were in that area to detect drug deals, you must have associated his standing on the street with drug dealing, am I right officer?

Police Officer: Not exactly. I still had an eye for other crimes, not just drug dealing.

Defence: In any case, the defendant became a suspect immediately you saw him standing on the street....

Contained in interrogation of this type is the defence's interpretation of how police officers view suspicion. The defence describes black localities as being more likely to be subjected to police surveillance and the black inhabitants as being more vulnerable to police suspicion. By asking why the police officers conducted their observations in specific areas - occupied by the marginalised sections of society, mainly the black population, the defence draws attention to police employment of selective procedures in their daily occupational activities. This implies that the selection of certain areas to watch means that certain groups of people would be liable to suspicion and in turn more vulnerable to arrest and prosecution. Indeed, the message that the defence tries to convey to the judge and jury is that the police suspicion of black defendants, based on their gesture, is not indicative of a drug offence, instead, such suspicion is determined by the police stereotypical classifications that structure their perceptions and influence their response to the behaviours that they encounter. The police, as the defence subtly suggests, are guided by these typifications in their conception of what conduct is suspicious, which group of people are drug offenders, what areas are popular for drug offences and so forth.

A Deviational Stratagem

Another aspect of common-sense action pursued by the defence in a contested trial is contained in the formulation of stories that have no direct correspondence with the objective reality of the drug offence case in question. In this context, the specific issue of an alleged drug offence is at some stages in the claims-making process abandoned and its place is occupied by stories that highlight alleged mistreatment received by defendants at the hands of the police during arrest. Unpleasant remarks made by the police about defendants constitute one such alleged ill-treatment. In the one white defendant's case where the defence mentions the occurrence of such police attitude, the remark which is described as abusive is given very minimal attention by the defence. In some black defendants' cases where police use of unpleasant language is alleged, the remarks are presented as abusive - and racist when words such as "black" and "nigger" are incorporated in the language. Alleged racist remarks are raised into sensational focus and invariably, the terms of reference are reversed in the sense that the factors relevant to the fundamental issue - the drug offence allegation - remain dormant.

Allegations of physical assault on defendants form another justification that is saturated with an interpretational matter that partly obscure the subject of a drug offence. Assault was alleged in one case involving white defendant and it was in the course of giving evidence under examination by the defence that the defendant stated that he was manhandled by the police, however, the defence made no issue of the allegation, and whilst cross-examining police officers, no mention of this accusation was made. Rather than view an allegation of police brutality on black defendants as an issue external to the drug offence case, the defence makes a noticeable reference to it as a supporting essential for the construction of innocence. By drawing clear attention to the alleged police use of violence in dealing with black defendants, the defence seemingly mean to morally degrade the police officers involved. And above all, the adoption of this mechanism portrays an attempt to persuade the jury to rely upon the long lasting and widespread stories about police brutality on black people, in order to make sense of the defence's claim. The menace of assault on black people by the police has been extensively acknowledged, including complaints made by black people that the police usually engage in discriminatory practices such as physical assault and racial insults when relating to them (Humphrey and John, 1971; Humphrey, 1972; Solomos, 1988a; Cashmore and McLaughlin, 1991).

In the claims-making process, allegations of police use of violence and racist language are in black defendants' cases placed within an external 'reality' by drawing upon the widely provided information that reveal how black people suffer physical assault and verbal insults at the hands of the police. During cross-examination, police officers involved in black defendants' cases, where such allegations are made, face an elaborate interrogation. This is illustrated in the following sample questions asked a police officer by the defence:

Q1   Throughout the incident, you and your fellow officers physically assaulted the defendant?

Q2   You manhandled him at the initial place of arrest, did you not?

Q3   Officer, were you not the one that grabbed the defendant by the neck...and pulled him into the flat as soon as the door was opened?

Q4   You called him a black 'scaghead' and asked him where he hid the drug?

Q5   The defendant said that you were the one that called him a black 'scaghead'?

Q6   Why would he pick you out of eleven officers to be the one that called him a black 'scaghead'?

Q7   If you did not call him a black 'scaghead', which of the other officers did?

Q8   When the defendant was arrested, you handcuffed him, why was that? He could not have possibly escaped from eleven officers?

Q9   The assault on him continued in the police vehicle and at his home?

Q10   After being physically assaulted, the defendant complained of severe pains on his body especially in his groin, did he not?

Q11   I can understand that. The doctor was a police doctor, am I right (in reference to the police officer's statement that the defendant was medically examined by a doctor and there was no trace of bruises)?

Q12   Why did he need a doctor if he did not sustain bruises from the assault by you and your colleagues?

Q13   You tried to shove his head into the toilet...and then tried to sprinkle the heroin into his mouth?

In other black defendants' cases where physical assault and racial insults by the police are alleged, each of the arresting police officers is exposed to a form of questioning that is suggestive of police racism. In the above case, the question of assault dominated the interrogation of other prosecution witnesses. Some police officers who were on duty at the police station when the defendant was taken in were questioned and so was the police doctor who medically examined the defendant. The police doctor claimed that no physical injury was identified on the defendant indicating that the police did not use violence on the defendant. In relation to this, the defence interrogates the doctor:

Defence:	....As you can see doctor, the defendant is very black in complexion. Any redness or mark on his body will be difficult to notice without a thorough medical examination. Doctor, how long did the examination take?
Doctor:	I am not sure but I checked him and there was no injury.
Defence:	....The examination, I understand lasted for about two minutes?
Doctor:	Perhaps. I examined the areas that he complained he had pains.
Defence:	The defendant told you that he was badly beaten by the arresting officers and complained of aches and pains all over his body but you only examined his face?
Doctor:	He said he was having headache, pains in his face and shoulders and I examined those areas.
Defence:	....He told you that he was having pains in his groin, did he not doctor?
Doctor:	Yes.
Defence:	And what did you do about that?
Doctor:	I suggested that he took some pain reliever.
Defence:	So you did not have him remove his clothes for a proper medical check up?
Doctor:	I didn't think there was any need for that....

It is not only during cross-examinations of prosecution witnesses that allegations of police brutality on black defendants and racial insults are made crucial issues. In the examination of black defendants, the defence also reproduces the widespread allegations of police racist activities and how the police in the execution of their duties ill-treat and brutalise black people. This is illustrated in the following questions asked a black defendant by the defence:

Q1   You saw the officers running after you and you ran faster, then what happened?

Q2   You fell because you felt something hit you on the head. You did not slip and fall as the officers have told us?

Q3   What happened when you fell?

Q4   PC X was on top of you while you were lying on the road?

Q5   When did you realise that what hit you on the head was a truncheon?

Q6   Go on (meaning continue with the story on assault).

Q7   Were you still lying on the road when you were being physically assaulted?

Q8   When you say they swore at you, what exactly did they say?

Q9   Which of the officers called you a black bastard?

Q10   You sustained a serious head injury from the truncheon that was thrown at you by one of the officers. In fact you received six stitches that left you with a scar on your head. Could you lower your head so that the jury can see the scar?

Q11   You were handcuffed and taken to the police station. What happened when you got to the station?

Centralising allegations of police brutality and racist remarks in black defendants' cases may be aimed at conveying racial meanings to the responders with the view to making them, particularly, jury feel sympathetic towards a black defendant. On the contrary, this defence strategy of establishing innocence could well be viewed and interpreted negatively by those whose favour the defence intends to win, after all, it deviates from the key issue as a court staff noted in one such case:

> He (that is, the defendant) is not doing himself any good by saying that the police assaulted him. His barrister should know better....What he's doing is wasting the court's time. Why would the police beat him?...At the end, he's being tried for a drug offence....Whether the police assaulted him or not is irrelevant in this case.

For the defence, however, employing a mechanism whereby an issue unrelated to the subject of concern is centralised, is one of the subjective elements vital to the development of the claim of innocence in drug offence trial of black defendants.

The next chapter will demonstrate the judicial response to the various claims made by the prosecution and the defence in the claims-making process, and in the process, show the role of discretion and extra-legal ingredients on the actions of individual judges.

6 In Response: The Judge

Here the activities of judges in the claims-making process is specifically encompassed in order to understand the role of the judiciary in the social construction of guilt and innocence in black and white defendants' cases. Cole (1973, p.182) states that the judge more 'than any other actor in the system...is expected to embody the symbol of justice, insuring that due process rights are respected and that the defendant is fairly treated'. Griffith (1985, p.193) adds:

> In the traditional view, the function of the judiciary is to decide disputes in accordance with the law and with impartiality.... Impartiality means not merely an absence of personal bias or prejudice in the Judge but also the exclusion of 'irrelevant' considerations such as his political or religious views. Litigants expect to be heard fairly and fully and to receive justice. Essentially, this view rests on an assumption of judicial 'neutrality'....He must act like a political, economic, and social eunuch, and have no interest in the world outside his court when he comes to judgement.

Chapter four has shown how the judge subscribes to the prosecution's decision to drop drug trafficking offence charges in white defendants' cases. In contested trials, judicial response to the disparate claims made by the competing claimants differs according to variations in the racial origin of defendants. Individual judges do not view comparable claims from analogous perspectives and similar issues raised by the prosecution on the one hand and the defence on the other, to support their differing claims stimulate contrasting judicial response - to what seems to be, more often than not, to the detriment of black defendants. Turk (1969, p.12) has noted that although judges operate the same legal function, they 'are not necessarily consistent with one another or with themselves in their judicial decisions, with type of case held constant...'. Some judges' response to competing claims reveals a feeling of indifference regardless of the race of defendants, and other judges' response show attitudes that reflect their own ideologies, moral perspectives and so forth. This second form of response, in black defendants' cases, often appears to work to the disadvantage of this group of defendants. In contrast, judicial attitudes towards competing claims concerning white defendants are overall far more favourable in the sense that the response to cases involving defendants of this racial group is usually expressed in a neutral form, or even in a supportive rather than an unsupportive manner.

Judges have extensive discretionary powers and according to Pattenden (1982, p.170) 'many of the Judge's discretionary powers enable him consciously or unconsciously to influence the outcome of a trial'. We shall see how individual judges exercise their discretion at specific stages in the social construction process and how through their actions, portray views that concur with that of the prosecution or the defence to the apparent or subtle detriment or advantage of defendants.

Judicial Response to Competing Claims and Justifications

The focus is on specific justifications for competing claims which evoke a judicial response in the social construction process. Firstly, the judicial reaction towards competing claims and justifications regarding drug trafficking and how such a response is located within the context of race. Secondly, judicial response to issues of violence and sexuality - which the prosecution raises and portrays as immoral and offensive. These issues which have no direct bearing on the drug offence charges in question are made meaningful by the prosecution and confined to black defendants. Thirdly, the defence strategies highlight allegations of police brutality on defendants, arrest of defendants based on 'false' police suspicion and speculation, and police engagement in drug planting (to be discussed later in this chapter). In some contexts, race is a relevant factor in both the defence claims-making activity and the judicial response to these allegations by the defence.

Judicial response is revealed in two major forms. One is verbal and the other, non-verbal. Verbal response is reflected in questions raised and remarks made by judges during the prosecution and defence claims-making activities, and in the judges' summing-up. Non-verbal gestures which may indicate an agreement or disagreement with certain justifications are shown by way of shrugs, shaking of the head, nodding, raising of eyebrows, cynical smiles, tuts, expression of boredom and so forth. It is not impossible for individual judges, through their verbal and non-verbal responses, to give jurors indications of their conceptions and consequently determine the outcome of a case thus favouring one claim and not the other.[1] Pattenden (1982) has claimed that although it would be a miscarriage of justice if a judge takes sides with either the prosecution or the defence, a judge could try charting the direction of a case to favour either the prosecution or the defence (also see Gordon, 1983). Like the prosecution and the defence, Bennett and Feldman (1981, p. 3) note that judges 'who receive legal training must rely on some common-sense means of presenting legal issues and cases in ways that make sense to jurors, witnesses, defendants and spectators'. In drug trials, it may be through such 'common sense means of presenting legal issues and cases' that individual judges convey their beliefs to the jury so as to direct the result of a case to whichever side they want. However the case may be, the defendant is the one who is either advantaged or disadvantaged.

The observations of drug offence trials show indications that judges express their views, verbally and/or non-verbally in a way that may have an overall impact on drug cases, although such an expression of views is not universally manifest. It is more likely for a negative judicial interference to occur when barristers, witnesses and judges differ in their views. Such incompatibility, which is shown to be more evident in the defence - defence witnesses - judges interaction, is confined to cases concerning black defendants. Conflict is less likely between judges and the prosecution which may be synonymous with an existence of a high level of shared understanding between these two groups of legal members over the justification stratagems adopted by the prosecution. Judges, on the other hand, may find certain issues raised by the defence in black defendants' cases sensitive and improper, therefore, resulting in a conflict between the two groups of legal participants. Even when competing claimants, in similar black and white defendants' cases, justify their disparate claims with issues that are similar and 'relevant' to their different claims, the judicial response tend to agree with the prosecution's justifications whilst disapproving of those of the defence - when the defendant is black. Such agreement and disagreement are shown in the sort of statements made by individual judges during competing claims ,in the questions asked and the manner in which they are asked. In summing-up and in the form of non-verbal gestures. The prosecution and defence claims-making activities involving white defendants arouse a pattern of judicial response that is often more of a display of indifference, which leaves the decision to either convict or acquit entirely to the jury. Such judicial response, for example, takes the form of simple silence and when comments are made or questions asked, they seem to be basically aimed at clarifying ambiguities in evidence given by witnesses without demeaning either of the claimants. Obviously, judicial interventions through questions and comments are not always geared towards favouring the prosecution, however, the judiciary can raise questions to 'underline the defendants' guilt' (Jones, 1990, p.55) - as is seemingly evident in black defendants' cases.

Not every judge show signs of having the potential to sway the jury to either side of his/her preference. In spite of defendants' disparate racial backgrounds, some judges seem to remain neutral, displaying non-suggestive response during a trial. With such judges, intervention takes the form of asking questions to elucidate equivocalities in witnesses' evidence for the benefit of all the members, or to ensure that the judge is making an accurate note of what is being said. Summing-up is merely a reproduction of the evidence given by witnesses with no emphasis added. Judges' reply to competing claimants' arguments - whether biased against one group in favour of the other, or neutral, may be established by diversified factors. The collective or single potency of their personal attitudes, beliefs, knowledge and similar factors may affect their order of response. Worth noting is that a negative or positive judicial reaction towards cases during trials could be provoked to a reasonable extent by the level of emphasis given to certain issues by the prosecution and the defence. It appears that the manner in which cases are addressed by the prosecution and the defence play a part in ascertaining how judicial responses contrast favourably or unfavourably according to a defendant's racial background.

A Case of Drug Trafficking: Judicial Response

> "Get the dealer!" That is the cry today as the demands for change in the drug laws erupt on all sides. Soft on the user, hard on the dealer, that is the theme. And why not? Who is more indignant, more evil than the drug peddler? Can there be a criminal more loathed and feared than the pusher who is thought to seduce children into a life of slavery? He is the demon who spreads crime and corruption in the slums, who controls the minds and bodies of others by exploiting the cravings he has himself created. These are the images the drug peddler conjures up in the public mind (Blum, 1977, p.223).

In Britain, the picture we get of the drug trafficker and the drug user is similar to that portrayed above. As already indicated, the media have played a significant role in putting the drug problem on the agenda and political debates have contributed in making drug use a visible social problem. The immense frustration, despair and torment suffered by that those who have to cope with problem drug users, that is, relatives, friends and so forth, is shown in diverse literature on drug use, particularly, heroin use (Dorn et al., 1987; Dorn and South, 1987). At one end of the spectrum, public sympathy moves towards the drug user/addict and at the other end is the issue of the origin of the drug use problem with numerous fingers pointing at the 'evil' drug trafficker as the cause. Pearson (1987a, p.4) states that common stereotypes of heroin addiction 'will often describe the problem as originating with "evil pushers" who set out to trap helpless victims in the snares of heroin misuse...'. Pearson (ibid., p.9) adds, '...the most widely publicised image of how someone first encounters heroin...depicts a "pusher" driving down to school gates in a flash car and handing out free samples of "sweeties" in order to get children hooked...'. But in spite of the incorrectness in the stereotypic image of the 'pusher' as someone unscrupulous who in different ways deliberately get people hooked on drugs, Pearson (ibid.) claims that such 'sensational images refuse to get away, perhaps because they help to reinforce the view that people who become involved with heroin are passive victims of a wicked conspiracy which sets out to trap them unwittingly into addiction'.

Judges share public feelings about drug use and drug trafficking and express such feelings during drug offence trials. Considering the enormous amount of public, official and media attention that the drug problem receives, the judiciary could not be unaware of the feelings of social and moral instability that permeates Britain. In the words of Quinney (1970, pp 142-3):

> conceptions of crime are constructed and diffused in the segments of society by means of communication....Whenever the concept of crime exists, conceptions of the nature of crime also exist. Images develop concerning the relevance of crime, and the relation of crime to the social order.

Judges' feelings, mirrored in their language, become a reflection of their own concerns aroused by national publicity about drug use and drug trafficking. On the issue of drug trafficking, judges and the prosecution often adhere to similar views and are invariably mutually supportive. The judiciary view drug trafficking as heinous, the prosecution (not in all cases) portrays drug trafficking and the alleged drug traffickers as 'evil' and the police visualise drug trafficking as a serious social problem worth fighting. Judges hold conservative views (Box, 1981; Griffith, 1985), the police are puritanical and conservative in their political views (Box, 1981) and have middle class aspirations (Humphrey, 1972); both the police and the judiciary are 'guardians of public morality' (Box, 1981), and like the police and the prosecution, it is the judge's responsibility to ensure that stability is restored in society. It is therefore the drug traffickers against whom action should be taken. The problem drug user, as most studies of drug use have shown, is white. In contrast, constant media attention has been given to black localities as areas of drug trafficking with black people as the perpetrators of drug trafficking. Pearson (1987a) has noted how common cannabis dealing is in black communities, whereas, heroin dealing is virtually unknown to these communities, and in a form contradicting Pearson's observation, Dorn et al. (1992) make mention of black people's deep involvement in heroin dealing. Regardless of drug type, media coverage of black crime fosters a negative stereotype of black people and drug trafficking: the 'Yardies' dominate the image of the 'evil' drug trafficker.

In judges' application of their knowledge and conceptions to drug trafficking cases, a bifurcation of response into negative and positive emerges depending on the race of defendants, and such differing responses tally with the popular images of the drug trafficker and the problem drug user. If problem drug users are often known to be white, then it is this racial group of people who constitute the helpless victims of the 'evil' drug trafficker widely acknowledged as black. Prior to a jury's verdict, selective judgements and discretion are employed by judges in portraying a defendant as a drug trafficker so that even when black and white defendants stand trial for drug trafficking, the drug trafficker label is not universally bestowed upon the two racial groups of defendants.

Two specific 'agreed upon' grounds for pressing a drug trafficking offence charge give rise to judicial response in the social construction process. They are: (1) proceeds of drug dealing, and (2) quantity of drug in the context of the reason behind its existence. As the next two subsections will reveal, judicial response in relation to the above issues is advantageous both to the prosecution and the defence but a difference lies in the fact that the defendants are not equally favoured. Judicial response appears to work in favour of the prosecution when cases concern black defendants, and seems to be rendered more persuasive by the lack of 'intense' defence counter definitions of the prosecution's own interpretations of these issues. In both black and white defendants' cases, those two issues do not attract conflicting explanations from the defence and the defendants but in spite of the basic consensus in the justifications for these objects, judicial disagreement occurs specifically in black defendants' cases.

Judicial feelings about drug trafficking become apparent at the sentencing stage, albeit in black defendants' cases, where the characterisation of drug trafficking is imbued with social judgements which are directed at the moral order and to social stability; judges' statements are in accord with Young's (1977, p.119) observation of the 'stereotype that sees the drug taker essentially as an immature, psychologically unstable young person corrupted by unscrupulous pushers' and drug use as an act 'not freely chosen but a result of corruption of innocence' (ibid., p.122). Illustrated in the words of a Judge whilst sentencing a black defendant are such representations:

> Do you realise that the drugs that you are selling are
> causing misery and suffering to the people that the

> drugs are being supplied and encourages crime in order
> for those people to purchase these drugs?

In the above statement and others, there is a demonstration of judicial feeling of protectiveness towards those who fall prey to drug traffickers popularly considered to be responsible for destroying the lives of drug users. As Griffith (1985, p. 185) states:

> Judges like the rest of us are not all of a piece, that they are liable to be swayed by emotional prejudices, that their 'inarticulate major premises' are strong and not only inarticulate but sometimes unknown to themselves. The Judges seldom give the impression of strong silent men wedded only to a sanctified impartiality. They frequently appear - and speak - as men with weighty, even passionate, views of the nature of society and the content of law and of their partial responsibility for its future development.

Also shown in the language of judges is an awareness of the problem which drug users/addicts pose to those close to them. In placing blame for the pain inflicted on relatives and friends of problem drug users on the drug trafficker, the convicted black defendant is thus portrayed by judges as a heartless criminal who deliberately goes out of his/her way to exploit and ruin the lives of innocent drug addicts and those close to them, therefore, he should be condemned and not be spared by the law:

> You deserve imprisonment. By supplying drugs to
> users, you are shortening their life expectancies
> thereby causing anxiety and worries in the families of
> the drug users. It will be in the interest of the public to
> put away the likes of you.

> Considering the appalling danger and misery caused by
> such drugs in our society, I have no hesitation in using
> the full weight of the law in sentencing you to....

Public interest is recruited into the judicial response as a justification for a custodial sentence and a specific length of custodial sentence, and to add legitimacy to judicial remarks against drug trafficking. Griffith (1985, pp 199 & 234) points out that:

the judicial conception of public interest...concerns first, the interest of the state (including its moral welfare) and the preservation of law and order, broadly interpreted...and thirdly the promotion of certain political views normally associated with the conservative party....The Judge defines the public interest, inevitably, from the viewpoint of their own class. And the public interest, so defined, is by a natural, not an artificial, coincidence, the interest of others in authority, whether in government, in the city or in the church.

It is in the sentencing of black defendants that this public interest become an important explanation for punishing drug traffickers.

Defendants' assets: proceeds or non-proceeds of drug trafficking?

A defendant's possessions are not alleged to be his/her profit from drug trafficking only to ascertain that s/he engaged in drug trafficking. The whole issue of a defendant's possessions and their alleged link to drug trafficking is also made important so that an asset confiscation order will be applied by the court under the 1986 Drug Trafficking Offences Act, once the defendant is convicted. The provisions of the DTOA expect the court to make determinations of a defendant's proceeds from drug trafficking prior to sentencing. Courts are allowed 'to make assumptions that any property appearing to the court to have been held by the defendant the previous six years was derived from drug trafficking; that any expenditure made by him was from drug money; and all property received by him was free of any other interests' (Sallon and Bedingfield, 1993, p. 168). The provisions effect 'the recovery of the proceeds of drug trafficking and other provision in connection with drug trafficking...'. (Home Office, 1986b, pp 1-2), and as Tyler (1986, p.352) states, the 'declared object' of the 1986 DTOA 'is to prevent major league traffickers from retaining their proceeds after being apprehended'. The Act is further aimed at preventing drug trafficking and deterring those with the intention of committing drug trafficking offences from doing so.

Judges upon whom the enforcement of the 1986 DTOA is entrusted, at this stage, exercise their discretionary powers to either confiscate or not to confiscate defendants' assets 'established' to be their proceeds from drug trafficking, and to map out what assets should or should not be confiscated. Whether or not a defendant made a profit from drug trafficking is a question that is not universally addressed in a similar manner by judges. The difference in the way that a judge perceives a defendant's possession in the context of drug trafficking is exhibited in his/her reply to competing claims and justifications. The judicial conception of this issue is usually consistent with that of the prosecution whose argument significantly focuses on the link between defendants' belongings and drug trafficking. Such agreement between judges and the prosecution may partly stem from the level of attention drawn by the prosecution to the joint issue of a defendant's economic conditions, the supposed proceeds of drug trafficking and the drug trafficking allegation. If the prosecution questions, in detail, a defendant's economic circumstances in the context of drug trafficking and in doing so introduces familiar imageries applicable to the defendant, the prosecution seemingly provides room for judges to air their own views on the matter - which tend to move in a direction that is favourable to the prosecution. The onus is apparently placed on the defendant to prove that his/her assets are unrelated to drug trafficking. Conversely, if a defendant is not subjected to in-depth prosecution interrogation regarding the economic conditions-asset-drug trafficking link, judges apparently do not introduce gestures that are suggestive of a link between the defendant's asset and his/her supposed involvement in drug trafficking.

As shown in Chapter four, black defendants form the primary target for the prosecution's 'intense' interrogation regarding this subject with the logic being that an unemployed or a self-employed black defendant could not possibly acquire certain possessions through legal means. The underprivileged economic position of black people is not a hidden issue and the belief that this handicap incites crime among this racial group is widely acknowledged. Unemployment and poverty in inner cities, where a vast majority of black people reside, have generated a stereotype of those localities as areas where crime, including drug trafficking, is endemic. Therefore, no difficulty is posed to the prosecution to deviously bring to the limelight the popular ideology which holds that the black population is exposed to economic conditions that foster criminal behaviour. Further represented in the prosecution's justification is the negative stereotypic image of black people as parasitical layabouts who 'sponge' on social security and at the same time threaten the stability of the social order by way of their criminal behaviour of which drug trafficking is a part.

It is not impossible that judges adhere to ideologies about race and lowly status nor to the belief that black people are predisposed to crime. Indeed, judges show an awareness and knowledge of the supposed connection between 'blackness' and crime, as well as, the widespread explanation that black people's involvement in criminal activities emanate from their peripheral economic position. Young (1977, p.117) has noted that 'a person in a position of power vis-à-vis the deviant tends to negotiate reality so that it comes to fit his preconceptions', as derived from stereotypical information of deviants purveyed via the media industry and so forth. Young uses the police to instance how such a difference in power positions of law enforcers and deviants facilitates the former's contribution to the consolidation (by labelling certain groups or class of people as deviants) of the stereotypical media portrayal of deviants. Judges who, like the police, are assigned a special role in the social control process may be viewed in like manner: they too may reproduce their knowledge of criminals and drug traffickers - as furnished by the media dissemination of information about criminals and drug traffickers.

In assessing black defendants' account on the subject of proceeds of drug trafficking, the judicial response artfully mirrors what the prosecution has extensively construed as illogical and unacceptable. What 'we know' about race and deprivation appears to act as a resource from which judges partly produce images of race and drug trafficking, and invariably, drug trafficking appears acceptable to judges as a logical explanation for the existence of black defendants' possessions. Whilst giving evidence, black defendants witness judicial intervention in the form of questions and remarks which probe the link between black defendants' assets and their employment status, and embedded in such response are indications of doubts in the defendants' story - revealed in ways that cast them as drug traffickers. Being in receipt of unemployment benefits makes the issue of proceeds of drug trafficking more significant in black defendants' cases and the line of argument cunningly pursued by the prosecution vis-à-vis this form of economic condition is further magnified by judicial intervention which move in a similar direction:

> In the case of a black male defendant whose alleged proceeds of drug trafficking were £104, clothes, jewellery and a car he owned, the defendant's account of how he came to have these possessions evoked a form of judicial response - both verbal and non-verbal - that may have put the defendant at a disadvantage. As the defendant told the court during cross-examination that relatives and friends assisted him financially, raising of eyebrows and cynical smiles remained common forms of non-verbal gestures expressed by the Judge whilst looking at the jury. The defendant claimed to have borrowed part of the £104 from a girlfriend and in relation to this, the Judge asks:

Will this girlfriend of his be here to testify that she gave him the money?

The defendant claimed that he had broken up with her and had lost contact. On raising eyebrows and looking at the prosecution, the Judge asks:

> If this is the case, how can we be sure that the money was given to him by the lady?

Like the prosecution, judges view with suspicion the employment status of self-employed black defendants - even when a black defendant considers the self-employed job stable enough as to warrant no absolute need for state benefits. Ingeniously, judges pay attention to the general notions of race, deprivation and crime, and characterise irregular employment in black defendants' cases as a precondition for the committance of a drug trafficking offence. The case of a black male defendant alleged to have made a profit of £360 from drug trafficking exemplifies this point:

> The defendant 'accounted' for the money by claiming that he withdrew £100 from his girlfriend's building society account and that the remaining was his profit from a car sale. When the defendant stated that he withdrew money from his girlfriend's account, the Judge questions:

Judge:	Is the account jointly owned?
Defendant:	No.
Judge:	Does she know that you withdrew money from her account?
Defendant:	Yes

The prosecution told the court that a total of £415 was withdrawn by the defendant from his girlfriend's account. In response to this, the Judge comments:

> It is unbelievable that she allowed you to frequently withdraw money from her account (this comment has similar implications with the prosecution's claim that the defendant withdrew money from the girlfriend's account because the money in the account actually belonged to him).

In relation to the money in the defendant's account which the prosecution said was less than £100, the Judge intervenes thus:

Judge:	You said that you have been in this business for three years?
Defendant:	Yes.
Judge:	For a business that yielded no profit, what purpose did it serve to keep it open? (this question concurs with the prosecution's allegation that the defendant used his second-hand car business as a cover for his drug trafficking transactions.)
Defendant:	Things were not always bad.
Judge:	Your evidence shows that the business was very unreliable, how could it have been your main source of income? (implying that the defendant made money through other means, in this case, drug trafficking.)

It also happened in this case that the defendant whilst being interviewed at the police station failed to inform the police that part of the £360 was money that he withdrew from his girlfriend's account. This piece of evidence was heard in court for the first time. The Judge asked the defendant why he did not give the police this explanation, the defendant replies:

> I was confused. I didn't know what was going on.

In response, the Judge states:

> But you must be used to the police station (this remark seems to have been designed to point out to the jury that the defendant had prior arrest and conviction record and was after all the criminal-type.).

The judicial concern is not only limited to the connection between black defendants' assets and drug trafficking which is perceived within the frame of economic marginalisation. Equally significant is the part that judges play in bringing black defendants' alleged criminal behaviour and past deviant conduct into focus, for by indirectly unveiling a black defendant's past contact with the criminal justice system, the drug offence charge is made less likely to be questioned by the jury. The above case shows that even when a black defendant's actions may have no criminal motive, they are none the less amplified and presented in a definite criminal context. Whilst in-depth prosecution questioning culminates in the criminalisation of black defendants, judicial reaction further assists in emphasising it.

Black and white defendants are similarly hit by economic deprivation, yet, this factor remains confined to black defendants by judges in their assessment of the association of assets with drug trafficking. In no white defendant's case is the alleged proceeds of drug trafficking negatively questioned by a judge nor are comments and non-verbal gestures that appear to underline a white defendant's guilt made by judges in relation to this issue. It should be remembered that white defendants did not face 'intensive' prosecution interrogation and secondly, not all the white defendants associated with proceeds of drug trafficking were involved in a jury trial. In any case, where jury trials are encountered by white defendants alleged to have made a profit from drug trafficking, their employment status is not made an issue in the judicial understanding of this subject. In some cases, white defendants' accounts of the source of their assets is clearly acceptable to judges, for example, self-employment - as illustrated below - is counted on by the judge as a logical source of a white defendant's asset:

> A white defendant had a drug trafficking offence charge pressed against him. The charge to which he pleaded not guilty was dismissed on the sole direction of the Judge. The police found £750 in the defendant's home and the money was alleged to be his profit from drug trafficking. Whilst interrogating one of the police officers, the defence related the £750 to payment received by the defendant for a building job. The Judge responded positively to the defence's claim irrespective of the amount of money involved. In dismissing the drug trafficking offence charge, the Judge states:

> From the evidence I have heard, the defendant could account for the money he was known to possess....I am satisfied that he did not make any profit from drug supplying.

With white defendants, the defence experiences no negative encounters with judges over the issue of proceeds of drug trafficking, and accordingly, these defendants are clearly or seemingly advantaged. Jury trials are limited in white defendants' cases and unlike their black counterparts, asset confiscation orders pose less threat to them. The 1986 DTOA is more likely to create a notable difference in the sentencing of black and white defendants since its implementation is more likely to be felt by black defendants considering that more black defendants encountered a contested jury trial and were equally alleged to have profited from drug trafficking. Only those defendants believed to have made profits from drug trafficking are subjected to asset confiscation orders.

Quantity of drug: significance and purpose

As already shown, a notable defence for black and white defendants who negate the prosecution's allegations that the drugs found in their possession or control were for commercial purposes is the explanation linking the drugs to personal use and so forth. The defence considers such explanations logical because as Young (1977, p.120) observes, 'the police, the courts and the laws themselves distinguish between possession and sale of drugs'. Whilst the law is lenient towards those in possession of controlled drugs, it is harsh on those who sell them. The personal use of drugs or sharing drugs with friends on a social basis constitute an explanation that could be acceptable to the court. In the magistrates' court, such accounts are condoned by magistrates given that in some cases, defendants render accusations of drug trafficking absurd by providing this excuse. In such cases, the defendants were white and in each case, a shared understanding of the prosecution, the defence and the magistrate favours this mitigating factor:

> A white male defendant charged with possession of eighteen tablets of amphetamines with intent to supply denied drug trafficking and instead claimed that the drugs were for him and his friends. In presenting the case, the prosecution stated that he "agreed that the tablets were to be shared with friends". He added that the defendant "didn't seem to have made any commercial gain from drugs". Similarly, the defence stated that the defendant "only takes amphetamines when he is at a social gathering with friends". In agreement with the prosecution and the defence, the Magistrate comments: "fair enough. He only supplied to his friends and no financial gain was made, 100 hours community service for a year...".

In the Crown Court, black and white defendants' accounts regarding the presence of drugs are not plagued by ambiguity, nevertheless, the judicial response to these explanations does not represent the consensus of the judges. The group of defendants that are affected by the discrepancy which shrouds much of the judicial response to the justifications are the black defendants. What happens to be similar straightforward explanations given to the 'same' object by black and white defendants are viewed differently - in a method that reveals differential classifications of drug users and drug traffickers. Whereas qualities ascribed by judges to drug trafficking in terms of its overall link to profit making purposes are brought to bear in cases concerning black defendants, judges do not show disagreement with claims which construe white defendants, accused of drug trafficking, as mere drug users. In such cases, a common step that judges take in relation to explanations which link drugs to personal use or to the purpose of sharing with friends is to greet them with indifferent judicial silence during the claims-making activity; and during judges' summing-up, the disparate justifications are neutrally summarised to the jury. On occasions, similar attitude is extended to black defendants. Otherwise, a subtle or clear objection to black defendants' justifications for having a controlled drug in their possession or control is shown. Either that these explanations call for discrediting judicial non-verbal gestures or they give rise to remarks and questions that seem to work in favour of the prosecution. Usually, a supposedly large amount of drug gives justification for such response. That black defendants are viewed with uncertainty as victims of the drug industry is shown in the following judicial response during a claims-making activity by the prosecution:

> A black male defendant claimed that he was a drug user, refuting the prosecution's allegation that he had five ounces of a class A drug with the intention of selling it in order to make a profit. The Judge interrupts:

> Why would a drug user purchase that amount of drug at one time?

Defendant:	I am an addict.
Judge:	(shaking his head in disapproval) I wouldn't have thought that a drug addict would store such an amount of drug just for his own use.
Defendant:	(silence)
Judge:	How do you cope in prison with your addiction? Are you supplied drugs (the defendant was in custody on remand)?
Defendant:	No

The defendant also claimed that he sometimes shared drugs with his girlfriend.

The case of a black male defendant alleged to be in possession of 84.14 grams of herbal cannabis with intent to supply gives further illustration to this point:

As the prosecution claimed that the quantity of drug
was large and was indeed for sale, the defendant denied
the allegation thus:

Defendant: No. I smoke three fags or more a day and that can last me for
               about three months.

The Judge at this point interferes:

               Pardon?

Defendant: Your Honour, the cannabis was for my own use. I smoked three
               or more a day and that amount could have lasted me for three
               months.
Judge: Why would you have a quantity of drug that would last you for
               three months?
Defendant: I grew cannabis....I saved money by growing them myself but
               they were not for sale. I used to give some to my friends.
Judge: You supplied drugs to your friends, did they pay you for the
               drugs?
Defendant: No.

The Judge tutted in distrust.

Similar black and white defendants' cases sometimes attract blatant
judicial responses that clearly unveil two opposite views to the 'same'
justifications for the presence of drugs. In a case involving a white defendant
charged for drug trafficking, the Judge accepted the defence's story that the drug
in question was meant for the defendant's own consumption and that of his
friends. The defendant and his friends were said to be drug addicts. The Judge in
this case made a decision to dismiss the drug trafficking offence charge and end
the trial irrespective of the quantity of drug involved - which did not matter for
the defence had stated that the defendant was a heavy drug user. In a similar case
involving a black defendant, the 'sharing with friends on a non-commercial basis'
explanation stimulated a verbal rejection from the Judge - which was legitimised
by introducing legality into the response. These cases are clarified below:

               The white defendant faced a charge of unlawful
               possession of a controlled drug and a charge of 'intent

to supply'. The amount of drug involved was 3 ounces of cocaine. The defendant pleaded guilty to the charge of 'possession' and not guilty to the charge of 'intent to supply'. On cross-examining a police officer, the defence maintained that the cocaine found in the defendant's control was for his own use and that of his addict friends.

After the interrogation of the police officer, the Judge sent the jury away so that he could have a dialogue with the barristers. The Judge stated that he would direct the jury to find the defendant not guilty on the charge of 'intent to supply'. According to the Judge, "there is no direct evidence to suggest supply except the quantity of drug found. That evidence is not enough if the defendant and his friends whom he shared drugs with are drug addicts".

In the case of a black male defendant charged with unlawful possession of 4 grams of cocaine with intent to supply, a guilty plea was entered for the 'possession' charge and a not guilty plea entered for the 'intent to supply' charge. The defence was that the drug was for the defendant's own personal use and that of his girlfriend whom he supplied drugs on a non-commercial basis. The defence further claimed that both the defendant and his girlfriend were addicts. Whilst summing-up, the Judge advised the jury not to consider the defence's claim that the defendant supplied drugs to another on a non-commercial basis:

Members of the jury, I should let you know that it is still unlawful to supply drugs even if the drugs were supplied to a friend without receiving money in return.

The image cast in the above two cases emphasises the relativity in the judicial conceptions of the defence's 'personal use or sharing with friends' justification for the presence of drug. Sharing drugs with a friend was a behaviour deemed undesirable by the Judge that heard the black defendant's case and his verbal response to this justification was therefore negative which was given credence by the expression of language in a form of legality - whereby the law was used to justify the action. Similar behaviour in the white defendant's case was ratified by another Judge as understandable so that the prosecution's claim of drug trafficking in this case was hindered by the Judge's concurrence with the defence's justification. In such white defendants' cases where judicial agreement with the defence is apparent (as demonstrated above) or where there is an overt agreement between the judge, the prosecution and the defence (as instanced by the dropping of drug trafficking offence charges against some white defendants), the drug trafficking offence is reconstrued as less serious by limiting the perceived social harm caused by the offence to individual defendants and few friends. The white defendants' crime is internalised rather than externalised - they inflict harm on themselves and on their friends and not on others, after all, the drugs were for them and their friends to use, and no harm is caused on a broader scale.

This raises the question as to the extent to which such disparity is determined by the existing popular ideologies of drug use and drug trafficking - to which judges may subscribe - as the judicial response appears consistent with an identification of drug trafficking with un-Englishness and conversely, a recognition of a link between race and drug trafficking. The prosecution's role in relation to this issue is also relevant here if account is taken of the extent to which the judicial confinement of the drug trafficker image to black defendants may be related to the prosecution's form of 'detailed' interrogation of black defendants in a way which seems to precipitate a situation that leaves wide room for individual judges to apply their knowledge to this group of defendants - as forming the drug trafficking class rather than mere drug users/addicts as they claimed to be. As far as the significance of an amount of drug or the reason behind its existence is concerned, white defendants on a jury trial are not subjected to the prosecution's 'hostile' interrogation approach which their black counterparts face. Likewise, the judicial response to white defendants' cases follow similar direction. The defence's contribution is also vital in light of the racial variations in emphasis placed on this issue. Unlike cases involving black defendants, the defence seems comfortable to emphatically define white defendants as drug users and some instances of such definitions portray this group of defendants as 'preys to wicked pushers who play on their naiveté and inexperience' (Young, 1977, p.118) despite the charge of a drug trafficking offence instituted against them. Race is sometimes clearly intertwined with such defence's representations of drug trafficking in white defendants' cases- as the case below demonstrates - which not only highlight the extent of defence's perceptions of racial imageries but brings to mind that such characterisation could influence or strengthen judicial conceptions of drug trafficking within the context of race:

A white female defendant charged with a drug
trafficking offence denied the allegation and claimed
that the drug in question was for her own personal use.
In the process, she stated that she bought the drug from
a black drug dealer. In his closing argument, the
defence did not hesitate to tell the jury that "the
defendant has related to this court that she purchased
the cannabis from a local black drug dealer". The
defence pointed out how the defendant started using
cannabis "to cope with her marital problems. She is a
woman that has undergone a lot of stress in her life".

It is ironical that such references that identify black people as drug traffickers are
made by the defence in the attempt to establish innocence in white defendants'
cases.

The overall pattern of claims-making activities of the prosecution and
defence is vital to our understanding of why judicial response to white
defendants' cases rests on the premise that drug dependence and so forth
constitute key causative factors for the existence of drugs, with the quantity
whether 'large' or 'small' being inconsequential, whereas, drug trafficking is
visualised as characterising the presence of drugs in black defendants' cases,
particularly, if the amount is classed as substantial. No doubt, the racial disparity
that impinge in a central way on the judicial responding activities may be
attributed to the identified factors amidst other possible factors.

The Prosecution and Immorality: Judicial Response

Chapter four has shown how the subject of immorality - identified with drug
offending behaviour in the prosecution justification process - is ingeniously
stretched by the prosecution to incorporate certain alleged actions unrelated
directly to the alleged drug offence. Black defendants form a specific group
whose alleged immoral behaviour in the particular contexts of sexuality, violence
and filthiness is accentuated by the prosecution. What this section discusses is
how two specific behavioural patterns - violence and sexuality - purported by the
prosecution to be abnormal and offensive, stimulate a mode of judicial response
that lends significance to the allegations. Bottomley (1973, pp 143-4) points out
that:

one of the most common personal characteristics of Judges...which has been suggested as a likely influence upon their decisions is that of their social class background. Virtually all studies show Judges...come from predominantly middle-class or professional backgrounds, and often hold relatively conservative political views. Their general socio-economic status contrasts sharply with that of the vast majority of convicted offenders appearing before them for sentence.

In relation to the prosecution's presumed contravention of morality norms by black defendants, judges, in accordance, show notable agreement with the prosecution. 'Black sexuality' which is introduced by the prosecution as evidence of abnormality and a threat to the moral order, is seemingly perceived in an analogous manner by judges. It is in relation to the allegation of the use of violence on the police by black defendants during police-suspect encounter, that a patent indication of a disapproving judicial response materialises. But inasmuch as police officers' accounts of a scuffle that erupted between them and white defendants during contact is unmentioned by the prosecution, violence remains an issue that is ignored by judges in those cases. Likewise, conducts which could be termed as signs of sexual immorality amongst white defendants are not portrayed as such by the prosecution and similarly, judges do not view this racial group of defendants as violators of any sexual norm. It could be argued that judicial reactions towards such 'out of the ordinary' conducts in black defendants' cases may be related, to an extent, to the degree of prominence given to them by the prosecution so that the more negative the attention that the prosecution gives a particular conduct perceived as immoral, the more probable it is for a discrediting judicial intervention to occur and assign a deviant status to the conduct.

Violence on the police

Violence represents a basic violation of the person; the greatest personal crime is 'murder', bettered only by the murder of a law-enforcement agent, a policeman. Violence is also the ultimate crime...against the state. It thus represents a fundamental rupture in the social order. The use of violence marks the distinction between those who are fundamentally of society and those who are outside it. It is coterminous with the boundary of 'society' itself....The basis of the law is...to protect the individual...and the state against those who would 'do violence' to them. This is the basis of law enforcement and of social control (Hall et al., 1978, p.68).

As 'part of the machinery of authority within the state', judges 'cannot avoid the making of political decisions' (Griffith, 1985, p.195). Griffith (ibid., p.196) cites Lord Devlin as stating that 'in the criminal law the Judges regard themselves as at least as much concerned as the executive with the preservation of law and order'. Judges adhere strongly to the maintenance of law and order, the protection of the social order, and the preservation of 'appropriate' moral standards. To see to it that the authority is not threatened, and law and order not endangered, the judicial support is likely to go for police powers in the enforcement of the law. As Reiner (1985) states, the police are microcosmic perpetrators of the mainstream values and morals. Both the police and the judiciary aim at maintaining law and order in the 'public interest', therefore, it would be a threat to the legal institutions and to the state if those who preserve the interest of the public by maintaining law and order are physically assaulted by 'ordinary' members of society.

In their evidence during drug trials, police officers allege assault on them by black defendants, a claim which the prosecution lifts into visibility in a form that cast black defendants as representing a threat to the social fabric. Allegations of physical attack on police officers by black people is not a new story. Claims have been made by the police that black people, particularly, black youths are hostile and aggressive towards them; the police have alleged rudeness, insolence or verbal abuse by black people. Violent clashes between the police and black people, resulting in police officers being attacked and injured, have dominated political debates and received extensive media attention. The public disorders of 1958, 1976, 1981 and 1985 represent examples of such violent disputes between these two groups of people and from such events, alongside violent street crime, have emanated the rapid racialisation of violence in political and official discourse. To the police, violence, disruption and race are positively correlated (Matthews and Young, 1986), and to the courts, black people constitute a law and order problem (Gordon, 1983). That black people detach from mainstream values of British society and despise the police, are troublemakers, disruptive, a social problem and violent constitute a widely acknowledged portrayal which the media have played a significant role in providing (Solomos, 1989; Hall et al., 1978; Hartman and Husband, 1974). A clear relationship between race and violence is also depicted in the media representation of inner cities as 'no-go-areas' in the context of the violence associated with these localities. The court, as Hall et al. (1978) point out, forms one of the providers of such information, especially crime news, to the media.

Judges do not have to have personal contacts with black people to be able to specifically define their behaviour, for judges, in any case, seem to have knowledge of the widespread belief that the black population form the dangerous class and characterise a threat to law and order; they show an awareness of the link between race, crime and violence, and the conception of black localities as criminal and violent areas. In 1975, Judge Gwyn Morris was reported by the Daily Mail (16 May 1975 cited in Hall et al., 1978, p.333; also see Gordon, 1983, p.96) to have voiced his opinion on how the black presence has contaminated the British society. Embedded in his comment whilst sentencing five black people for mugging offences, is an image of the police, for instance, as upright maintainers of law and order on the one hand, and a link between race and violence on the other:

> Within memory these areas were peaceful, safe and agreeable to live in. But the immigrant resettlement which has occurred over the past 25 years has radically transformed that environment. Those concerned with the maintenance of law and order are confronted with immense difficulties. This case has highlighted and underlined the perils which confront honest, innocent and hardworking, unaccompanied women who are in the street after nightfall. I notice that not a single West Indian woman was attacked.

It appears as no suprise to judges when police officers accuse black defendants of subjecting them to physical assault and accordingly, they disapprove of the use of violence on the police in spite of the allegation being denied by the black defendants concerned. As the case below demonstrates, judges view the use of violence on the police as an act against national interest, as expressive of an attack on law and order which the police represent:

> A black male alleged to have used violence on two police officers refuted the allegation and instead claimed that he was the one that fell victim to the physical assault by the police officers. As the defendant denied the allegation of assault on the officers, the Judge intervenes:

Judge: The officers have said that you attacked them as they were carrying out their assigned duty, now you are telling us that they assaulted you.

Defendant: That is true sir.

Judge: You must know that physical assault on a police officer is a criminal offence.

Defendant: They assaulted me. I didn't do it to them.

Judge: Are you saying that the officers have lied to this court?

This judicial intervention occurred during the prosecution interrogation of the defendant. Prior to that, the Judge had shown indications of disagreement with the defence when the police officers were being cross-examined in relation to the defendant's allegation of police brutality. The allegation of police brutality was reversed by the Judge who did not fail to remind the jury that it was the defendant and not the police officers who was violent.

It is in black defendants' cases that an alleged use of violence on the police is highlighted by judges as a threat to law, order and social stability; it is in those cases that judges show that they subscribe to the value of social stability and that they are equally devoted to its preservation. The prosecution's consistent claim of physical assault on the police by black defendants may be synonymous with a belief that the court detests the use of violence on law enforcement officers (Humphrey, 1972), especially, when the alleged attackers are 'noted' for violence. Aside the absence of a disapproving judicial response - verbal or non-verbal - to encounters between the police and white defendants which, as the police alleged, were not completely devoid of physical violence towards the police, the use of abusive language such as "fuck off" by white defendants constitutes another similar prosecution allegation that evokes a non-detrimental judicial response. Judges, in those cases, are not judgmental neither do they immoralise such behaviour.

Except for one black defendant, none of the other black defendants was charged for physically assaulting a police officer, yet, it was a conduct notably alleged by the prosecution and enhanced by judges. The fact that physical assault on a police officer is alleged and highlighted in a drug trial when it does not constitute an official charge was questioned by a black defendant:

> If I dragged the officer, why didn't they charge me with
> assault? A little touch on a police officer is assault.
> Why was I not charged for assault if I dragged him
> and struggled with him (see Chapter 4)?

Studies have shown that assaulting a police officer is a charge commonly instituted against black people (Humphrey, 1972; Scraton, 1987; Gordon, 1983).

The issue of sexuality

Despite sexual immorality not forming an official reason for prosecuting black defendants, it is a subject that the prosecution raises to strengthen a drug offence allegation brought against this group of defendants, and subsequently becomes behaviour which judges believe to deviate from morally 'appropriate' standards which middle and upper class judges 'observe'. The courtroom is less likely to be the first and only place where information about 'black sexuality' is made known to judges. In fact, its knowledge beyond the courtroom has been widespread for decades and during drug trials, this specific issue of 'black sexuality' merely reappeared in the courtroom drama. Gilroy (1987b, p.79) draws attention to the popular association of race with sexuality, noting that a different form of concern about the criminal behaviour of black settlers which was assumed in the late 1940s and 1950s clustered 'around a distinct range of anxieties and images in which issues of sexuality and miscegenation were often uppermost'. Such concern was expressed by politicians and others who felt that it was their responsibility to preserve the English way of life in the interest of the nation by 'waging war' against those who not only violate the law but jeopardise the English moral standards. Judges have given support to 'the conventional, established, and settled interests' when it comes to significant social issues such as moral behaviour and 'they have reacted strongly against challenges to those interests' (Griffith, 1985, p.233).

Prostitution is popularly believed by the police, for instance, to be an act that black men engage in (Humphrey, 1972; Cashmore and McLaughlin, 1991; Gilroy, 1987b). This belief surfaces during the prosecution claims-making activity in the interrogation of black defendants - a scenario that is also applicable to the issue of promiscuity addressed in Chapter four. These aspects of sexuality which are brought to the attention of the responders are not welcomed with an indifferent judicial response but are instead amplified by judges through verbal and non-verbal gestures. In the eyes of judges, promiscuity is an abnormal behaviour and is therefore regarded with disapprobation; it is cast as an indication of the collapse of the moral order of society so that those black defendants whose sex life the prosecution constructs in a negative light are further portrayed by judges as morally disreputable, corrupt and deviant. An example of how judges illuminate the prosecution's subtle connection between 'black sexuality', immorality and crime has been shown in Chapter four in a drug case involving a black male defendant. In that case, the Judge demanded that the tape of a recorded interview between the police and the defendant be played to verify whether or not the defendant, as the prosecution alleged, did tell the police that his girlfriends pay him "after gratifying them sexually". The Judge's suggestion, as it appeared, was not aimed at favouring the defendant as the request was followed by cynical smiles and raising of the eyebrows whilst looking at the jury. Non-verbal gestures seemingly form a common judicial method of confirming the prosecution's revelation and presentation of 'black sexuality' as inappropriate and unacceptable. Also, questions are raised in a way that suggests an agreement with the prosecution's intricate claim of sexual immorality amongst black defendants as the following case further illustrates:

> A black male defendant was charged with unlawful
> possession of a controlled drug with intent to supply.
> The defendant was arrested in a flat that was raided by
> the police following police observation of the flat. In
> refuting the prosecution's allegations, the defendant
> stated that the only reason he was at the flat was to
> meet a lady that he met at a public house the previous
> day. The defendant had a girlfriend. What seems to be
> a negative interpretation was given to the fact that the
> defendant had a girlfriend and still made an
> appointment to meet another woman:

Prosecutor:	On the day that you met this lady at the pub, did your girlfriend know that you were going to a pub?
Defendant:	She knew I was going to see some friends. I didn't know I was going to be at the pub.
Prosecutor:	Does she know about the lady you met at the pub?
Defendant:	Yes, when I was arrested.
Judge:	Is this lady you met at the pub the same one you arranged to meet at the flat where you were arrested?
Defendant:	Yes.
Judge:	(with a disapproving facial expression) Your girlfriend only knew about your arrangement to meet with this lady after you had been arrested.

Promiscuity and dishonesty on the part of the defendant were brought to bear in the above case as the defendant was made by the prosecution and the Judge to look like he was cheating on his girlfriend.

In another case concerning a black male defendant, sexual immorality was also unveiled during the prosecution's interrogation of the defendant.

Although the interrogation was geared towards establishing that part of the defendant's possessions was his profit from drug trafficking, the form of questioning at the same time revealed a sexually immoral picture of the defendant which the Judge acknowledged:

Prosecutor:	...you have two children from two previous relationships and one from the lady that you presently live with?
Defendant:	Yes.
Judge:	Do these children live together with you?
Defendant:	Only the one from my girlfriend.
Judge:	So the other two are staying with their different mothers?
Defendant:	Yes (the Judge frowned in disapproval).
Prosecutor:	Do you give financial support to those two children?
Defendant:	(pause) Sometimes.

Unlike black defendants' cases, the issue of sexuality evokes no judicial interest and condemnation in white defendants' cases. We should remember that the prosecution presents not as immoral nor deviant the behaviour of white defendants who, for instance, show evidence of promiscuity, and likewise, judges do not apply their definitions of appropriate norms about sexuality in those cases. The following case will illustrate an apparent judicial reluctance to attach a deviant label to what was a promiscuous behaviour of a white defendant:

> A white male defendant told the court a story of how he admired one of two plain clothes WPCs in the public house where he was arrested, and decided to "chat her up". The defendant who claimed that he had a steady relationship with a girl, did not know that the lady he admired was a police officer on observation with her colleague in the public house. It was when the police raided the public house and arrested the defendant that he realised that the lady he "fancied" and "chatted up" was a police officer.

Rather than express a negative response to the defendant's story, the Judge, the prosecution, the defence, jurors and others present in court found it amusing, in spite of the evidence of what would be classed as sexual immorality in the defendant's conduct. This piece of evidence which was given during examination by the defence was not directly or indirectly referred to by the prosecution and the

Judge. Other white defendants are not questioned about sexuality when their sexual behaviour show similarities to that of their black counterparts. It is in black defendants' cases that the judicial response to sexuality suggest a disagreement with a sexual lifestyle which is believed to deviate from the 'agreed upon' norms of sexuality. A behaviour seems to be categorised as sexually immoral by the application of meanings derived from the prosecution's and judges' own knowledge about sexuality and race.

The Defence and the Moral Degradation of Prosecution Witnesses: Judicial Reaction

In a disparate form, the defence addresses specific subjects in black and white defendants' cases that aim at morally denigrating prosecution witnesses, that is, police officers to the advantage of defendants. As shown in Chapter five, police arrest of defendants based on what the defence sees as unreasonable suspicion and speculation is one line of argument employed by the defence although its presentation differs in black and white defendants' cases. Also, the defence significantly allege police brutality on defendants - albeit in black defendants' cases. One allegation that the defence prominently put forward, with no significance attached to race, is drug planting. Drug planting is alleged in cases where defendants reject the prosecution's allegation of unlawful possession or control of a controlled drug and in such cases, the defence presents police officers' engagement in drug planting as the main reason behind the defendants' appearance in court.

Allegations of police brutality and drug planting generate a distinction in the judicial response that is consistent with both the defence's style of argument and the defendants' racial background. Conflicting notions erupt between judges and the defence in relation to the alleged police use of violence on black defendants and similarly, drug planting, although alleged by the defence in black and white defendants' cases, produces a judicial response that specifically shows a disagreement with defence barristers representing black defendants. Inconsistency is embedded in the judicial response to the defence's moral degradation tactics and as will be shown, this inconsistency appears to have salience with racial stereotyping. Still, not every defence allegation of abnormal police conduct notably attract an opposing judicial reaction in black defendants' cases. In a reverse situation where the defence claims as wrongful the arrest of a defendant on grounds of unreasonable police suspicion and assumption, judges treat such allegation with tacit indifference - in both black and white defendants' cases. One evidence of a conflict between the defence and a judge regarding this subject is instanced by a case involving two black defendants, and in that case, the defence's attempt to gain judicial acceptance of the view on arrests that were premised on unwarranted police suspicion, was met with success

Police brutality

To the judiciary, accusing the police of using violence on defendants is like pointing an accusing finger at the law - a vital part of Englishness. In the claims-making process, the defence tries to enrol judges and the jury into discrediting an alleged inappropriate police behaviour - the use of violence - in their dealings with black defendants during police-suspect encounter. And in response, judges maintain a rigid position outside the slightest approval of this allegation.

It is not unknown that there have been grave accusations levelled against the police for using brutal and racist methods on black people. That black people sustain injuries as a result of police brutality is a matter that has also been widely publicised but as Humphrey (1972, p.39) states:

> no black person - and very few whites - has ever successfully claimed that police beat him up inside a station. The only time a claim of police beating has succeeded has been when there was an independent witness in the street who happened to see the occurrence. There are no "independent witnesses" inside a police station and the injuries an arrested person receive are held to be the result of his attacking the police, falling down the stairs, and the like.

Chigwada (1991) states that over half of the £500,000 that the Metropolitan Police paid out to wronged citizens in 1989 went to black people as compensation for wrongful police behaviour - in the form of assault, drug planting and so forth. Allegations of police brutality on black people have been claimed to be hardly believed by the court. In reference to the magistrates' court, the Roach Family Committee (1989, p.209) reports:

> There is some indication that many complaints made by black defendants, often in court, were virtually dismissed without further investigation. An important reason for this seems to have been a view taken by the police and courts that black people were inherently unreliable and excitable. Noisiness, excitability and general excess of emotion figured very frequently in police descriptions of events leading up to the arrest and appearance in court of black people, usually on charges of assault and obstruction.

The observations of drug offence trials at the Crown Court feature similar portrayals of black people indicated above. It appears surprising to judges that a racial group of people who are 'known' to be violent and aggressive, non-compliant and disrespectful to the law, would claim that they were brutalised and treated with contempt by the police. The police are described by judges as visible representatives of authority, who in carrying out their authorised duties come in contact with antagonism, aggression and resentment from certain members of the public. Such societal members try to make the police bear the brunt of any conflict situation that arise between them and the police. Complaints made by black defendants and their defence barristers about police brutality therefore receive judicial disapprobation; it is an allegation not heeded by judges. In the following statement by a judge, which suggests such judicial disagreement, it is portrayed that it is this sort of suspects that make police work more difficult by way of their false allegations against the police. Whilst summing-up in a black defendant's case, the Judge states:

> The police are a professional body doing a very strenuous job to keep the peace and maintain law and order, and they do not have to use violence on people when carrying out their duty.

After a verdict had been reached by the jury, the Judge adds:

> I commend the police in their professionalism in giving evidence under very strenuous circumstances and I hope your Chief Inspector will hear of my commendation.

As claims regarding police brutality went on in the above case, a non-verbal expression of boredom was shown by the Judge whilst the defence interrogated police officers, and as the defendant described how he was 'brutalised' by the police, the Judge constantly shook his head in disbelief; derogatory looks and cynical smiles were exchanged between police officers. In rejecting the police brutality allegation, the Judge questions the defendant thus:

> Why would the police physically assault you?

A doctor has given evidence stating that she examined you and located no injuries but you have denied that such examination was conducted. If you were in so much pain, why didn't you consult your doctor?

Prior to this, the Judge had questioned a police officer about the alleged use of violence on the defendant:

Judge: Was the defendant assaulted by any of the officers?

Police Officer: No your Honour. That is ridiculous, it is never done in the force.

Judge: If you witnessed a fellow officer behaving in such manner, what would you do?

Police Officer: I will definitely report the officer to a superior (the Judge nodded in agreement).

Even if the police do use violence in dealing with suspects, judges seem to believe that there must be a legitimate reason for such police conduct:

> In the case of a black defendant where it was alleged by the defence that the police threw a truncheon at the defendant causing him a head injury, the police officers' basic story was that the defendant, who was said to be trafficking in drugs, started running as soon as he saw them in an unmarked police vehicle. The police officers claimed that they ran after him and that the defendant sustained the head injury as a result of the 'fact' that he slipped and fell, banging his head on the road. The defence maintained that the defendant did not slip and fall as the police claimed but fell because a truncheon hit him on the head. Frequent raising of eyebrows was displayed by the Judge in disbelief as this line of argument was being pursued by the defence. The Judge eventually asked the defence:

Judge: Mr D, the defendant started running away from the police, did he not?

Defence: I agree with you your Honour but I do not consider throwing a truncheon at his head to be a reasonable method of stopping him.

Judge: The officers have said that he slipped and fell.

The Judge in the above case supported the police officers' story. Again, it may have been justifiable to the Judge if the police threw a truncheon at the defendant in order to stop him from running. This judicial approach to allegations of police brutal behaviour probably gives support to Griffith's (1985) observation that the judiciary support police practices even when such practices are beyond the powers of the police and contradict the rule of law, and to Humphrey's (1972) view that the police have knowledge of the fact that courts tolerate brutality that black people receive at the hands of the police. As state representatives, police use of violence is justified since 'the state, and the state only, has the monopoly of legitimate violence...'. (Hall et al., 1978, p.68). Of course, the 1984 Police and Criminal Evidence Act (PACE) provide the police with 'the power to use force in stop-and-search on the street...'. (Scraton, 1987, p.158). That power given to the police to keep the peace is acknowledged by judges, in effect, to allege that those who maintain law and order pose a threat to social stability generates obvious judicial resentment.

The non-direct relevance of the allegation of police use of violence on black defendants to the specific issue of drug offending behaviour under consideration also justify an opposing judicial approach to the defence's claim. In the above case, the Judge disregards the allegation by indicating that it does not constitute the sole subject of inquiry. The relevance of the police brutality allegation to the drug offence trial is questioned:

Judge: (to the defence during interrogation of a police officer) Mr D, are these questions all relevant? Remember we are not dealing with an assault case.

Judges react to allegations of police brutality on black defendants in a fashion that suggests that they are showered with such complaints and are, therefore, used to them. They do seem to comprehend the defence's imputation of racial meanings and may perceive such defence strategy as a shield behind which the defence and the defendants hide in order to generate sympathy and avoid a conviction. As they sense the defence's subtle attempt to assign the police brutality accusation to a social context - by placing it within a frame of racial meanings believed to be familiar to the jury - judges introduce a contrasting stratagem which indicates to the jury the need to disregard the defence's allegation as unfounded thus upholding the constant stand taken by the police that such allegations by black people are false.

Drug planting

When defendants deny the prosecution's allegation of unlawful possession or control of a controlled drug, the fundamental defence is that of drug planting by the police and a subsequent police fabrication of the story of unlawful possession or control. The drug planting allegation surfaces in black and white defendants' cases, and addressed in similar ways by the defence. Despite that, judicial communication of discontent with the allegation specifically appears in black defendants' cases and is overt. In similar situations involving white defendants, a judicial expression of indignation is not witnessed. Perhaps, the discrepancy in the judicial reaction to the 'same' complaint made by black and white defendants stems from judges knowledge and existing interpretive framework which seem to strongly govern the manner in which they view information provided by the defence and defendants about police officers' involvement in drug planting. Judges show an awareness of the widespread allegation, both within and outside the court, that the police engage in drug planting, and particularly, plant drugs on black people out of prejudice and charging them thereafter for committing a drug offence. Allegations have been made by black people that the police plant drugs on them and as Chigwada (1991, p.137) notes 'many courts have awarded damages to black defendants for being framed or having drugs planted on them by the police'. The role of the press in unveiling such police misconduct is also observed by Chigwada (1991).

In drug offence trials, judges acknowledge that news is made available to the public by the media and that the media play a vital role in the formation of public opinions and beliefs. The media is a 'source of social knowledge, ideas, and beliefs for those exposed to them' (Giddens, 1991, p.428); it is through the use of the media of the press and other communications media that information about other groups of people is derived (Young, 1977; Hall et al., 1978); and invariably, the media assist in the confirmation of people's prejudices and solidify pre-existing stereotyped information about others (Young, 1977). Apparently demonstrated in the social construction process is a judicial awareness of the possible interference of an external influence - in terms of bodies of knowledge - in the jury's interpretation of alleged police drug planting practices on black defendants. In a case involving a black male defendant, the Judge's definition of the media as such outside influence provides an example:

> The defendant was charged with 'possession with intent to supply'. He pleaded not guilty to the two count charge. The defence was that the drug in

question was planted in his car by the police. Whilst summing-up, the Judge advises the jury:

It is a serious allegation when the police are accused of drug planting. There have been a lot of criticisms in the newspapers that the police plant drugs and practice injustice. You should not believe that members of the jury....Why should the police tell lies?

The Judge in the above case not only expressed his own knowledge of the allegation of drug planting to flow from the mass media but also assumed its broader knowledge to emerge from the media industry. Because the Judge was of the impression that the jury could assign to the defence's allegation of drug planting meanings derived from their knowledge of the police and drug planting, as provided by the media, he openly declared his view and asked the jury not to make a causal inference from their supposedly pre-existing beliefs.

A sentiment echoed in the language of judges is that the police have a deep sense of moral responsibility and as maintainers of the normative order, their primary duty is to enforce the law, not break it; the police need not frame a suspect in the course of crime control activities. Below is another example of how judges verbally show disagreement with the defence's allegation of drug planting, indicating what appears to be an invitation of the jury to disregard the defence's claim:

A black defendant constantly maintained during examination that the drugs found on him and at his home were planted by the police. Shaking his head in disagreement, the Judge asks the defendant:

Where did the officers get the drugs from to plant on you?

Defendant:	I don't know your Honour.
Judge:	If you thought that the drugs were planted on you, why did you not report that at the police station?
Defendant:	I was scared of receiving more hiding your Honour.
Judge:	(to the defence) I don't understand. What did he say Mrs P?
Defence:	He meant he did not report because he did not want to be beaten by the police.
Defendant:	But I told them that the drug was not mine even at the station.

The Judge in the above case had earlier shown disagreement with the defence's claim of drug planting during interrogation of police officers. When the defence accused one of the police officers of trying to sprinkle heroin into the defendant's mouth, the Judge found the accusation out of line with his ideology and looking at the defence in disbelief questions:

> Mrs P (that is, the defence), why would the police want to destroy their evidence?

Defence: Your Honour, the defendant said that they tried to shove heroin down his throat.

Judge: That is unbelievable. I can't imagine the officers trying to destroy their evidence.

Without waiting for the Judge to finish his statement, the defence continued with her next question to the police officer. The interruption by the defence provoked the Judge who shouted: "Mrs P could you let me finish". A brief silence in the courtroom followed after which the defence unremorsefully apologised to the Judge for her behaviour.

The verbal interaction between the Judge and the defence in the above case was not only characterised by opposing viewpoints but also demonstrated indications of an authority relationship in the interaction process. Due to the fact that the Judge was infuriated by the way he was interrupted by the defence, there occurred an obvious display of judicial authority. The Judge did not hesitate to remind the defence of his superior power position and the defence in turn showed knowledge of the non-egalitarian power positions that they both occupied.

The prosecution and the police try to deconstruct allegations of drug planting and as the illustrations above have shown, black defendants' allegations of police engagement in drug planting reveal a form of response undertaken by judges, which is congruent with the prosecution's overall pattern of claims-making in the bid to establish a black defendant's guilt. By clearly rejecting any allegation of police drug planting practices, it is as though a conclusion has been drawn by the judge about the guilt of the defendant. The defence appears to stand little or no chance, under this circumstance, to favourably make his/her claim of innocence stick.

Police suspicion

In virtually all cases, regardless of the defendants' racial background, no judgmental judicial response was evoked in relation to the defence's logic that unwarranted police suspicion and assumption led to the arrest of the defendants. One case involving two black defendants, nonetheless, exhibits a remarkable verbal fight between the defence (two barristers) and the Judge as to whether or not to define the defendants as drug offenders. The case, which was discontinued during the course of the proceeding, turned out to be a judge-directed acquittal on the grounds of wrongful arrest and prosecution aroused by the merest pretext of false police suspicion and conjecture. According to the Judge, the case by legal standards lacked evidential sufficiency. This judicial point of view and response draws attention to Gandy's (1988, p.12) observation that:

> unless a crown prosecutor is satisfied that there is admissible, substantial and reliable evidence that a criminal offence has been committed by an identifiable person, a prosecution should not be started or continued.

And to McConville and Baldwin's (1981, p.185) view that:

> though claims are made that proceedings are instituted only against those who have at least a case to answer, some defendants against whom the prosecution has little or no incriminating evidence are nevertheless arrested, charged and placed on trial.

In the preceding chapter, the defence in the argument about unnecessary police suspicion and presumption, implies that racist ideas had a practical effect on the police response to black defendants' behaviour leading to arrest. As the defence argues, the defendants became objects of police suspicion and invariably had their activities placed under police scrutiny. In fostering this line of argument, the defence appears to draw upon widely provided information on how police operational practices involve persistent targeting of black localities as high crime areas. The following description of the case - mentioned above - shows how the Judge may have tried to dismiss the defence's intricate suggestion that the arrest of black defendants is synonymous with the subjection of black people to police discriminatory practices. After an extensive debate between the defence and the Judge, the Judge agreed with the defence's contention that unreasonable suspicion and conjecture were central in the arrest and prosecution of the black defendants - even though race may have been incorporated into the defence's argument:

The two black defendants, one male and one female, appeared as co-defendants. The male defendant was charged with supplying a class A drug to another - to which he pleaded not guilty. The female defendant was charged with possession of a class A drug and concerned with supplying a class A drug to another. She pleaded guilty to the 'possession' charge and not guilty to the drug trafficking offence charge. The police were on observation in the locality where the male defendant was arrested. According to the police, they saw the male defendant supply "something", which they believed was drug, to another black male. The defendant was arrested; £200 was found in his rear trouser pocket and £55 in his car. The man to whom it was alleged the drug was supplied was said to be riding a bicycle and had been under police observation before he got to the defendant. The police added that the man had already been into four places including public houses before approaching the defendant. The police also claimed that while the defendant was parked (in his car), a black man and two white ladies walked up to him and a conversation started between the four. In relation to the female defendant, the police acted on information they claimed to have received regarding her involvement in drug trafficking with the male defendant. The police went to her flat and she was seen standing by her front door talking to one of the white ladies that the officers had seen talking to the male defendant. The female defendant's flat was searched and inside her jacket pocket was found two rocks of crack cocaine, and £55 - alleged to be her proceeds from drug trafficking.

Whilst cross-examining police officers involved in this case, the defence perceived speculation and false police suspicion as causative factors in the arrest of the defendants; they did subtly assert that the police on the basis of their prejudice made a poor judgement. After the interrogation of the police officers, the defence asked to discuss a point of law with the Judge. The jury was sent out. The barrister representing the female defendant argues:

Your Honour, the prosecution has no evidence against my client. The prosecution evidence is based on mere speculation....My client was not seen with him (that is, the male defendant) at all during the observation and was not under police observation of any sort. There is no evidence to prove that she had anything to do with Mr K (that is, the male defendant) as regards supplying drugs. The only reason she was accused of being concerned in supplying drugs is that one of the officers that visited her flat recognised one of the white ladies who had earlier been seen having a conversation with Mr K. The officers assumed that my client was involved in supplying drugs because she was seen talking to the same lady. That is no evidence your Honour.

Judge: Why is it not evidence? What are you driving at Mr G?

Defence: Your Honour, the white lady was seen with my client after she had been seen with Mr K on the evening of the police observation. If this white lady was seen with Mr K after she had been with my client, the prosecution allegation that my client directs customers to meet Mr X in his car outside...would have made sense.

Judge: ....We have heard that the money and the drugs were found inside the same pocket of the lady's jacket. Is that not enough evidence to prove that she sells drugs?

Defence: That is not the issue your Honour. The allegation is that she directs customers to Mr K and is therefore concerned in the supplying of drugs. Even if she had the drugs and the money inside the same pocket, it could be a coincidence and still does not support the allegation put forward by the prosecution....She has pleaded guilty....At no point did she deny being in possession of the drugs. She also accounted for the money....Your Honour, there still is no strong evidence to prove the allegation except that the white lady came in-between.

Here the Judge took the role of the prosecution in disputing the defence's assertion that the arrest and prosecution of the defendant was grounded on speculation. The defence and the Judge argued at length: neither side was willing to give in without a contest. The Judge, like the prosecution and the police, considered as evidence the fact that the same white lady was seen with the defendant after being seen with the male defendant; the presence of the drug and money inside the same jacket pocket added relevance to the Judge's line of argument, it was enough evidence for the Judge who persistently placed it within the context of drug trafficking. The Judge sheds light on his knowledge and conception of events that constitute a drug offence.

The barrister representing the male defendant presents, as his primary defence, the argument that the arrest and prosecution of the defendant were embodied in false police suspicion and assumption rather than evidence. This point of view also gave rise to a debate with the Judge. The defence states:

> ...it was dark on the day the officers carried out the observation. PC O and PC W have told us that they did not see what was passed on to Mr Y by my client. PC B said that he did not see the defendant give something to Mr Y. The prosecution has failed to prove that the defendant received money from Mr Y....A drug deal was assumed to be going on between the two men because the officers believed that my client handed something over to the other man. Your Honour, the officers for no rational reason, were suspicious of these men even before they came in contact with each other....None of the officers saw my client receive anything from Mr Y and yet the monies that he had in his car and on his person are assumed to be his proceeds from drug dealing....No drug-related item was found on the defendant or in his car.

The Judge interrupts:

> Where did the man on a bicycle get the drug from if he did not get it from the defendant? The officers saw the defendant give to this other man something that they believed was drugs. When the man was stopped by the officers, a drug was found in his possession.

Defence: He had been into four places before getting to the defendant. He was out of the officers' view at these points and was even out of their view for sometime after he had left the defendant. He could have got the drug from any of those places.

Judge: According to the officers, he had the drug in his right hand....If he got the drug from any of those places that he branched into, he wouldn't in the real world have the drug in his hand and ride a bicycle. He must have got the drug from the defendant, had it in his right hand and immediately rode not far away before he was stopped by the police.

Defence: How can we be sure that he had it in his right hand all through? The drug could have been in his pocket....The officers did not tell us exactly where the drug came from. They only told us that Mr Y put the drug which he had in his right hand inside his mouth. Your Honour, it was dark on that evening....Mr Y could have got the drug from somewhere else, put it away and on being stopped by the police, he brought it out with his right hand and put it in his mouth.

The debate went on and at a point, the Judge asked the prosecution to comment on the issue. The prosecution states:

> Mr Y on that evening went to that road to buy drugs
> and Mr K was there to sell drugs to him.

Judge: (waved the prosecutor off with his hand) That is an assumption Mr C. You cannot put that to the jury to draw inferences.

Afterwards, the defence's claim won the approval of the Judge. The incompatibility in the views held by the Judge and the defence was resolved in favour of the defendants. In the presence of the jury, the Judge rejected the prosecution's claim and indirectly condemned the infiltration of false suspicion and speculation in police operational practices. The Judge says to the jury:

> ....The Law demands that when a defendant is brought
> before the court by the prosecution, the prosecution
> must be prepared to prove beyond reasonable doubt
> that the defendant is guilty. In this case the prosecution
> has not succeeded in doing so. No strong evidence has
> been put forward by the prosecution to support the
> allegation against the defendants. As evidence is
> lacking in this case, I intend to dismiss the case. The

> trial will not continue. You may now go members of
> the jury.

In this case where a judge-directed acquittal was effected, the Judge in stating that the prosecution evidence did not meet objective legal standards, pointed out the relevance of objectivity and accuracy in police evidence. The absence of these criteria in the police evidence characterised the judicial justification for disregarding the prosecution evidence - which the Judge claimed was shrouded with doubts and speculations. Regardless, the dismissal of this case was not initiated by the Judge but dismissal emerged from a process of claims-making between the defence and the Judge - with the former arguing for, and the latter arguing against, an acquittal. There seemed to be no challenge from the prosecution to give support to the Judge's opposing claim thereby making the defence's claim acceptable to the Judge.

The focus of the next chapter is extended to embrace an attempt to understand the jury's response to the competing claims and judicial actions in the social construction process.

Note

1   Although reasons, not related to a drug offence case, could account for the non-verbal gestures expressed by judges, other legal actors and participants, they may have an effect on the outcome of a case.

7 The Verdict

Variations that occur in drug trials involving black and white defendants have been examined from a social constructionist perspective that views the court process within the context of claims-making. As indicated, the pattern of disparity found in the trial process is consistent with 'non-legalistic considerations' (Box, 1981) introduced during a trial by legal participants in the claims-making activity. Revealed is a situation whereby lawyers use their discretion in deciding what claims to make, how to make those claims and in what 'cases' to make them; likewise, judges exercise their discretion in their decision to consider a claim acceptable or unacceptable. In the event of exercising their legally-provided discretion, these legal actors allow their actions and decisions to be guided by their human elements. Consequently, pieces of information presented before the jury are informed by knowledge, stereotypes, myths and imageries - with the effect that black and white defendants are cast in different lights - in similar cases. The process of social construction and claims-making may explain the prosecutorial decision making activity which resulted in more blacks than whites having a more serious drug offence charge instituted against them; it may explain how it is that more blacks than whites went through a contested trial and may well explain how more blacks than whites came to be convicted by the jury and subsequently imprisoned for a drug offence.

In questioning how a jury comes to be convinced beyond any reasonable doubt of an 'appropriate' verdict or decision, the intention is not to assign specific stocks of knowledge, ideologies, personal opinions, attitudes and similar subjective criteria to jurors and thereafter claim that their decision making activity is guided to whatever extent by extra-legal considerations. Despite that, discretion is not eliminated from a jury's duty. Jurors' legally-provided discretion is a fundamental and unavoidable part of the legal order (Hawkins, 1992). Therefore, they may perform their duties entirely within the realms of the law whether or not their decisions are subjectively bound. In the drug trials observed, the factors that determined the juries' satisfaction beyond reasonable doubt of a defendant's guilt or innocence, or their inability to reach a verdict were beyond my observation and knowledge. But whatever the criteria upon which the decisions of the juries were based, the consequence of their decisions surfaces in disparate verdict decisions by race. Irrespective of similarities in drug cases, black defendants faced more convictions than their white counterparts.

It should be recognised, nevertheless, that the information that different participants provide jury members is supposed to be their guideline towards an 'appropriate' verdict. How then did the juries utilise the information which the prosecution (and the prosecution witnesses), the defence and (the defence witnesses), and judges conveyed to them? In questioning how the juries interpreted the language of competing claimants and judges, and on the basis of their interpretations, made a decision, attention will be drawn to questions raised by jury members during deliberation - which were read out in open court by the judge. Those questions and the answers that judges, the prosecution and the defence unanimously agreed to give to the questions may unearth some factors that may have influenced the juries' decisions.

Summary of the Social Construction and Claims-making Activity

In addressing the problem of the disproportionate presence of black people in the criminal statistics, the two broad explanations for the problem were subsequently disclosed in Chapter one. One views the problem of disproportion in terms of high black crime rate attributed, fundamentally, to the socio-economic deprivation that is experienced by the black community. Conversely, the tone of other studies is critical of the police and the courts for their supposed discriminatory practices towards black people. Such lines of argument give credence to the claims-making activity in the courtroom.

Drug trials entail the use of discretion; they entail the perpetuation of popular beliefs about race, deprivation and crime; they entail the solidification of images of race, sexuality, violence and filth; they involve the reproduction of allegations of police discriminatory practices, police brutality, police use of racist language and drug planting. These imageries, which assist the prosecution and the defence in their effort to prove their case, and judges in guiding the claims-making activity, have received wide attention as reflected in documented studies, political debates and mass media coverage. In black and white defendants' cases, stereotypical images of black and white people do not merely inform the discretionary choice of issues to discuss by the prosecution and the defence but also shape the description of those issues. In effect, an absence of similarity and consensus - according to a defendant's racial background - lies within the rhetoric used by the prosecution and the defence to interpret an alleged drug offence. And also represented in the judicial reaction to the trials is such dissimilarity.

Chapter two has examined the gradual emergence of the link between race and drugs, with the racialisation of drug trafficking during the 1980s. In the

1960s, the shifts in debates and perceptions on drugs associated drug use with the working class and working class areas, and in the 1980s, this question of deprivation was emphasised as discussions arose over the demand and availability of drugs. Those areas of high unemployment and similar indications of socio-economic deprivation have been described in terms of drug use/trafficking (Dorn et al., 1992; Pearson, 1987b) and the image of the drug user/trafficker portrayed with the socio-economically deprived in mind. Within this context, race has remained prominent in official, media and public discourses on drugs. In the claims-making process, the prosecution (and the police), the defence and the court show knowledge of this popular ideology. Chapter four has shown how the typification of black defendants as drug traffickers remains, on the one hand, a dominant representation in the prosecution's language and on the other, the prosecution deconstructs the drug trafficker image in white defendants' cases by describing the defendants in relation to drug use. The similarity in the socio-economic circumstances of black and white defendants notwithstanding, the prosecution subtly introduces familiar cues as race and deprivation to support his/her allegation of drug trafficking in black defendants' cases by prioritising the economic accountability of black defendants to construct them as drug traffickers whilst pursuing the defendant's assets - proceeds of drug trafficking claim.

The discretionary powers given to the prosecution (and the police) are applied during claims-making to their definition of assets as proceeds of drug trafficking, items as drug-related paraphernalia, as well as the meanings that they give to quantities of drugs and separate wraps of drugs vis-à-vis drug trafficking and straight possession. These criteria which seem not be determined in advance lack precise definition in terms of their relationship to a particular drug offence. How are proceeds of drug trafficking determined? What quantity of drug and drug-related paraphernalia are indicative of drug trafficking? How many separate wraps of drugs indicate drug trafficking? Given the non-existence of an accurate clarification of these criteria in relation to drug trafficking and straight possession, and the accordance of wide discretion to the prosecution (and the police), these participants are indirectly allowed to inject their prejudices, stereotypes, ideologies and so forth into their discretionary decisions to ascertain these factors. Variations will occur in the mode that these criteria are determined with the subsequent effect of conviction and imprisonment being differentially faced by defendants.

The defence in Chapter five reinforces the view of the drug offender within the context of race and deprivation as indicated in the different racially underlined patterns of representation in the magistrates' court, and in the Crown Court, in the notable interest in challenging and redefining certain elements associated with drug trafficking in white defendants' cases, whilst undermining the significance of the 'same' elements, which constitute the core of drug trafficking allegations, in black defendants' cases. Basically, the defence takes two different routes in defending black and white defendants - even when similarity exists in the drug offence charges. Challenging, specifically, a drug offence allegation is the primary interest of the defence in white defendants' cases as exhibited, for instance, in how drug trafficking allegations are refuted by stressing a link between white defendants and drug use. In a reverse situation, the moral degradation of police officers forms the central focus of the defence in black defendants' cases as it is only in those cases that the police are 'intensely' laid open to questions that show them as retreating from the direction of 'true' accountability of police-suspect encounter prior to, or during, arrest. The defence (and black defendants) allege police brutality, police use of racist remarks, police deliberate surveillance of black localities and police unnecessary suspicion of black defendants. In making these allegations - some of which have no direct bearing on the allegation of a drug offence - the defence perpetuates beliefs about police racist and discriminatory practices towards black people. Much as this defence strategy seems to aim at evoking the jury's sympathy, it reinforces certain imageries which stimulates a disapproving judicial response, for example, the allegation of police brutality. Could this defence tactic have done more harm than good to black defendants' cases?

Drug planting is another defence allegation meant to disprove the prosecution's drug offence claim. This finds relevance in both black and white defendants' cases as the defence claims that the drugs in question were planted on the defendants by the police. Yet, it provokes a judicial disapproval specifically evident in black defendants' cases as shown in Chapter six.

The prosecution also adopt the moral degradation tactic which is, however, confined to black defendants' cases. White defendants are exonerated from 'in-depth' questioning in every aspect of the prosecution drug offence interrogation, and unlike their black counterparts, they are not subjected to moral character assassination. In addition to constructing the drug trafficker image in black defendants' cases, the prosecution applies to black defendants racial stereotypes of violence, sexuality and filth. These images are as old as the slave trade (Walvin, 1971; Folarin, 1977; Craton et al., 1976; File and Power, 1981) and have been revived following black immigration into Britain. The black pimp who lives off the immoral earnings of white women, the aggressive black wo/man who is a threat to law and order, the dirty black wo/man (Hiro, 1992; Gilroy, 1987b; Chiqwada, 1989) are popular descriptions of black people subtly echoed by the prosecution in the claims-making process in order to morally degrade black defendants.

On the part of judges, this pattern of prosecution - irrelevant to the specific allegation of a drug offence - is not considered out of line with the heart of the trial as Chapter six demonstrates. Whereas the defence's allegation of police brutality on black defendants fails to win the support of judges, the prosecution's allegation of violence by black defendants on the police gains a favourable response from judges. Whether or not the black defendants accused of physically assaulting the police, did so or not, is another issue altogether. The crucial point is that this information is channelled through the court by the prosecution, and acknowledged by judges hence indicating their knowledge of race and violence. The label ascribed to black people as violent, aggressive and disruptive by the police (Carlen, 1976; Gilroy, 1987b) and the wider society seemingly underpin the judicial response that discredits the police brutality allegation made in the defence of black defendants. Meanwhile, the prosecution's imputation of sexual immorality to black defendants - in the form of prostitution and promiscuity - is further shared by judges whose verbal and non-verbal responses portray a resentment of such conduct by the defendants.

Chapter six has also describe how judges react to allegations of drug trafficking made by the prosecution. As the prosecution emphatically portray black defendants - and not their white counterparts - as drug traffickers, judges show an acceptance of the argument which the prosecution propagates. Like the prosecution and the defence, judges find drug use an unfortunate but pitiable characteristic feature of white defendants. This shared understanding between these participants over the categorisation of a drug user and a drug trafficker is tantamount to popular images of drug use - which is most commonly related to white people - and drug trafficking - which is popularly associate with black people. The law attributes a lesser degree of seriousness to illegal drug use and in contrast, drug traffickers are loathed and harshly treated. In black defendants' cases where the image of the drug trafficker is created, judges visualise a devastating effect of drug trafficking in a language similar to that of the prosecution. This perceived social harm that results from drug trafficking justified a custodial sentence for all the black defendants convicted by the jury. For the few white defendants found guilty of drug trafficking, a custodial sentence did not apply in all the cases.

A reasonable number of white defendants charged with a drug trafficking offence were exempted from jury trials as a result of negotiation and bargaining between the prosecution and the defence who redefined the significance of drug trafficking in those cases. The explanations which relate the existence of drugs to those white defendants' personal use or for the purpose of sharing with friends on a social basis is equally condoned by judges. One may mistakenly argue that the prosecution and the court succumbed to these explanations in white defendants' cases because the defendants basically pleaded guilty to drug trafficking inasmuch as they agreed to having the intention to supply to friends. And accordingly, they should have their penalties reduced because by pleading guilty, they expressed remorse and reduced '...the pressure on the workload and cost of the courts' (Hood, 1992, p.182). But, these explanations, commonly provided by black and white defendants, are considered unacceptable by the prosecution and judges in cases concerning black defendants. Besides, rarely did defendants plead guilty to trafficking in drugs for commercial purposes so that in those white defendants' cases, what may seem to be a change of plea from not guilty to guilty to drug trafficking is in fact an outcome of offence redefinition by the prosecution. 'Supplying' and 'intent to supply' charges are devoid of their drug trafficking meaning when it is claimed that the defendants, for non-commercial reasons, supplied drugs to, or intended to share drugs with, their friends. In the white defendants' cases where such explanations are given in the magistrates' court to refute a drug trafficking allegation, they are also considered an understandable justification by magistrates.

At various stages in the social construction process, judges exercise their discretion, power, ideological perspectives and so forth but their response to a case may also depend to a reasonable extent on how the case is presented by the prosecution and the defence. If a differential mode of claims-making by race occurs when the prosecution and the defence justify drawing conclusions from their varied evidence, it may subsequently entail a variation in the way that judges view black and white defendants' cases. As a powerful force in the shaping of jurors' consciousness about a case, the judicial conception of a case is likely to affect jurors' own perception of the case. As has been noted, similar cases attracted disparate racially-based jury verdicts. But as far as guilty pleas are concerned in both the Crown Court and the magistrates' court, similar sentences were often dished out to black and white defendants for similar drug offences - irrespective of the difference in the racial background of the defendants.

Reaching a Final Decision: The Jury

> I don't trust that man, you know the one with a bad leg. Every time my case is going well, he spoils it, that is when he wants to stretch his leg. I don't trust him

> man! You can see by the look on his face that he thinks
> I am guilty. He's bad luck, real bad luck (A statement
> made by a black defendant in reference to a white
> juror).

Black defendants, their relatives and friends express dissatisfaction with the selection of certain white jurors whose looks and age they believe signify conservatism. The belief that those jurors would opt for a definite guilty verdict decision on the basis of their race is held by black defendants. As Hagan (1988) observes, criminal injustice is more likely to be perceived by blacks than whites. Complaints are also made about the racial composition of the juries as some cases show an all white jury and the absence or scanty representation of black jurors constitutes a cause for concern. In cases where black defendants or/and their relatives and friends were apprehensive of the jury, the defendants were convicted.

Previous chapters have shown how the prosecution and the defence impart information on similar black and white defendants' cases in a language that is believed would be of value to the jury in its decision to reach a guilty or a not guilty verdict. The preceding chapter has also argued that on the one hand, some judges adopt an indifferent approach to trials and cases are summarised in accordance with the different representations, and on the other, individual judges clearly or seemingly air their views in favour of the prosecution or the defence. The disparity by race that surfaces in the mode of presentation of similar cases by the prosecution and the defence, in the pattern of response to similar cases by individual judges has been disclosed. In view of the verdict decisions, I am inclined to ask how cases with similarities received interpretations from the juries amounting to differential outcome according to race. Jurors are faced with a mass of information on cases and in addition to absorbing the different versions of a case presented by the prosecution and the defence, jurors are expected to adhere to the judge's directions on the law and assimilate his/her review of a case in summing-up. Of the pieces of information elicited during trials, which ones swayed the juries' approach to their ultimate verdict?

Much of the strength of the prosecution's case rests on the inferences which the juries are invited to draw from defendants' supposed criminal, deviant and immoral behaviour, and their economic circumstances vis-à-vis the specific allegation of drug trafficking. The defence, in addition to negating the specific issue of a drug offence allegation, morally degrades prosecution witnesses. The justifications used by the prosecution and the defence do not find relevance in all the cases as some are only significant in black defendants' cases and some others, although applied in both black and white defendants' cases, are not accorded a form of presentation that suggests a similar desire to win a conviction or an acquittal. It is not unlikely for jurors to notice any sign of reluctance or eagerness on the part of the prosecution and the defence to actively demonstrate the guilt or innocence of a defendant (McCabe and Purves, 1974).

The prosecution and the defence justifications are couched in a language that has racial and stereotypical implications and this raises the question as to whether the juries recognised the meanings that underlay the justifications for the varied claims. And if they did, the extent to which their decisions on a verdict were influenced by them. The prosecution devotes much time to stories about black defendants' conduct, introducing as evidence of present guilt, the defendants' moral standards. Violence, abusiveness, sexuality and filthiness form imageries embedded in the responsibility of the prosecution to persuade the jury to convict a black defendant. McCabe (1975) has drawn attention to how jurors' moral assessment of defendants forms a great part of their discussions during deliberation, whereas, the prosecution witnesses rarely have their character subjected to questioning and criticism by the jury. The prosecution approaches the drug trafficking allegation by basically addressing its profit making purpose and further giving solidity to this claim by referring to the quantity of drug involved, the presence of drug trafficking items and the splitting of drugs into separate portions. But projected as a fundamental justification for black defendants' alleged involvement in drug trafficking is the imagery of race socio-economic deprivation and drug trafficking. All the black defendants who entered a not guilty plea for 'intent to supply' what the prosecution emphatically construe as a large quantity of drugs wrapped in separate portions for sale, and having assets supposedly derived from drug trafficking activities, were convicted by the jury.

Working on a jury's emotions is a vital tool of the defence's trade. Jurors have also been said to allow their sympathy for the defence witnesses to sway them very firmly against a clear assessment of the evidence as it is presented before them (Barber and Gordon, 1976). The drug user/addict defendant who had drugs to all intents and purposes for his own use or to share with friends on a social basis, the defendant whose alleged proceeds of drug trafficking are 'in fact' the fruit of his/her own legitimate labour and so forth, the defendant who was physically and verbally abused by the police, the defendant who had drugs planted on him by the police, and the defendant who was subjected to unnecessary police suspicion are portrayals of defendants expressed in the language of the defence to persuade the jury into reaching a not guilty verdict. Some of these themes are emphasised in white defendants' cases, and some others, represented in racial symbols, find importance only in black defendants' cases.

The prosecution and the defence take interest in telling the juries juicy stories in the form of information that is clearly condemnatory of a witness' conduct which does not necessarily bear relevance to the drug offence allegation in question.. The juries seem to find the stories more sensational when judges, in addition to giving legal guidance, air their own views about them, for example, in their resentment of allegations of drug planting and in underlining the 'serious' nature of a drug trafficking allegation. The court process places claims within a social context of knowledge, stereotypes and similar elements to which the juries are exposed to and may have already been conversant with. Jurors, drawn from different ranks of society, have no legal training, and as Bennet and Feldman (1981, p.3) argue:

> If trials make sense to untrained participants, there must be some implicit framework of social judgements that people bring into the courtroom from everyday life. Such framework would have to be shared by citizen participants and legal professionals alike.

What the prosecution, the defence, the witnesses and judges seem to do is reproduce, in a language that jurors are expected to understand, what 'we already know' about black and white people as racial groups, in terms of their relationship with crime, deviancy, criminal justice and so forth. Whether the juries' final decisions were wholly or partly influenced by an attribution of the expected meanings to the varied justifications and judicial response is another issue. But, studies have shown that although jurors pick up their materials from the trial process and information presented before them, their stand for either a conviction or an acquittal of a defendant is related to their knowledge, preconceived ideas, experiences, moral beliefs and personal attitudes (Bankowski, 1988; Marshall, 1975; McCabe and Purves, 1974; Barber and Gordon, 1976), their common sense which they are expected to exercise (Walker, 1975), and even their personal opinions of the prosecution, the defence, the judge and the witnesses (Barber and Gordon, 1976).

Some claims produce what seems to be an expression of boredom and a lack of interest among members of some juries and such claims, presented by the defence, lie in questions directed at police officers regarding events that took place leading to an arrest. In claiming to establish certain facts of a case, the defence emphatically raise questions such as "how far away were you from the defendant when you noticed that he was holding plastic bags", "how many yards away", "how was the defendant holding the plastic bags"??? In black defendants' cases, this defence stratagem calls for a display of an expression of boredom among some judges who also intervened by stating that the defence was dragging the case to unnecessary lengths. Jurors reactions lean towards this form of judicial response. The drug trials show that jurors watch a judge's reactions and more often than not, jurors' non-verbal response to the events that take place in the courtroom move in line with the atmosphere in the room, influenced to a large extent by the judge. In making decisions on their alternative verdicts, how did the juries attend to the judges questions and comments during trials, and their instructions during summing-up?

Jurors are said to have their own beliefs on what judges think about a case and with whom their sympathy lies (Barber and Gordon, 1976); some juries have reached their verdicts in accordance with their belief that such verdicts were expected of them by the trial judge (Bankowski, 1988). Judges' summing-up (comprising the directions on the law and summary of a case) makes an influential contribution to jurors' understanding and interpretation of a case (Barber and Gordon, 1976; McCabe and Purves, 1974). Juries' reliance on a judge's guidance is illustrated in the following question asked a judge by a jury (during deliberation) in a drug trafficking case:

Do we have to find the defendant guilty?

This question suggests, amidst other possible explanations, a reasonable lack of the jurors' understanding of the task assigned to them or an absence of a complete assimilation of the case - that they put their trust in the judge to make the decision for them. The incapability of a jury to absorb the opposing representations made by claimants, to ascertain the facts of a case mostly clouded with uncertainty, to follow the complicated events that take place in a courtroom and comprehend legal principles such as 'beyond reasonable doubt' is noted by Barber and Gordon (1976) as a difficulty that impinge upon jurors' attempt to unravel the mystery surrounding a case. In such circumstances, personal conceptions and similar subjective factors direct the jurors' assessment of the credibility of competing claims (ibid.). Moreover, a judge's form of response to a case, particularly, when manifest in favour or disfavour of a defendant could be of great assistance to a jury in drawing a conclusion (Gordon, 1983).

Some juries in the drug trials requested that further evidence be provided to support that already brought out during trial. These juries seemingly believed that there were missing pieces in the evidence made known to them and in their search for hard, unambiguous and clear evidence about the facts of the case to be proved, the juries raised questions:

Case A: The jury asked if the defendant's fingerprints were found on the cigarette packet containing the drugs. The defendant in this case denied being in possession of drugs and drug trafficking.

Case B: The jury asked (1) whether the defendant's fingerprints were on the wraps and matchbox in which the wraps of drugs were contained, (2) what the message one of the police officers received on his radio about the defendant was, (3) why the man who was with the defendant when he was arrested did not testify, and (4) where the defendant dropped the matchbox.

After a brief discussion between the presiding judges, the prosecution (and police officers) and the defence, the juries received replies that seem not to have exactly answered all their questions. In relation to case A, the answer was that the defendant stepped on the cigarette packet which was squashed so that no fingerprints were detected. In case B, the answer to question 1 was that it was a rainy day and the matchbox was wet; for reasons only known to the police as it seemed, questions 2 and 3 could not be answered as the jurors were told; question 4 received an answer that pinpointed the distance between where the matchbox was dropped and where the defendant was stopped. Still, the answers were useful in their decision to reach a guilty verdict in case A and a not guilty verdict in case B. The above questions discloses what 'facts' juries could consider to be important in a case, whether or not the 'facts' are made available to them.

In the social construction process, different juries may apply, in different ways, information presented before them in their comprehension of similar but different cases. How the juries differently or similarly define a case and the extent to which subjective elements and legal principles are introduced amounting to a final decision may cohere with what and how information is presented before them by the prosecution and the defence, and how judges respond to the various claims. But because of the legal restrictions on speaking with jurors, this assessment must remain as speculation so caution must therefore be exercised in drawing any definite conclusions that point the jury in favour of the prosecution or the defence.

Conclusion: Appeal for Further Research

This book has tried to address the issue of black overrepresentation in criminal statistics by establishing how social construction in the court process constitutes an aspect of the overall problem of disproportion, how through the social activities of barristers and judges in the trial process, assumed or factual actions of black defendants are more likely to be designated as indicative of a drug offence. Major studies on the problem of disproportion have focused on *why* black people are over-represented in the criminal statistics whilst giving limited attention to the social processes by which this problem arises.

For one, studies of race and sentencing have tend to limit information available in the trial process by looking at substantial inventories of variables such as nature of offence, age, previous convictions and plea status, and subsequently reveal the likelihood by which each of the variables influence the court disposal of defendants based on race. Those analyses have remained important to our comprehension of the overrepresentation of black people in the criminal statistics but whilst addressing the facts is vital, how the criminal justice process affects the facts is not to be taken for granted. What those studies have fundamentally addressed is the issue of direct discrimination and accordingly, the introduction of an ethnic monitoring system in the criminal justice system under Section 95 of the 1991 Criminal Justice Act is concerned with preventing any direct existence of discrimination on racial grounds, ethnic origin or colour. In relation to the court, this policy is a step in the right direction, however, it overlooks the potential significance of indirect discrimination in the processes that lead to conviction, sentencing and the production of criminal statistics. The analysis adopted in this book seeks to persuade the reader to look at the problem of disproportion from a different perspective - that which examines *how* the problem emerges from the process of social construction and claims-making activities that take place in the courtroom arena. Its key argument is that it is in this process of social construction and claims-making that there occur an indirect form of racially-based discrimination which is subtle, covert yet powerful.

In examining how the problem of disproportion emerges, it has been found that the existing conflicting accounts of race, crime and criminal justice are significant and linked systematically to the drug trial process. For example, issues on race, deprivation and crime apparently form part of the social construction process and so are some criteria used in studies of race and sentencing. Such variables that find relevance in studies of race and sentencing do not mechanically determine the outcome of a case but are, instead, subjectively influential in the claims-making process during which their role is socially constructed, for instance, offence seriousness. This book which contains a description of claims-making activities, has focused on the details of discourse and the effect that discourse has or may have on the outcome of black and white defendants' cases. Although the claims-making process takes place within the framework of a situational context, whereby participants' actions are oriented to that of one another, their discourse reflects and reproduces the picture of the wider society. As racial awareness informs the claims-making activities, the trial process becomes partisan with race as a significant factor. The pattern that the social construction of guilt and innocence takes, evolves into the production of a scenario that deviates from the actual facts of a case in that the claims-making activities of legal members is concerned with the manipulation and persuasion of the jury on the logicality of a case, rather than its truth. In essence, barristers rely on their skills in introducing extra-legal criteria when interrogating witnesses, and judges and perhaps jurors, penetrate into the realm of discretion and subjectivity in the course of giving legitimacy to their response.

Criminal statistics is, therefore, not a fixed and mechanical phenomenon and accepting criminal statistics as an indication of criminality obscures the subjective influences in the criminal justice process as a whole thereby projecting a robotic image of the system. Much as this analysis suggests that the activities of legal members place black defendants in a more likely position of being over-represented in the conviction and prison statistics, the scope of this study is small and in view of this limitation, hypothetical statements can only be made vis-à-vis the applicability of the conclusions to other courts. Notwithstanding that, the study creates an opening to an inquiry that addresses the in-depth embodiment of sociological factors in the court system. Until full recognition is given to *how* the criminal justice process affects the formation of criminal statistics, the position of black people in the criminal statistics may not be fully understood.

Bibliography

Adler, P. and Adler, P.A. (1980) 'Symbolic Interactionism', in J.D. Douglas (ed), *Introduction to the Sociologies of Everyday Life*, Boston: Allen and Bacon.

Agozino, B. (1997) *Black Women and the Criminal Justice System*, Aldershot: Ashgate.

Ashworth, A. (1994) *The Criminal Justice Process*, Oxford: Clarendon Press.

Auld, J., Dorn, N. and South, N. (1986) 'Irregular Work, Irregular Pleasures: Heroin in the 1980s', in R. Matthews and J. Young (eds), *Confronting Crime*, London: Sage.

Awiah, J., Butt, S. and Dorn, N. (1990) '"The Last Place I Would Go": Black People and Drug Services in Britain', *Druglink*, 5, 5: 4-15.

Baldwin, J. and McConville, M. (1977) *Negotiated Justice*, London: Martin Robertson.

Bankowski, Z. (1988) 'The Jury and Reality', in M. Findlay and P. Duff (eds), *The Jury Under Attack*, London: Butterworths.

Banks, T. (1977) 'Discretionary Justice and the Black Offender', in C. E. Owens and J. Bell (eds), *Blacks and Criminal Justice*, Massachusetts: Lexington Books.

Banton, M. (1972) *Police Community Relations*, London: William Collins & Sons.

Barber, D. and Gordon, G. (eds) (1976) *Members of the Jury*, London: Wildwood House.

Barker, A.J. (1978) *The African Link: British Attitudes to the Negro in the 17th and 18th centuries*, Britain: Frank Cass.

Barnett, S. (1977) 'Researching Black Justice: Descriptions and Implications', in C. E. Owens and J. Bell (eds), *Blacks and Criminal Justice*, Massachusetts: Lexington Books.

Bean, P. (1974) *The Social Control of Drugs*, London: Martin Robertson.

Bean, P. and Pearson, Y. (1992) 'Cocaine and Crack in Nottingham, 1989/90 and 1991/92, in J. Mott (ed), *Crack and Cocaine in England and Wales*, Home Office RPU Paper 70, London: HMSO.

Becker, H.S. (1963) *Outsiders: Studies in the Sociology of Deviance*, New York: Free Press.

Bennet, T. (ed) (1991) *Drug Misuse in Local Communities: Perspectives Across Europe*, London: The Police Foundation.

Bennett, W.L. and Feldman, M.S. (1981) *Reconstructing Reality in the Courtroom: Justice and Judgement in American Culture*, New Brunswick: Rutgers University Press.

Benyon, J. (ed) (1984) *Scarman and After*, Oxford: Pergamon.

_____ (1986) *A Tale of Failure: Race and Policing*, Policy Papers in Ethnic Relations, 3, University of Warwick.

Benyon, J. and Solomos, J. (eds) (1987) *The Roots of Urban Unrest*, Oxford: Pergamon.

Berridge, V. (1984) 'Drugs and Social Policy: The Establishment of Social Control in Britain, 1900 -1930', *British Journal of Addiction*, 79: 17-29.

_____ (1988) 'The Origins of the English Drug "Scene" 1890-1930', *Medical History*, 32: 51-64.

_____ (1989) 'Historical Issues', in S. MacGregor (ed), *Drugs and British Society*, London: Routledge.

Berridge, V. and Edwards, G. (1981) *Opium and the People: Opiate in Nineteenth-Century England*, London: Allen lane.

Best, J. (1987) 'Rhetoric in Claims-making: Constructing the Missing Children Problem', *Social Problems*, 34, 2.

_____ (ed) (1989) *Images of Issues: Typifying Contemporary Social Problems*, New York: Aldine De Gruyter.

Bewley, T.H. (1966) 'Recent Changes in Patterns of Drug Addiction in the United Kingdom', *Bulletin of Narcotics*, 18, 4.

Black, D. (1991) 'The Recent History of British Drugs Policy', in T. Bennett (ed), *Drug Misuse in Local Communities: Perspectives Across Europe*, London: The Police Foundation.

Blom-Cooper, L. and Drabble, R. (1982) 'Police Perception of Crime: Brixton and the Operational Response', *British Journal of Criminology*, 22, 2.

Blum, R.H. (1977) 'Drug Pushers: A Collective Portrait', in P.E. Rock (ed), *Drugs and Politics*, New Jersey: Transaction Books.

Blumberg, A.S. (1969a) 'The Practice of Law as Confidence Game: Organizational Cooptation of a Profession', in W. J. Chambliss (ed), *Crime and the Legal Process*, New York: McGraw-Hill.

_____ (1969b) 'The Criminal Court as Organization and Communication System', in R. Quinney (ed), *Crime and Justice in Society*, Boston: Little, Brown and Company.

Blumer, H. (1971) 'Social Problems as Collective Behaviour', *Social Problems*, 18, 3.

Bottomley, A.K. and Pease, K. (1986) *Crime and Punishment: Interpreting the Data*, Milton Keynes: Open University press.

Bottomley, K.A. (1973) *Decisions in the Penal Process*, Oxford: Martin Robertson.

Bottoms, A.E. (1967) 'Delinquency Among Immigrants: A Further Note', *Race*, 9, 2.

Box, S. (1971) *Deviance, Reality and Society*, London: Holt, Rinehart and Winston.

_____ (1981) *Deviance, Reality and Society*, 2nd edn, London: Holt, Rinehart and Winston.

Box, S. and Hale, C. (1986) 'Unemployment, Crime and Imprisonment, and the Enduring Problem of Prison Overcrowding', in R. Matthews and J. Young (eds), *Confronting Crime*, London: Sage.

Brooks, A. (1987) *Key Facts: Ethnic Population*, London Borough of Lambeth: Directorate of Town Planning and Economic Development.

Brown, C. (1984) *Black and White Britain: The Third PSI Report*, London: Heinemann.

Brown, I. And Hullin, R (1992) 'A Study of Sentencing in Leeds Magistrates' Courts: The Treatment of Ethnic Minority and White Offenders', *British Journal of Criminology*, 32: 41-53.

Brown, J. (1977) *Shades of Grey: Police/West Indian Relations in Handsworth*, Cranfield Police Studies.

Brown, S. (1991) *Magistrates at Work*, Milton Keynes: Open University Press.

Burr, A. (1987) 'Chasing the Dragon: Heroin Misuse, Delinquency and Crime in the Context of South London Culture', *British Journal of Criminology*, 27, 4.

Cain, M. and Sadigh, S. (1982) 'Racism, the Police and Community Policing: A Comment on the Scarman Report', *Journal of Law and Society*, 9, 1.

Caplan, P. (ed) (1987) *The Cultural Construction of Sexuality*, London: Tavistock.

Carby, H.V. (1982) 'Schooling in Babylon', in Centre for Contemporary Cultural Studies (ed), *The Empire Strikes Back*, London: Hutchinson.

Carey, T.J. (1978) *Introduction to Criminology*, New Jersey: Prentice-Hall.

Carlen, P. (1976) *Magistrates' Justice*, London: Martin Robertson.

_____ (1988) *Women, Crime and Poverty*, Milton Keynes: Open University Press.

Cashmore, E. and Troyna, B. (eds) (1982) *Black Youth in Crisis*, London: George Allen and Unwin.

Cashmore, E. and McLaughlin, E. (1991) 'Out of Order', in E. Cashmore and E. McLaughlin (eds), *Out Of Order*, London: Routledge.

Chambliss, W.J. (ed.) (1969) *Crime and the Legal Process*, New York: McGraw-Hill.

Chigwada, R. (1989) 'The Criminalisation and Imprisonment of Black Women', *Probation Journal*, 36, 3.

_____ (1991) 'The Policing of Black Women', in E. Cashmore and E. McLaughlin (eds), *Out of Order*, London: Routledge.

Cicourel, A.V. (1976) *The Social Organization of Juvenile Justice*, London: Heinemann.

Clare, J. (1984) 'Eyewitness in Brixton', in J. Benyon (ed), *Scarman and After*, Oxford: Pergamon.

Clarke, M. (1990) *Business Crime*, Cambridge: Polity.

Clinard, B.M. (1968) *Sociology of Deviant Behaviour*, New York: Holt, Rinehart and Winston.

Cloward, R. and Ohlin, L. (1961) *Delinquency and Opportunity*, London: Routledge and Kegan Paul.

Cohen, A.K. (1955) *Delinquent Boys: The Culture of the Gang*, Chicago: Free Press.

Cohen, P. and Bains, S.H. (eds) (1988) *Multi-Racist Britain*, London: Macmillan.

Cole, G.F. (1973) *Politics and the Administration of Justice*, Beverly Hills: Sage.

Conrad, P. and Schneider, J.W. (1980) *Deviance and Medicalization: From Badness to Sickness*, St Louis: C.V. Mosby.

Cooney, M. (1994) 'Evidence as Partisanship', *Law and Society Review*, 28, 4.

Cross, M. (1982) 'The manufacture of Marginality', in E. Cashmore and B. Troyna (eds), *Black Youth in Crisis*, London: George Allen and Unwin.

Craton, M., Walvin, J. and Wright, D. (1976) *Slavery, Abolition and Emancipation: Black Slaves and the British Empire*, London: Longman.

Crow, I. and Cove, J. (1984) 'Ethnic Minorities and the Courts', *Criminal Law Review*, 413-417.

Crow, I. and Simon, F. (1987) *Unemployment and Magistrates' Court*, London: NACRO.

Dahrendorf, R. (1959) *Class and Class Conflict in Industrial Society*, England: Routledge and Kegan Paul.

Davis, K.C. (1971) *Discretionary Justice: A Preliminary of Enquiry*, Urbana: University of Illinois Press.

Davis, M., Croall, H and Tyrer, J. (1995) *Criminal Justice*, London: Longman.

Day, M. (1989) 'Naught for Our comfort', in E. Russell (ed), *Black People and the Criminal Justice System*, London: The Howard League for Penal Reform.

Deedes, W. (1970) *The Drugs Epidemic*, London: Tom Stacey.

Demuth, C. (1978) *'Sus': A Report on the Vagrancy Act 1824*, London: Runnymede Trust.

Dholakia, N. and Sumner, M. (1993) 'Research, Policy and Racial Justice', in D. Cook and B. Hudson (eds), *Racism and Criminology*, London: Sage.

Dodd, D. (1978) 'Police and Thieves on the Streets of Brixton', *New Society*, 16 March.

Donald, T.R. (1956) *Criminology*, New York: Macmillan.

Dorn, N., Murji, K. and South, N. (1992) *Traffickers: Drug Markets and Law Enforcement*, London: Routledge.

Dorn, N., Ribbens, J. and South, N. (1987) *Coping with a Nightmare*, London: ISDD.

Dorn, N. and South, N. (1985) *Helping Drug Users*, Hants: Gower.

_____ (eds) (1987) *A Land Fit for Heroin?*, London: Macmillan.

Downes, D. and Rock, P. (1988) *Understanding Deviance*, Oxford: Clarendon.

Eaton, M. (1986) *Justice for Women*, Milton Keynes: Open University Press.

Emerson, R.M. (1991) 'Case Processing and Interorganizational Knowledge: Detecting the "Real Reasons" for Referrals', *Social Problems*, 38, 2.

Field, F. and Haikin, P. (eds) (1971) *Black Britons*, London: Oxford University Press.

File, N. and Power, C. (1981) *Black Settlers in Britain 1555-1958*, London: Heinemann.

Finigarette, H. and Hasse, A. (1978) *Mental Disabilities and Criminal Responsibility*, California: University of California Press.

Fludger, N. (1981) *Ethnic Minorities in Borstal*, Directorate of Psychological Services, Prison Department, London: HMSO.

Folarin, S. (1977) *Black People in Britain 1555-1833*, London: Oxford University Press.

Foy, S (1996) 'Getting a Grip', *Criminal Justice Matters*, 24: 8-9.

Frank, J. (1949) *Courts on Trial: Myth and Reality in American Justice*, New Jersey: Princeton University Press.

Frohmann, L. (1991) 'Discrediting Victims' Allegations of Sexual Assault: Prosecutorial Accounts of Case Rejections', *Social Problems*, 38, 2.

Gandy, D. (1988) 'The Crown Prosecution Service: Its Organisation and Philosophy', in H.J.E. Williams (ed), *The Role of the Prosecutor*, Hants: Avebury.

Garfinkel, H. (1967) *Studies in Ethnomethodology*, Englewood Cliffs: Prentice-Hall.

Gay, P. (1989) *Getting Together: A Study of Self-Help Groups for Drug Users' Families*, London: Policy Studies Institute.

Giddens, A. (ed) (1991) *Introductory Sociology*, London: Macmillan.

Gilroy, P. (1982a) 'Police and Thieves', in Centre for Contemporary Cultural Studies (ed), *The Empire Strikes Back*, London: Hutchinson.

_____ (1982b) 'The myth of Black Criminality', in M.Eve and D.Musson (eds), *The Socialist Register*, London: Merlin.

_____ (1987a) 'The myth of Black Criminality', in P. Scraton (ed), *Law, Order and the Authoritarian State*, Milton Keynes: Open University Press.

_____ (1987b) *There Ain't No Black in the Union Jack*, London: Hutchinson.

Glanz, A. and Taylor, C. (1986) 'Findings of a National Survey of the Role of General Practitioners in the Treatment of Opiate Misuse: Extent of Contact with Opiate Misusers', *British Medical Journal*, 293, 6544: 427-30.

Glaser, D. (1974) 'Interlocking Dualities in Drug Use, Drug Control and Crime', in J.A. Inciardi and C.D. Chambers (eds), *Drugs and the Criminal Justice System*, London: Sage.

Glatt, M.M. (1974) *A Guide to Addiction and its Treatment*, Lancaster, England: Medical and Technical Publishing Co.

Gordon, P. (1983) *White Law: Racism in the Police, Courts and Prisons*, London: Pluto.

Gouldner, A.W. (1970) *The Coming Crisis of Western Sociology*, London: Heinemann.

Graef, R. (1990) *Talking Blues*, London: Fontana.

Green, P. (1991) *Drug Couriers*, London: The Howard League for Penal Reform.

_____ (ed) (1996) *Drug Couriers: A New Perspective*, London: The Howard League for Penal Reform.

Griffith, J.A.G. (1985) *The Politics of the Judiciary*, 3rd edn, London: Fontana.

Gusfield, J.R. (1981) *The Culture of Public Problems: Drinking-Driving and the Symbolic Order*, Chicago: The University of Chicago Press.

Gutzmore, C. (1983) 'Capital, "Black Youth" and Crime', *Race and Class*, 25, 2.

Hagan, J. (1988) *Structural Criminology*, Cambridge: Polity.

Hall, S., Critcher, C., Clarke, J., Jefferson, T. and Roberts, B. (1978) *Policing the Crisis*, London: Macmillan.

Hall, T. (1989) 'Black People, Crime and Justice', in E. Russell (ed), *Black People and the Criminal Justice System*, London: The Howard League for Penal Reform.

Hansen, T. (1989) *Coping with Drug Abuse*, London: Incorporated Catholic Truth Society.

Haralambos, M. and Holborn, M. (1990) *Sociology*, London: Unwin Hyman.

Hartman, P. and Husband, C. (1974) *Racism and the Mass Media*, London: Davis-Poynter.

Hartnoll, R. (1989) 'The International Context', in S. MacGregor (ed), *Drugs and British Society*, London: Routledge.

Haw, S. (1985) *Drug Problems in Greater Glasgow*, London: Chamelion.

Hawkins, K. (1992) 'The Use of Legal Discretion: Perspectives from Law and Social Science', in K. Hawkins (ed), *The Uses of Discretion*, Oxford: Clarendon.

Heaven, O. (1997) 'Foreign Nationals in UK Prisons: The Role of FPWP and Hibiscus', in J. Braggins (ed), *Tackling Drugs Together: One Year On*, London: ISTD.

Henman, A., Lewis, R. and Malyon, T. (1985) 'Junkie Babies v. the Merchants of Death', in A. Henman, R, Lewis and T. Malyon (eds), *Big Deal: The Politics of Illicit Drug Business*, London: Pluto.

Hepple, B. (1968) *Race, Jobs and the Law in Britain*, London: Penguin.

Hill, C.S. (1967) *How Colour Prejudiced is Britain?*, London: Panther.

Hiro, D. (1992) *Black British White British*, London: Paladin.

Hobson, W. (1975) *A Theory and Practice of Public Health*, London: London University Press.

Holzner, B. (1972) *Reality Construction in Society*, Cambridge: Schenkman.

Home Office (1983) 'Crime Statistics for the Metropolitan Police District Analysed by Ethnic Group', *Home Office Statistical Bulletin*, 22/83, London: Home Office.

_____ (1984) 'Crime Statistics for the Metropolitan Police District Analysed by Ethnic Group, 1977-1983', *Home Office Statistical Bulletin*, 22/84, London: Home Office.

_____ (1985) *Tackling Drug Misuse*, 1st edn, London: HMSO.

_____ (1986a) 'The Ethnic Origin of Prisoners: The Prison Population on 30 June 1985 and Persons Received, July 1984-March 1985', *Home Office Statistical Bulletin*, 17/86, London: Home Office.

_____ (1986b) *Drug Trafficking Offences Act 1986*, London: HMSO.

_____ (1989a) 'The Ethnic Group of Those Proceeded Against or Sentenced by the Courts in the Metropolitan Police District in 1984 and 1985', *Home Office Statistical Bulletin*, 6/89, London: Home Office.

_____ (1989b) *Misuse of Drugs Act 1971*, London: HMSO.

_____ (1992) *Race and the Criminal Justice System*, London: HMSO.

_____ (1993) 'The Prison Population in 1992', *Home Office Statistical Bulletin*, 7/93, London: Home Office.

_____ (1994a) 'The Ethnic Origins of Prisoners', *Home Office Statistical Bulletin*, 21/94, London: Home Office.

_____ (1994b) *Tackling Drugs Together*, London: HMSO.

_____ (1994c) *Police, Drug Misusers and the Community*, London: HMSO.

Hood, R. (1992) *Race and Sentencing*, Oxford: Clarendon Press.

Howe, D. (1973) 'Fighting Back: West Indian Youth and the Police in Nottingham', *Race Today*, 5, 11.

Hudson, B. (1989) 'Discrimination and Disparity: The Influence of Race on Sentencing', *New Community*, 16, 1.

_____ (1993) 'Racism and Criminology: Concepts and Controversies', in D. Cook and B. Hudson (eds), *Racism and Criminology*, London: Sage.

_____ (1996) *Understanding Justice*, Buckingham: Open University Press.

Humphrey, D. (1972) *Police Power and Black People*, London: Panther.

Humphrey, D. and John, G. (1971) *Because They're Black*, Harmondsworth: Penguin.

Hunte, J. (1966) *Nigger Hunting in England?*, London: West Indian Standing Conference.

Inciardi, A.J. and Chambers, D. (eds) (1974) *Drugs and the Criminal Justice System*, London: Sage.

Indian Workers' Association (1987) *The Regeneration of Racism*, Southhall: Indian Workers' Association.

Inner London Probation Service (1982) *Probation and Aftercare in a Multi-Racial Society: A Working Party Report*, London: Inner London Probation Service.

_____ (1991) *Race and the Pattern of Drugs Misuse*, London: Inner London Probation Service.

Institute of Race Relations (1979) *Police Against Black People*, London: Panther.

Jamieson, A., Glanz, A. and MacGregor, S. (1984) *Dealing with Drug Misuse: Crisis Intervention in the City*, London: Tavistock.

Jefferson, T. (1988) 'Race, Crime and Policing: Empirical, Theoretical and Methodological Issues', *International Journal of the Sociology of law*, 16, 521-539.

_____ (1991) 'Discrimination, Disadvantage and Policework', in E. Cashmore and E. McLaughlin (eds), *Out of Order*, London: Routledge.

Jefferson, T. and Walker, M. (1990) 'Ethnic Minorities in the Criminal Justice System', *Criminal Law Review*, 83-95.

John, G. (1970) *Race in the Inner City*, London: Runnymede Trust.

_____ (1980) *Projects versus Politics: A Report on the Political Cultures of Youth and Community Work with Black People in British Cities*, London: National Association of Youth Clubs.

_____ (1981) *In the Service of Black Youth*, London: National association of Youth Clubs.

Jones, A. (1990) *Jury Service*, London: Robert Hale.

Kalunta-Crumpton, A. (1996) 'The Influence of Race and Unemployment upon Prosecution of Drug Traffickers', *Probation Journal*, 43, 4: 182-186.

_____ (1998) 'Claims-making and the Prosecution of Black Defendants in Drug Trafficking Trials: The Influence of Deprivation', *International Journal of Discrimination and the Law*, 3, 29-49.

Keith, M. (1991) ''Policing a Perplexed Society?': No-Go Areas and the Mystification of Police-Black Conflict', in E. Cashmore and E. McLaughlin (eds), *Out of Order*, London: Routledge.

Kettle, M. (1982) 'The Racial Numbers Game in Our Society', *New Society*, 30 September.

King, J.F.S. (1969) *Probation and After-Care Service*, London: Butterworths.

King, M. and May, C. (1985) *Black Magistrates*, London: Cobden Trust.

King, R. (1974) 'The American System: Legal Sanctions to Repress Drug Abuse', in J.A. Inciardi and C.D. Chambers (eds), *Drugs and the Criminal Justice System*, London: Sage.

Kitsuse, J. and Spector, M. (1975) 'Social Problems and Deviance: Some Parallel Issues', *Social Problems*, 22, 5.

Lafree, G. (1989) *Rape and Criminal Justice: The Social Construction of Sexual Assault*, Belmont, CA: Wadsworth.

Lambert, J.R. (1970) *Crime, Police and Race Relations*, London: Oxford University Press.

Landau, S. (1981) 'Juveniles and the Police', *British Journal of Criminology*, 21, 1.

Landau, S. and Nathan, G. (1983) 'Selecting Delinquents for Cautioning in the London Metropolitan Area', *British Journal of Criminology*, 23: 128-149.

Lawrence, E. (1982) 'Just Plain Common Sense: The 'Roots' of Racism', in Centre for Contemporary Cultural studies (ed), *The Empire Strikes Back*, London: Hutchinson.

Lea, J. and Young, J. (1982) 'The Riots in Britain 1981: Urban Violence and Political Marginalisation', in D. Cowell et al. (eds), *Policing the Riots*, London: Junction Books.

_____ (1984) *What Is To Be Done About Law and Order*, Harmondsworth: Penguin.

_____ (1993) *What Is To Be Done About Law and Order*, London: Pluto.

Leigh, L.H. (1982) *The Control of Commercial Fraud*, London: Heinemann.

Levi, M. (1987) *Regulating Fraud*, London: Tavistock.

Lewis, R. (1985) 'Serious Business: The Global Heroin Economy', in A. Henman, R. Lewis and Malyon, T. (eds), *Big Deal*, London: Pluto.

Lindesmith, A.R. (1965) *The Addict and the Law*, Bloomington: Indiana University Press.

MacGregor, S. (1989a) 'The Public Debate in the 1980s', in S. MacGregor (ed), *Drugs and British Society*, London: Routledge.

_____ (1989b) 'Choices for Policy and Practice', in S. MacGregor (ed), *Drugs and British Society*, London: Routledge.

Mackay, R and Moody, S. (1996) 'Diversion of Neighbourhood Disputes to Community Mediation', *Howard Journal of Criminal Justice*, 35, 4.

Mair, G. (1986) 'Ethnic Minorities, Probation and the Magistrates' Courts', *British Journal of Criminology*, 26, 2.

Manis, G.J. (1976) *Analysing Social Problems*, New York: Praeger.

Marshall, G. (1975) 'The Judgement of One's Peers: Some Aims and Ideals of Jury Trials', in N.Walker (ed), *The British Jury System*, Cambridge: Institute of Criminology.

Matoesian, G.M. (1993) *Reproducing Rape*, Cambridge: Polity.

Matthews, R. and Young, J. (eds) (1986) *Confronting Crime*, London: Sage.

Mays, J.B. (1970) *Crime and its Treatment*, London: Longman

McBarnet, D. (1983) *Conviction: Law, the State and the Construction of Justice*, London: Macmillan.

McCabe, S. (1975) 'Discussions in the Jury Room: Are They Like This?', in N. Walker (ed), *The British Jury System*, Cambridge: Institute of Criminology.

McCabe, S. and Purves, R. (1974) *The Shadow Jury at Work*, Oxford: Basil Blackwell.

McClintock, F. (1963) *Crimes of Violence*, London: Macmillan.

McConville, M. and Baldwin, J. (1981) *Courts, Prosecution and Conviction*, Oxford: Clarendon.

_____ (1982) 'Influence of Race on Sentencing in England', *Criminal Law Review*, 652-658.

McConville, M., Sanders, A. and Leng, R. (1991) *The Case for the Prosecution*, London: Routledge.

Mehan, H. and Wood, H. (1975) *The Reality of Ethnomethodology*, New York: John Wiley and Sons.

Merton, R.K. (1957) *Social Theory and Social Structure*, Glencoe 111: Free Press.

Metropolitan Police (1990) *Extracts on Crime Statistics from the Commissioner's Annual Report*, London: Metropolitan Police.

_____ (1991) *Policing Brixton: The Annual Report of the Brixton Division of the Metropolitan Police*, London: MET.

Mhlanga, B. (1997) *The Colour of English Justice*, Aldershot: Ashgate.

Miles, R. (1978) *Between Two Cultures?*, Bristol: SSRC.

Miles, R. and Phizacklea, A. (1984) *White Man's Country: Racism in British Politics*, London: Pluto.

Miller, E.M. (1986) *Street Woman*, Philadelphia: Temple University Press.

Mirza, H., Pearson, G. and Phillips, S. (1991a) *Drugs, People and Services in Lewisham*, Final Report of the Drug Information Project, London: Goldsmiths College, University of London.

Mirza, H.S., Philips, S. and Pearson, G (1991b) 'Drug Misuse in a South London Borough', in T. Bennett (ed), *Drug Misuse in Local Communities: Perspectives Across Europe*, London: The Police Foundation.

Morris, T. (1989) *Crime and Criminal Justice Since 1945*, Oxford: Basil Blackwell.

Moxon, D. (1988) *Sentencing Practice in the Crown Court*, London: HMSO.

Murji, K. (1996) 'Enforcing Demand Reduction', *Criminal Justice Matters*, 24: 6-7.

Musto, D. (1973) *The American Disease: Origins of Narcotic Control*, New Haven: Yale University Press

NACRO (1986) *Black People and the Criminal Justice System*, London: NACRO.

_____ (1989) *Race and Criminal Justice*, London: NACRO.

_____ (1993a) *Evidence of the Links Between Homelessness, Crime and the Criminal Justice System*, Occasional Paper, London: NACRO.

_____ (1993b) 'Statistics of Notified Drug Addicts, UK, 1992', *NACRO Criminal Justice Digest*, 78, London: NACRO.

_____ (1993c) 'Drug Offenders, United Kingdon, 1991', *NACRO Criminal Justice Digest*, 75, London: NACRO.

Newcombe, R. (1987) 'High Time for Harm Reduction', *Druglink*, 2, 1.

Newman, D.J. (1969) 'Pleading Guilty for Considerations: A Study of Bargain Justice', in W.J. Chambliss (ed), *Crime and the Legal Process*, New York: McGraw-Hill.

Norman, J. (1971) *How to Cure Drug Addicts*, London: Tom Stacey.

Norris, C., Fielding, N., Kemp, C. and Fielding, J. (1992) 'Black and Blue: An Analysis of the Influence of Race on Being Stopped by the Police', *British Journal of Sociology*, 43: 207-24.

Osborne, S. and Bright, J. (1988) *Policing Housing Estates*, London: NACRO.

Parker, H., Bakx, K. and Newcombe, R. (1986) 'Heroin and the Young', *New Society*, 24 January.

Parker, H., Newcombe, R. and Bakx, K. (1988) *Living with Heroin*, Milton Keynes: Open University Press.

Parker, H., Sumner, M. and Jarvis, G. (1989) *Unmasking the Magistrates*, Milton Keynes: Open University Press.

Pattenden, R. (1982) *The Judge, Discretion, and the Criminal Trial*, Oxford: Clarendon.

Pearson, G. (1987a) *The New Heroin Users*, Oxford: Basil Blackwell.

_____ (1987b) 'Social Deprivation, Unemployment and Patterns of Heroin Use', in N. Dorn and N. South (eds), *A Land Fit for Heroin?* London: Macmillan.

_____ (1989) 'Heroin Use in its Social Context', in D. Herbert and D. Smith (eds), *Social Problems and the City: New Perspectives*, Oxford: Oxford University Press.

_____ (1995) 'Drug Problems and Criminal Justice Policy in Britain', in N. South (ed), *Drugs, Crime and Criminal Justice*, vol.2, Aldershot: Dartmouth.

Pearson, G., Gilman, M. and McLver, S. (1987) *Young People and Heroin*, Aldershot: Gower.

Peck, D.F. and Plant, M.A. (1986) 'Unemployment and Illegal Drug Use: Concordant Evidence from a Prospective Study and from National Trends', *British Medical Journal*, 293: 929-932.

Penal Affairs Consortium (1996) *Race and Criminal Justice*, London: Penal Affairs Consortium.

Pfohl, S. (1977) 'The Discovery of Child Abuse', *Social Problems*, 24: 310-324.

_____ (1978) *Predicting Dangerousness*, Toronto: Lexington Books.

Philips, M. (1976) 'Brixton and Crime', *New Society*, 8 July.

Pitts, J. (1986) 'Black Young People and Juvenile Crime: Some Unanswered Questions', in R. Matthews and J. Young (eds), *Confronting Crime*, London: Sage.

_____ (1993) 'Theoreotyping: Anti-Racism, Criminology and Black People', in D. Cook and B. Hudson (eds), *Racism and Criminology*, London: Sage.

Plant, M. (1987) *Drugs in Perspective*, London: Hodder and Stoughton.

_____ (1989) 'The Epidemiology of Illicit Drug-use and Misuse in Britain', in S. MacGregor (ed), *Drugs and British Society*, London: Routledge.

Platt, A.M. (1969) *The Child Savers*, Chicago: The University of Chicago Press.

Pryce, K. (1979) *Endless Pressure*, Harmonsdworth: Penguin.

Punch, M. (1979) *Policing the Inner City*, London: Macmillan.

Quinney, R. (1970) *The Social Reality of Crime*, Boston: Little, Brown and Co.

Ramsay, M. (1982) 'Mugging: Fears and Facts', *New Society*, 26 March.

Rankin, D. (1991) *Changing Shape*, Southwark Council: Planning Division Development Dept.

Reid, S.T. (1979) *Crime and Criminology*, New York: Holt, Rinehart and Winston.

Reiner, R. (1985) *The Politics of the Police*, Brighton: Wheatsheaf Books.

Rex, J. (1982) 'West Indian and Asian Youth', in E. Cashmore and B. Troyna (eds), *Black Youth in Crisis*, London: George Allen and Unwin.

Richards, M., McWilliams, B., Batten, N., Cameron, C. and Cutler, J. (1995) 'Foreign Nationals in English Prisons: II. Some Policy Issues, *Howard Journal of Criminal Justice*, 34, 3.

Roach Family Support Committee (1989) *Policing in Hackney 1945-1984*, London: Karia/RSFC.

Roberts, B. (1982) 'The Debate on "Sus"', in E. Cashmore and B. Troyna (eds), *Black Youth in Crisis*, London: George Allen and Unwin.

Roberts, K. (1984) 'Youth Unemployment and Urban Unrest', in J. Benyon (ed), *Scarman and After*, Oxford: Pergamon.

Roshier, B. (1989) *Controlling Crime*, Milton Keynes: Open University Press.

Roggiero, V. and South, N. (1995) *Organised Crime and Drug Markets: Images of Illegal Drug Markets in the Late Modern City*, A Working Paper 1, BSA.

Runnymede Trust and the Radical Statistics Race Group (1980) *Britain's Black Population*, London: Heinemann.

Runnymede Trust (1990) *Black People, White Justice?*, London: Runnymede Trust.

Ryan, W. (1976) *Blaming the Victim*, New York: Vintage Books.

Sacks, H. (1972) 'Notes on Police Assessment of Moral Character', in D. Sudnow (ed), *Studies in Social Interaction*, New York: The Free Press.

Sallon, C. and Bedingfield, D. (1993) 'Drugs, Money and the Law', *Criminal Law Review*, 165-173.

Sanders, A. (1994) 'From Suspect to Trial', in M. Maguire, R. Morgan and R. Reiner (eds), *The Oxford Handbook of Criminology*, Oxford: Clarendon Press.

Scarman, Lord (1981) *The Brixton Disorders 10-12 April 1981: Report of an Inquiry by the Rt Hon. The Lord Scarman*, London: HMSO.

_____ (1982) *The Scarman Report*, London: Penguin.

_____ (1987) 'The Quest for Social Justice', in J. Benyon and J. Solomos (eds), *The Roots of Urban Unrest*, Oxford: Pergamon.

Schneider, C.E. (1992) 'Discretion and Rules: A Lawyer's View', in K. Hawkins (ed), *The Uses of Discretion*, Oxford: Clarendon.

Scraton, P. (ed) (1987) *Law, Order and the Authoritarian State*, Milton Keynes: Open University Press.

Shalice, A. and Gordon, P. (1990) *Black People, White Justice?*, London: Runnymede Trust.

Sherman, H.J. and Wood, J.L. (1979) *Sociology*, New York: Harper and Row.

Simpson, J. (1969) 'Man to Man', *The Job*, 1, 3.

Smellie, E. and Crow, I. (1991) *Black People's Experience of Criminal Justice*, London: NACRO.

Smith, D. and Gray, J. (1983) *Police and People in London*, vol.1V, London: Policy Studies Institute.

_____ (1985) *Police and People in London: The PSI Report*, Aldershot: Gower.

Smith, D (1994) 'Race, Crime and Criminal Justice', in M. Maguire, R. Morgan and R. Reiner (eds), *The Oxford Handbook of Criminology*, Oxford: Clarendon Press.

Solomos, J. (1988a) *Black Youth, Racism and the State*, Cambridge: Cambridge University Press.

_____ (1988b) 'Institutionalised Racism: Politics of Marginalisation in Education and Training', in P. Cohen and H.S. Bains (eds), *Multi-Racist Britain*, London: Macmillan.

_____ (1989) *Race and Racism in Contemporary Britain*, London: Macmillan.

_____ (1993) 'Constructions of Black Criminality: Racialisation and Criminalisation in Perspectives', in D. Cook and B. Hudson (eds), *Racism and Criminology*, London: Sage.

Solomos, J. and Rackett, T. (1991) 'Policing and Urban Unrest: Problem Constitution and Policy Response', in E. Cashmore and E. McLaughlin (eds), *Out of Order*, London: Routledge.

Sparks, R.F., Genn, H.G. and Dodd, D.J. (1977) *Surveying Victims*, Chichester: Wiley.

Spear, H.B. (1969) 'The Growth of Heroin Addiction in the United Kingdom', *British Journal of Addiction*, 64: 245-255.

Spector, M. and Kitsuse, J. (1977) *Constructing Social Problems*, Mento Park: Cummings.

Stanko, E. (1977) *These are the Cases that Try Themselves*. Unpublished PhD Thesis, The City University of New York.

Stein, S. (1985) *International Diplomacy, State Administration and Narcotics Control*, Aldershot: Gower.

Stevens, P. and Willis, F. (1979) *Race, Crime and Arrests*, London: HMSO.

Stevens, S., Crocker, C. and Byrne, A. (1988) *Key Facts: Employment*, London Borough of Lambeth: Directorate of Town Planning and Economic Development.

Stewart, T. (1987) *The Heroin Users*, London: Pandora.

Stimson, V.G. and Oppenheimer, E. (1982) *Heroin Addiction*, London: Tavistock.

Sutherland, E. (1961) *White Collar Crime*, New York: Holt, Rinehart and Winston.

Taylor, I., Walton, P. and Young, J. (1973) *The New Criminology*, London: Routledge and Kegan Paul.

Taylor, W. (1982) 'Black Youth, White Man's Justice', *Youth and Society*, November.

Thomas, D.A. (1979) *Principles of Sentencing*, London: Heinemann.

Tipler, J. (1985) *Juvenile Justice in Hackney*, Hackney: Research, Development and Programming Section, Social Services Directorate.

Turk, A.T. (1969) *Criminality and Legal Order*, Chicago: Rand Mcnally and Co.

Tyler, A. (1986) *Street Drugs*, Great Britain: New English Library.

Voakes, R. and Fowler, Q. (1989) *Sentencing, Race and Social Enquiry Reports*, Wakefield: West Yorkshire Probation Service.

Walker, M. (1987) 'The Ethnic Origin of Prisoners: The Prison Population on January 30, 1985 and Persons Received, July, 1984-March, 1985', *British Journal of Criminology*, 27, 2.

_____ (1988) 'The Court Disposal of Young Males by Race in London in 1983', *British Journal of Criminology*, 28, 4.

Walker, M., Jefferson, T. and Seneviratne, M. (1990) *Ethnic Minorities, Young People and the Criminal Justice System: Main Report*, Sheffield: Centre for Criminological and Socio-Legal Studies, University of Sheffield.

Walker, N. (ed) (1975) *The British Jury System*, Cambridge: Institute of Criminology.

Walker, N. (1985) *Sentencing*, London: Butterworth and Co.

Walvin, J. (1971) *The Black Presence*, London: Orbach and Chambers.

_____ (1973) *Black and White*, London: Penguin.

Weeks, J. (1985) *Sexuality and its Discontents*, London: Routledge and Kegan Paul.

West Midlands Probation Service (1987) *Birmingham Social Enquiry Report Monitoring Exercise*, West Midlands Probation Service.

Whitaker, R. (1969) *Drugs and the Law*, Canada: Mathuen.

Whitehouse, P.D. (1978) 'Ethnic Minorities', *West Midlands Probation Service Bulletin*, June.

Willis, C.F. (1983) *The Use, Effectiveness and Impact of Police Stop and Search Powers*, London: Home Office Research Unit.

Willis, J.H. (1969) *Drug Dependence*, London: Faber and Faber.

Willis, J. (1973) *Addicts: Drugs and Alcohol Re-examined*, Nairobi: Pitman.

Wood, J. (1988) 'Relations with the Police and the Public, and with Overseas Police and Judicial Authorities', in H.J.E. Williams (ed), *The Role of the Prosecutor*, Hants: Avebury.

Worsley, P. (ed) (1970) *Introducing Sociology*, Middlesex: Penguin.

Young, J. (1971) *The Drug Takers*, London: Paladin.

_____ (1977) 'Police as Amplifiers of Deviancy', in P.E. Rock (ed), *Drugs and Politics*, New Jersey: Transaction Books.

Young, M. (1991) *Inside Job: Policing and Black Culture in London*, Oxford: Clarendon.

Index

Advisory Council on the Misuse of
    Drugs 53
Agozino, B. x, xiii, 15
alcohol 32,52
Awiah, J. 52

Baldwin, J. x, 16, 74, 83, 84, 129,
    190
Barker, A. 119
Bean, P. 26, 29, 52
Becker, H. xiii, 56, 59, 60
Bedingfield, D. 50, 163
Bennett, W. 157, 204
Benyon, J. xiii, 3, 9, 11, 13, 123
Berridge, V. 24, 25, 26, 27, 31
Best, J. 21, 55, 61
Blair, Tony 44, 48
Blumberg, A. 83
Blumer, H. 55
Bottomley, A. 12, 65, 83, 174
Box, S. xii, xiii, 3, 6, 9, 18, 19, 59,
    65, 74, 160, 196
Brain Committee 33
'British system' of maintenance
    prescribing 29, 31, 32, 33,
Brittan, Leon 48
Broome Report 49
Brown, C. 3, 4
Burr, A. 22, 39, 40, 43, 74

Cain, M. x, xiii, 9, 10, 12, 15, 19
Cashmore, E. x, 7, 8, 13, 30, 51, 53,
    57, 152, 179
Chambliss, W. xiii, 83
Chicago School 5, 6
Chigwada, R. xiii, 8, 14, 19, 53,
    122, 126, 183, 187, 199
Cicourel, A. 56

claims-making 20-23, 55-70
Clare, J. 13
Cloward, R. xii, 6,
Cohen, A. xii
Condon, Paul
    Operation Eagle Eye 13
Conrad, P. 27, 55, 56, 59
Controlled Drugs (Penalties) Act
    1985 50
Cooney, M. 21, 85, 94
Cove, J. x, xii, 16
Crow, I. x, xii, xiii, xiv, 15, 16, 18,
    19

Dangerous Drugs Act 1920 28
Dangerous Drugs and Poisons
    (Amendment) Act 1923 28
Dangerous Drugs Act 1925 29
Dangerous Drugs (Prevention of
    Misuse) Act 1964 34
Dangerous Drugs Act 1965 35, 36
Dangerous Drugs Act 1967 33, 38
Day, M. x, 3, 17, 18, 54
Defence of the Realm (DORA) Act
    1916 27, 28
Demuth, C. xiii, 9, 11
Dholakia, N. 9, 15, 16, 18
Dodd, D. 36
Dorn, N. 22, 28, 29, 34, 35, 45, 49,
    50, 52, 74, 109, 111, 159, 160,
    198
Downes, D. xii, 6, 63,
drug dependency centres (DDUs) 33
Drug Trafficking Offences Act 1986
    50, 87, 163

Eaton, M. 56, 57
Edwards, G. 24, 25, 26, 27

Emerson, R. 84

Feldman, M. 157, 204
Frank, J. 61, 65
Frohmann, L. 74

Garfinkel, H. 58, 66
Gay, P. 39, 43
Gilroy, P. xii, xiii, 7,8,11,12, 36, 51,
    120, 123, 126, 179, 199, 200
Gordon, P. x, xiii, xiv, 11, 12, 14,
    15, 18, 157, 176, 177, 178
Gray, J. x, xiii, 9, 10, 74
Green, P. xi, 45, 46, 50
Griffith, J. 64, 66, 156, 160, 162,
    176, 179, 186
Gusfield, J. 58, 59, 63, 64

Hagan, J. xiii, 202
Hague Convention 25, 28
Hale, C. xii, xiii, 3, 6, 18, 19
Hall, S. 12, 30, 123, 175, 176, 177,
    186, 187
Hansen, T. 39, 43, 51
Harrison Narcotics Act 1914 28
Hawkins, K. 60, 196
Hellawell, Keith 43, 48
Henman, A. 47
Hiro, D. 3, 8, 9, 14, 30, 36, 199
Holzner, B. 112
Home Office x, xi, xii, xiv, 12, 18,
    27, 28, 30, 33, 34, 35, 41, 42,
    44, 46, 48, 49, 50, 53, 75, 109,
    163
Hood, R. x, xiv, 15, 16, 17, 18, 201
Howe, D. 30
Hudson, B. xii, xiv, 15, 16, 17, 18,
    19
Humphrey, D. x, 7, 12, 14, 36, 37,
    38, 97, 152, 160, 178, 179,
    183, 186
Hunte, J. 11
Hurd, Douglas 46

Indian Workers' Association 97
Inner London Probation Service 17,
    52
Institute of Race Relations 9, 10
Jamieson, A. 33
Jefferson, T. x, xiii, 10, 14, 18
John, G. 7, 11, 12, 36, 37, 38, 88,
    152

Kalunta-Crumpton, A. 51, 56, 74,
    75
Keith, M. x, 14
Kitsuse, J. 55, 57, 61, 63

Landau, xiii, 10
Lea, J. x, xii, 3, 6, 7, 9, 13
League of Nations 26, 29
Lewis, R. 25, 34, 47
Lindesmith, A. 25, 26, 31, 32

MacGregor, S. 32, 33, 40, 46
Major, John 44
Matthews, R. 19, 176
McBarnet, D. xiii, 19, 58, 62, 74,
    76, 83, 85
McCabe, S. 203, 204, 205
McClintock, x
McConville, M. x, 16, 21, 74, 83,
    84, 129, 190
McLaughlin, E x, 13, 30, 53, 57,
    152, 179
Medicines Act 1968 35
Merton, R. xii, 5
Metropolitan Police, 42, 54
Mhlanga, B. x, xiii
Miles, R. 120, 126
Mirza, H. 42, 46, 52, 111
Misuse of Drugs Act 1971 35, 38, 48
Murji, K. 50

Nathan, G. xiii, 10

National Association for the Care
and Resettlement of Offenders
(NACRO) x, xiii, 19
Newcombe, R. 40

Ohlin, L. xii, 6
opium wars 25
Oppenheimer, E. 25, 29, 30, 34

Parker, H. 22, 39, 40, 43, 51, 74
Pattenden, R. 157
Pearson, G 22, 24, 40, 43, 51, 52,
74, 159, 160, 198
Pfohl, S.55, 57
Pharmacy Act 1868, 26
Pease, K. 12
Pitts, J.x, xii, 3, 6, 7, 12, 14
Plant, M. 22, 27, 29, 31, 33-35, 41,
42, 43, 50
Platt, A. 65
Pryce, K. 36
Punch, M. 89
Purves, R. 203, 204, 205

Quinney, R. xiii, 20, 57, 60, 65, 160

Ramsay, M. 12
rastafarianism 36, 51
Reiner, R. 3, 8, 9, 15, 176
Rex, J. 51
Roach Family Support Committee
183
Rock, P. xii, 6, 63
Rolleston Committee Report 29
Runnymede Trust xiv, 3, 17, 18
Ruggiero, V. 52
Ryan, W. 7

Sacks, H. 145
Sadigh, S. x, xiii, 9, 12, 15, 19
Sallon, C. 50, 163
Sanders, A. 59, 74, 84
Scarman, Lord

Brixton riot 1981 4, 5, 6, 13
Schneider, C. 27, 55, 56, 59, 60
Shanghai Conference 1909 25, 26
Smith, D. x, xiii, 9, 10, 15, 18, 74
social construction 22-23
Solomos, J. x, xiii, 3, 4, 7, 8, 10, 11,
12, 13, 30, 123, 152, 176
South, N. 35, 45, 52, 81, 109, 111,
159
Spear, H. 29, 30
Special Patrol Group (SPG) 10
Spector, M. 55, 57, 61, 63
Stanko, E. 74
Stevens, P. x, xii, 3, 9
Stimson, V. 25, 29, 30, 34
Sumner, M. 9, 15, 16, 18
'Sus' 11, 14
Swamp 81 13

Troyna, B. 7, 8
Turk, A. 156
Tyler, A. 27, 28, 34, 163

United Nations 26
United States Marijuana Tax Act
1937 32

violent street crime
mugging 12, 13

Walker, M. x, xiv, 9, 15, 16, 18
Walvin, J. 119, 123, 126, 199
West Midlands Probation Service 17
Whitaker, R. 24, 31, 32
white-collar crime xiii
Willis, F. x, xii, 3, 9, 10
Willis, J. 24, 25, 27, 29, 30, 31, 32,
33

Young, J. x, xii, 3, 6, 7, 9, 13, 19,
37, 110, 161, 164, 169, 173,
176, 187